ETHNIC CHURCH MEETS MEGACHURCH

Ethnic Church Meets Megachurch

Indian American Christianity in Motion

Prema A. Kurien

NEW YORK UNIVERSITY PRESS
New York

NEW YORK UNIVERSITY PRESS
New York
www.nyupress.org

References to Internet websites (URLs) were accurate at the time of writing. Neither the author nor New York University Press is responsible for URLs that may have expired or changed since the manuscript was prepared.

ISBN: 978-1-4798-0475-7 (hardback)
ISBN: 978-1-4798-2637-7 (paperback)

For Library of Congress Cataloging-in-Publication data, please contact the Library of Congress.

New York University Press books are printed on acid-free paper, and their binding materials are chosen for strength and durability. We strive to use environmentally responsible suppliers and materials to the greatest extent possible in publishing our books.

Manufactured in the United States of America

10 9 8 7 6 5 4 3 2 1

Roshi, this one is for you!

CONTENTS

This project has been a very long time in the making and has evolved a great deal from the time I began the research in 1999. At that time, I undertook this research as part of a larger project focusing on the political mobilization patterns of the four major Indian immigrant religious groups in the United States—Hindus, Muslims, Sikhs, and Christians—around homeland issues. I had done some work on Hindus and Muslims and started my research on Indian Christians with the Mar Thoma church (part of the Syrian Christian tradition in Kerala that developed out of the contact with the Middle East in the early centuries of the Christian era) since some of its members and *achens* (pastors) had taken the lead in mobilizing the Indian Christian community in the United States to protest attacks against missionaries and Indian Christians taking place in several parts of India. I found very quickly that although Mar Thoma members were from Kerala state in India, known for its highly mobilized and politicized citizenry, most of the congregation was indifferent toward Indian national political developments. However, because of the close ties between the Mar Thoma home church based in Kerala and the U.S.-based diocese, church members were immersed in denominational politics. The mobilization of Indian American Christians in different parts of the United States around attacks against Christians in India soon petered out and was subsequently led by a national umbrella organization, Federation of Indian American Christian Organizations of North America, FIACONA.

Nonetheless, I continued with the research on the Mar Thoma church—the focus of this book—because I found it to be an excellent case study of the problems faced by ethnic churches in the United States. My prior research on Hindus of Indian background in the United States examined how the process of being transformed from a majority in India to a minority in the United States affected Hindu Indian Americans, and the ways in which various Hindu American organizations—religious, cultural, and political—attempted to address questions about minority status and identity outside their homeland (Kurien 2007). What interested me about the Indian Christian case was that it exemplified the reverse process from Indian Hindus, since Indian Christian immigrants move from being a small religious minority in India to becoming part of the majority religious group in the United States. My research showed that immigrant churches like the Mar Thoma face several challenges if they are to successfully institutionalize as an "ethnic" church in a context where Christianity is the majority religion. An important issue is how to retain the allegiance of the second and later generations to an "ethnic" Christianity in the face of the intense competition from American evangelical churches. In facing this challenge, it became clear that the transnational nature of the Mar Thoma denomination was its greatest asset, but also its biggest liability.

Beginning around 2007, a large literature on immigrant religion and civic engagement emerged in the United States that seemed to show that participation in religious institutions facilitated the civic incorporation of contemporary immigrants. This literature piqued my interest and led me to return to the topic of immigrant civic activism in my research. Discussions of civic involvement had come up spontaneously several times in my conversations with Mar Thomites before 2007, but from 2007 to 2009 I explicitly included questions on outreach and activism in my interviews.

Some Mar Thoma American theological scholars who read one of my journal articles from this project indicated that there had been many changes in the Mar Thoma church since my research had ended in 2009 (e.g., see Athyal 2015a). This was one of the questions in my mind when, in 2015, I undertook a last round of research to update my work before I completed this book. My 2015 conversations, particularly with second-generation lay members, showed me that although there had been some changes (which I have incorporated here), many of the fundamental issues that I had identified earlier still remained.

This book presents the perspectives and experiences of a variety of Mar Thomites in the United States (both immigrants and the second generation) as well as in Kerala and Bangalore in India, and also of Mar Thoma achens, and the Mar Thoma leadership (some Mar Thoma bishops and the Mar Thoma Metropolitan). Each of these constituencies had different viewpoints on Christianity and the church stemming from their own upbringing, influences, and involvements. These differences often led to tensions and criticisms, which I document in this book.

I realize that the Mar Thoma leadership is hurt by the critiques expressed by the members that I have presented in my publications and in this book, many of which are unjustified. But I want them to know that my intention was never to undertake a study that would criticize or undermine the Mar Thoma church. I appreciate much about the church and its leadership. My interest as a sociologist specializing in immigrant religion was to understand the effect of the contemporary American religious landscape on Christian immigrant groups. As a sociologist, it is my obligation to present the voices of the diverse groups in the congregation—I cannot simply present the point of view of the leadership. Although the Mar Thoma church has some unique features stemming from its historical background, many other immigrant churches and even mainline American churches are dealing with very similar issues in contemporary America. My hope is that my research and analysis will help the Mar Thoma church (and other immigrant churches with similar circumstances) understand some of the reasons for the intergenerational tensions and differences of opinion about religion, and bring about changes so it can continue to be relevant in the American context and to the new generation growing up in the United States.

My personal background has shaped this project in many ways. I am a Syrian Christian by birth who had a south Indian Protestant upbringing, since my paternal grandfather became a priest in a Protestant denomination, the Church of South India; traditionally, denominational lineage passes through the male line. My mother's family, however, originally belonged to the Mar Thoma church. My maternal grandfather's brother, who was a church historian of the Mar Thoma church, and subsequently my maternal grandfather, who was a priest, became leaders of the reformed side of the Mar Thoma from the late colonial period onward. They finally broke away from the Mar Thoma church in the early 1960s to form a separate denomination, the Saint Thomas Evangelical Church. Their goal was to eschew some of the rituals of the Mar Thoma church and hew more closely to the reformed evangelical position of the Church Missionary Society while still maintaining their ancient heritage. Until a few years ago, however, I had only a very hazy understanding of this history and learned about some of the painful details of this breakup only while conducting the archival research for this project.

Portions of the material presented in this book have been published in earlier form elsewhere. Chapter 3 is an amalgamated and revised version of two earlier publications: "Christian by Birth or Rebirth? Generation and Difference in an Indian American Christian Church," in *Asian American Religions: Borders and Boundaries*, edited by Tony Carnes and Fenggang Yang, 160–181 (NYU Press, 2004); and "Decoupling Religion and Ethnicity: Second-Generation Indian American Christians," *Qualitative Sociology* 35(4) (2012): 447–468. Chapter 5 draws from "Religion, Social Incorporation, and Civic Engagement: Second-Generation Indian American Christians," *Review of Religious Research* 55(1) (2013):81–104; and Chapter 6 is based on "The Impact of International Migration on Home Churches: The Mar Thoma Syrian Christian Church in India," *Journal for the Scientific Study of Religion* 53(1) (2014):109–129.

This book is the product of one and a half decades of work and I have accumulated many debts during the course of it. I gratefully acknowledge the funding of this research by fellowships from the Pew Charitable Trusts, the Louisville Institute, the American Institute of Indian Studies, and by several small awards from Syracuse University. I thank Mar Thoma Metropolitan Chrysostom for warmly welcoming me to conduct this research and for the long interview he allowed me to have with him in 2006. I am also particularly grateful to the many Mar Thomites and achens who invited me into their congregations and their homes, and who patiently answered my many questions. Others talked to me at length over the phone in the midst of their busy schedules, and yet others carved out time to talk to me at conferences jam-packed with sessions and events. Several Mar Thoma scholars and theologians in Kerala and in the United States provided crucial information about the Mar Thoma church's beliefs and practices, for which I am grateful. Some Mar Thomites read all or parts of the manuscript at different stages and provided thoughtful feedback which was critical in the shaping of this book. I especially thank Laurah Klepinger-Mathew, my research assistant, who conducted twenty of the interviews for this project in two different regions of the United States. I am also grateful to Jenna Sikka, who helped me with the references. My research and accommodation in India was made possible by the assistance and hospitality of relatives and friends—who I know have wondered why it has taken me so very long to produce my "Mar Thoma book."

R. Stephen Warner, Jacqueline Hagan, Donald Miller, Tim Fisher, Yasmin Ortiga, Mauricio Torres, and Robert Wuthnow offered comments that were critical to shaping various parts of the project. Comments and feedback I received at presentations at the department of sociology at Loyola University Chicago, as well as the University of North Carolina, the Princeton Theological Seminary, the Indian Christian Leaders conference in New Jersey, and several academic conferences were very important in helping me to think through key ideas. I benefited enormously from Margaret Case's patient editing of the chapters of the book. I particularly thank Jennifer Hammer of NYU press for soliciting my book, and for her patience and feedback while it was in development.

With Robert Wuthnow's support, I obtained affiliation with the Center for the Study of Religion at Princeton during the 2002–2003 academic year while on a fellowship from the Louisville Institute, which gave me access to the excellent holdings at Princeton University and the Princeton Theological Seminary. A Thomas Tam Visiting Professor position at CUNY in the 2014–2015 academic year, which came with a lighter work load and a much shorter commute, enabled me to finally complete this book. I am grateful to the Asian American/Asian Research Institute (AAARI) at CUNY for my position, and the support of Joyce Moy and Russell Leong during my time there.

My parents and husband were my bulwarks of support during the long period of research and writing. My parents visited me while I was doing the fieldwork and attended some Mar Thoma services with me, both in the United States and in India. They made arrangements for my field research in Kerala and in Bangalore and introduced me to several of their friends and relatives who were members of the Mar Thoma church. I left my husband and young son in the United States over the period of an entire summer in 2006 to conduct research in India, and my husband took over the full responsibility of child care and housekeeping without complaint.

I dedicate this book to my son. Work on it spanned the period from his infancy to his high school years. He was the reason that I felt it was important to understand the experiences of second-generation Indian

American Christians. During my fieldwork in the Mar Thoma congregation, I took him with me to Sunday services and other church events, where he was dandled and passed from lap to lap. Some Mar Thoma members were kind enough to visit me at my home so I could talk to them while babysitting my son. As a baby, he also traveled long distances over the weekend with me so I could meet with Mar Thoma members at their homes and conduct interviews. He and I went together to a Mar Thoma church family retreat. His presence during my fieldwork was a great icebreaker and helped people warm to me. If not for him, this research would not have been conducted.

Introduction

Indian American Christianity in Motion

"We were being shot down by the congregation, left and right. Then Sam started talking about the importance of being a true Christian, of having a personal relationship with Christ. As he was talking, you could see the steam rising in church." George, a second-generation Indian American, was talking about a showdown that occurred in his Bethelville parish, in a suburb in the United States, in 1999. The parish belongs to the Eastern Reformed Mar Thoma denomination based in Kerala, south India, part of the ancient Saint Thomas Syrian Christian church that traces its origin to the legendary arrival of Apostle Thomas on the shores of Kerala in 52 C.E. The tension between members of the first and second generations was about the meaning of being a Christian: "Finally, one of the uncles [in Indian culture men and women of the parent's generation are addressed as 'uncle' and 'aunty'] in the congregation jumped up and shouted, flailing his arms vigorously to make his point, 'How can you imply that we are not Christians? We are all Christians in this church. My father was a Christian, I am a Christian. I was baptized by the *Thirumeni* [bishop] himself. My son was born a Christian and will be a Christian all his life.'"

This confrontation epitomizes the differences between the models of Christianity embraced by first- and second-generation Indian Americans. Those who immigrated to the United States from Kerala have generally interpreted being Christian as the outcome of being born and raised in a Christian family, sacralized by infant baptism into the church community. Second-generation Mar Thoma Americans, on the other hand, have imbibed several of the ideas of American evangelicalism and have tended to view a Christian identity as the outcome of achieving a personal relationship with Christ, often beginning with a "born-again" experience.

There were several other fundamental differences in the way the immigrant and second generations understood what being Christian meant. Consequently, disputes and misunderstandings were common between the two generations in the church. These disputes have continued over the past fifteen years, but they have taken new forms as the second generation has grown older, and as a new wave of immigrants from India has become part of Mar Thoma American congregations.

This book examines how a new paradigm of ethnicity and religion is shaping contemporary immigrant religious institutions and the intergenerational transmission of religion. Drawing on multisited research both in India and the United States, including interviews and participant observation, it examines the pressures church members have faced to incorporate contemporary American evangelical worship styles into their practice, often at the expense of maintaining the ethnic character and support system of their religious community. The role of religion in the lives of contemporary immigrants and their children is very different from patterns established by earlier immigrant groups in the United States. Classic assimilation theory was based on the assumption of individualistic adaptation, whereby immigrants and their children were expected to shed their ethnic identities, adopt the behavior of white, upper-middle-class Protestants, and become Americans—although in the sphere of religion, they could maintain their ethnic traditions within American denominations. In contemporary society, in contrast, multiculturalism, spiritual seeking, and postdenominationalism have turned this paradigm on its head. The prevalence of multiculturalism as a social norm means that immigrants and their children find a place in American society by remaining ethnic and group-identified. Religion, on the other hand, has become de-ethnicized and individualized, particularly among Protestant groups, in a seeker-oriented society. In practice, becoming religiously "de-ethnicized" in a postdenominational society means shedding ethnic languages, theologies, and worship cultures, and adopting the language, theology, music, and worship practices of white, upper-middle-class evangelicals. Indeed, some younger immigrants and most of the second generation are gravitating toward American evangelical Christianity, helping to fuel the growing rise of evangelicalism both here and around the world.

The integration patterns of post–1965 U.S. immigrants and their descendants have thus become a mirror image of those of earlier European immigrants, with the religious and secular dimensions reversed. The children of European immigrants were expected to assimilate by becoming de-ethnicized in the secular and public sphere, but were able to retain their ethnic communities, language, and traditions in the sphere of religion. Members of the contemporary second generation are incorporated in U.S. society by maintaining their ethnic identities in secular contexts, but they tend to adopt a de-ethnicized, individualized, religious identity and practice. Since the native-born children of immigrants are the pivotal generation shaping the incorporation patterns of ethnic groups, their behavior has wide-ranging effects on ethnic religious institutions and the wider society. This book examines some of these effects by focusing on a case study of Mar Thoma Americans and their struggles and dilemmas in the process of establishing themselves and their church in the United States.

Specifically, this book looks at the shifts in the understandings of Mar Thoma members regarding their ethnic and Christian identity as a result of their U.S. migration and the coming of age of the American-born generation. In India, the church is based in Kerala, has its own Metropolitan (head of the church), and emphasizes its Indian identity. Until the arrival of European colonists in Kerala, the church maintained connections with the East Syrian church in Persia, and its liturgy was originally in Syriac, which explains why the church and its adherents are called "Syrian Christian." Syrian Christians are a well-established and respected ancient minority group in Kerala that is able to maintain its societal position and distinct subcultural identity based on religious affiliation.

In the United States, Indian Christians constitute around 18 percent of the Indian American population (Pew Research Center 2012). Syrian Christians from Kerala constitute the largest group of Indian Christians in the United States, and among Syrian Christian denominations, the Mar Thoma church is considered the best organized and most active (Williams 1996, 136–137). In India, Christians are a minority within a nation that is largely Hindu. Yet upon arrival in the United States they become religiously part of the Christian majority. This transition plays into their emerging identities as Christian Indian Americans and influences their religiosity in specific ways. In the United States, most Mar Thoma members identify as Protestant. In the postdenominational society of the United States, where Christianity is the majority religion, it becomes difficult for Syrian Christians to use religion as the locus of their ethnicity. They have to deal with the U.S. population's lack of familiarity with their ancient Indian Christian community—but more important, they have trouble transmitting the distinct liturgical, ritual, and ecclesiastical practices of the traditional church to their children.

There is a lot of literature on how nondenominational evangelicalism and the rise of American megachurches are "remaking" American mainline churches and American religious traditions (Ellingson 2007; Miller 1997; Roof 1999; Sargeant 2000). But American evangelicalism has also had a profound impact on the "ethnic" churches of recent immigrants. In the Mar Thoma case, the widespread prevalence and dominance of American evangelicalism created an environment in which the traditional practices of the Mar Thoma church seemed alien to its American-born generation. At the same time, parents and church leaders alike were finding it difficult to explain and justify their birth-ascribed, communal model of Christianity in the face of the personally achieved, individualistic model of evangelical Christianity that their children were being exposed to in their schools and colleges. Second-generation Mar Thoma Americans were influenced by nondenominational American evangelicalism and often rejected the "ethnic," denominational worship practices of the Mar Thoma. They argued that being a "closed" ethnic church was "not Christian." But their attempts to introduce nonliturgical praise and worship services in English, open to individuals of all backgrounds, were resisted by members of the immigrant generation for whom the church functioned as an extended family and social community. Consequently, many second-generation Mar Thomites have left the Mar Thoma church for large nondenominational churches once they reached adulthood. Others have attended both Mar Thoma and evangelical church services. Yet others have stayed in the Mar Thoma church, but worked to transform church practices to be closer to the evangelical church model.

Evangelical Christianity in the United States is not monolithic. Second-generation (and some first-generation) American Mar Thomites have participated in a variety of evangelical institutions including campus groups, Bible study fellowships, and an array of evangelical churches. Television, Internet, and radio ministries, Internet websites, and books provide other sources of influence. In interviews and conversations, however, the type of church that came up most frequently and to which the Mar Thoma church was compared, was the large transdenominational or nondenominational churches—the U.S. megachurches. Megachurches offer several services over the weekend, and sometimes even during the week, with slick multimedia presentations and contemporary music led by professional bands. They also have programming for a variety of age groups.

Describing the attraction of such churches, Vilja, a 1.5 generation (those born abroad who immigranted as young children) woman in her forties, explained that the youth in her Mar Thoma congregation liked "the short contemporary service, the music, pastors who are fluent in English, and sermons that are well put-together, and have life application." She mentioned that they also liked the fact that many of these pastors provided an outline of their sermon and the key points on a screen while they were speaking. Shobha, a second-generation Mar Thoma American who had left the Mar Thoma church, was enthusiastic about the large nondenominational church she attended along with her husband. "They have an amazing band, and amazing musicians. And we just love worshiping there. It brings a lot of people from the community in because it's like a free concert on Sunday morning—bagels and doughnuts too!"

Shobha's description of the service at the megachurch that she attended as a "free concert on Sunday" is very apt. In these churches, the carefully choreographed, emotionally charged productions with dramatic mood lighting, video enhancement, and professional music are designed to create a "collective effervescence" (Durkheim 1912) or uplifting atmosphere. This is probably why many of the Mar Thoma youth described such churches as being "on fire for Christ." They contrasted this type of worship experience with the sedate, formal service and the off-key congregational singing in the Mar Thoma churches. Evangelical megachurches are also structured very differently from the Mar Thoma church. While the Mar Thoma churches are small and community oriented, megachurches are large and impersonal—but many of the second generation I interviewed thought that the lack of community orientation of these evangelical churches actually helped to foster spirituality. Although the older, immigrant generation said that it was important for them to know "the person who is sitting next to me in the pew," the younger generation considered the social aspect of the Mar Thoma church a hindrance to being able to focus on God during the service. The services at megachurches are also much shorter than at the Mar Thoma church, which means that people could fit in many other activities during the day. If they went to a Mar Thoma church on the other hand, most of Sunday was spent on the commute, the service, and church activities. The financial obligations for Mar Thomites attending megachurches were also lower than at a Mar Thoma church. Due to these considerations, in the United States small, ethnic churches like the Mar Thoma face competition for their youth from the large megachurches that have become a ubiquitous part of the contemporary American Christian landscape.

The Mar Thoma case shows how the ideas and practices of second-generation American Christian evangelicals are bringing about changes in immigrant-dominated congregations. The second-generation members who remained in the church were caught between their criticisms of the "ethnic" character of the Mar Thoma church and its traditions, and their appreciation for the social support its warm community and familial relationships provided them as they were growing up. This dilemma was dealt with in different ways, but in the long run the Mar Thoma church is likely to be transformed by the evangelically influenced second generation.

At the same time, immigrants and their children may also be bringing about changes in American evangelical churches. Large American evangelical churches have recently started emphasizing multiracialism and have turned away from the homogeneity doctrine (Emerson 2009). The literature on multiracial congregations focuses largely on the integration of black members into white churches (Edwards 2008; Emerson and Smith 2000). However, it is likely that other racial minorities will be integrated within these churches in the long term; this is another reason to examine whether and how American evangelicalism can help new ethnic groups incorporate into the wider society.

This book, while showcasing these dynamics among the first and second generations in the United States, is also a case study of global religion. It examines how transnational processes shape religion in both the place of destination and the place of origin. Taking a long view, it examines how the forces of globalization, from the period of colonialism to contemporary large-scale outmigration, have brought about tremendous changes in Christian communities in the Global South. The engagement with the very different model of religion embodied by American evangelicalism is forcing the Mar Thoma denomination, and to some extent the larger Syrian Christian tradition in Kerala, to reshape its theology and practices. Previous encounters with Western Christianity going as far back as the sixteenth century have similarly transformed the ancient Kerala church at several key historical junctures. In June 1599, four centuries before the confrontation in the Bethelville church described above, a group of clerics and leaders from the Saint Thomas Syrian Christian church, which had remained unified for at least thirteen hundred years, was also dramatically confronted with a different model of Christianity. The group was herded into an ancient church in Diamper (present day Udayamperoor), Kerala, by Dom Alexis de Menezes, the archbishop of Goa, a south Indian territory then controlled by the Portuguese. Over the course of an eight-day synod, the Syrian Christians were made to abjure many of the central tenets and practices of their traditional East Syrian faith, adopt a Latinized East Syriac liturgy, and come under Portuguese *padroado* (patronage), the pope, and the Church of Rome. Several of their Syrian books, which were declared "heretical," were burned.

In the subsequent centuries, the Kerala Syrian Christian church saw big changes. In 1653, several thousand Syrian Christians, under the leadership of archdeacon Thomas, openly rebelled against the agreement of the Synod of Diamper and, holding onto ropes tied to a venerable stone cross, took an oath to sever their allegiance with the Latin Church. In 1665, the Syrian Christian church in Kerala formally split into two groups: Syrian Catholics, a group that remained under the See of Rome with a Latinized East Syriac liturgy, and the Syrian Orthodox dissident group that came under the leadership of a Syrian Orthodox bishop sent by the Church of Antioch and adopted a West Syriac St. James liturgy.

Beginning in the early nineteenth century, the encounter of Syrian Christians with British missionaries led to further divisions within the ancient church, particularly the creation of schisms between the Orthodox group and Anglican-influenced Syrian Christians. In 1889, a group led by Anglican-influenced priests of the Syrian Orthodox church broke away to form the first autonomous Indian church: the Mar Thoma denomination, blending an Orthodox worship style with a Reformed theology.

More recently, the international migration of Mar Thomites to the Middle East and the West has had profound impacts on the home church. The Mar Thoma leadership has modified some of its practices, particularly in parishes outside India, to meet the needs of the younger generation growing up away from the rural Kerala context. They are constrained, however, by the tradition, structure, and mission of the church. I argue that we need new frameworks to understand both the processes of religious change brought about through colonial encounters with groups that were already Christian, as well as the process of religious transformation in home communities that have been triggered by migration.

Theoretical Frameworks

Religion in Motion

Contemporary international migration and globalization of religions have together given rise to discussions of "religion in motion." However, the Mar Thoma case reminds us that global religious movements are much older than the contemporary world, and first emerged as a consequence of international trade, colonialism, and related missionary activities. There is literature on how colonialism and missionary activities affected the religious communities, practices, and ideas of colonized groups (Comaroff and Comaroff 1991, 1997; Copland 2007; Cox 2002; Oddie 2000) and, as discussed, other literature on the impact of international migration on religion. There has been little discussion, however, of cases where religion has undergone multiple movements of different types. Mar Thoma Syrian Christianity presents an excellent example of one such case and can help us to understand how religious encounters across several diverse social and cultural contexts shape the interpretation and institutionalization of religion.

In an incisive essay, Manuel Vásquez (2008) points out that understanding religion in motion means that we need to pay attention to the role of power in the production and movement of religion, as well as the multiple histories, understandings, and practices of religion. These considerations are important in the Mar Thoma case. For instance, the culture and identity, as well as the intra- and intergroup relationships of Syrian Christians, changed dramatically as a result of their assimilation into Hindu society, their encounters with the Portuguese, British, and Indian nationalism, and their international migration to the United States. In each case, these changes came about as the community and its leaders tried to adjust to or resist the dominant political and cultural forces in their environment.

Until the sixteenth century, Syrian Christians were integrated within Hindu Kerala society as a high-caste warrior group below only the Brahmins in status (Ayyar 1926:54–55; Frykenberg 2008). They participated in Hindu religious ceremonies and upheld Hindu pollution and purity rituals and rules (Bayly 1989). But they maintained a distinct religious identity from the Hindus, Muslims, and Jews in Kerala society by retaining their own "sacred language" (Syriac), avoiding the use or worship of icons, sustaining their ties with the Persian church in Babylon, and through their cult of Syrian Christian bishops from the Middle East, whom they considered to be saints. A well-known scholar of the early Saint Thomas Church in Kerala characterizes Syrian Christians in this period as being "Hindu in culture, Christian in religion, and Oriental in worship" (Podipara 1973, 107).

Syrian Christians in Kerala resisted Portuguese attempts at Latinization for decades, arguing that their prelate was the patriarch of Babylon, that they had never heard of the pope in Rome in all these centuries, and that they were bound by the "Law of Saint Thomas" and not the "Law of Saint Peter" (Gouvea [1606] 2003). But they were eventually incorporated into Roman Catholicism through a combination of deception and force at the Synod of Diamper, discussed above. The British Anglican missionaries who followed the Portuguese were less confrontational. Nonetheless, they tried to purge Syrian Christians of both Roman Catholic and Hindu influences in their attempt to restore the church to its "ancient purity." The British were able to gain some converts to their Anglican church and influence others like the Mar Thoma to reform their theology, but their efforts were rebuffed by many Catholic and Orthodox Syrian Christians who wanted to maintain their liturgy and traditions. Some changes adopted by Anglican-influenced groups, however, such as translating their Syrian liturgy into Malayalam (the language of Kerala state), were subsequently adopted by Orthodox and Catholic Syrian Christian denominations.

The large-scale migration of Syrian Christians to Malaysia, Singapore, and Sri Lanka (then Ceylon) started in the early decades of the twentieth century. By the post–World War II period, there was also a migration to countries in Africa. Initially limited to only a few migrants, out-migration to the Middle East picked up from the 1950s. Migration to the United States began in the early 1970s. As a result of these migrations, Syrian Christian churches like the Mar Thoma are now global, with dioceses and parishes around the world. Global migration in turn means that Syrian Christian churches now have several generations who are growing up outside Kerala and India. These generations have been demanding changes in the church. In the Mar Thoma case, migrants and their foreign-born children have new expectations of the church. As we will see, the Mar Thoma church has modified some of its practices to respond to the needs of members living overseas; many of these changes were also implemented in Indian metropolitan areas outside Kerala.

Immigrant Incorporation and Religious Change

Immigration and settlement in new societies often result in fundamental changes in religion, at both personal and organizational levels. Immigrants and their children now constitute over 25 percent of the U.S. population. Around two-thirds of post-1965 immigrants hail from Christian backgrounds (New Immigrant Survey 2003) and as such, are part of religious traditions that are well established in the United States. How do immigration and encounters with American coreligionists impact their understandings and practices of their Christian traditions? How might identifying as Christian shape their social and religious incorporation and those of their children into American society?

Contemporary theories of immigration have sought to differentiate the incorporation of earlier European arrivals in the United States from post-1965 groups, focusing on how the latter's nonwhite racial status might pose a barrier to their social integration (Portes and Zhou 1993; Basch et al. 1994; Alba and Nee 2003).[1] However, religion has traditionally been an important mode of incorporation for Protestant, Catholic, and Jewish immigrants (Greeley 1972; Herberg 1960; Warner 1993). Consequently, scholars have also begun to examine whether, as in the case of European immigrants, religion might help to link present-day immigrants and their children to institutions and groups in the wider society (Alba, Raboteau, and DeWind 2009; Foner and Alba 2008).

Classic assimilation theory in the United States, based on the experiences of the European immigrants who arrived in the country at the turn of the twentieth century, provided the canonical account of the process of immigrant integration until the 1960s (Alba and Nee 2003). According to this perspective, the maintenance of ethnicity and ethnic communities was a liability for the social and economic incorporation of individuals of European ancestry, since it prevented their chances of upward social mobility (Warner and Scrole 1945, 295). However, scholars such as Will Herberg (1960) and Andrew Greeley (1972) argued that the denominational structure of American religion provided second- and later-generation Europeans the means of locating themselves socially in the United States by developing "American" identities while maintaining their distinctness.

The large-scale immigration of the past four decades takes place in a new social and religious context. The civil rights, feminist, and ethnic movements of the 1960s laid the foundations for the development of cultural pluralism as a policy in education and subsequently as a political philosophy. Consequently, contemporary models of immigrant incorporation such as segmented assimilation and transnationalism turn the old assimilation paradigm "on its head" (Waters 1999, 5). Both these models, in slightly different ways, make the case that remaining ethnically identified and embedded in family, community, and transnational networks is beneficial for the economic and social incorporation of contemporary immigrants and their children, particularly for nonwhite groups (Basch et al. 1994; Portes and Zhou 1993; Waters 1999). Even those scholars who propose a modified assimilation paradigm recognize that immigrants obtain many benefits from maintaining their culture, ethnic institutions, and group ties (Alba and Nee 2003, 5–7).

At the same time that the maintenance of ethnicity has been embraced in secular spheres, however, there has been a retreat from inherited culture and traditions, or denominationalism, in the arena of religion (Wuthnow 1988; Miller 1997). The shift to postdenominationalism has been due to two factors, both tied to the "spiritual turn" in the West that took place over the same period, characterized by a "sacralization of the self" (Houtman and Aupers 2007). The first was the spread of a voluntaristic, anti-institutional, and consumerist religious climate that encouraged individuals to choose their religious tradition and to cobble together various religious doctrines and practices to satisfy their tastes. The second was the development of a therapeutic understanding of religion, the idea that religion should meet the psychological needs of individuals (Ellingson 2007; Miller 1997; Roof 1999; Sargeant 2000). Unlike a denominational society, which emphasizes that individuals are formed by, and live within, communities of memory, contemporary religious culture in the United States and in many other Western societies is individualistic and places importance on the autonomy and integrity of the inner spirit (Bellah et al. 1985; Hervieu-Léger 2006; Roof 1999, 83; Taylor 2007). Inherited traditions and rituals are seen as forces that alienate individuals from their authentic selves and are therefore liabilities (Heelas 1996; Houtman and Aupers 2007). There is also an emphasis on a textually based religion, with a minimalist theology, purified of most ritual observances (Hervieu-Léger 2006, 64).

In response to these larger changes, a new, "seeker-oriented" nondenominational, evangelical, Protestant church model developed in the United States, with informal, antiliturgical, and anticeremonial services. Such churches articulate an individualistic concept of religion that stresses personal salvation. The goal in attending church is to obtain "spiritual food" or sermons applicable to life, which, it is believed, helps individuals to "grow spiritually" and results in their becoming more loving, joyful, and free from stress. Since the goal of Christianity is believed to be to create a new community in Christ, ethnicity is often seen as a barrier to achieving a Christian identity (Jeung 2005). The ascendancy of nondenominational megachurches has resulted in a loss of membership, particularly the youth, in mainline Protestant denominations. In response, many have tried to adopt some of the music, worship practices, and also the theology of nondenominational evangelicalism (Ellingson 2007). Even Catholics and members of Orthodox churches have been affected by the individualistic, evangelical turn (Fisher 2005; Maurer 2010; Pew Research Center 2007).

How do these shifts in the patterns and expectations regarding ethnicity and religion affect the generational transition from "immigrants" to "ethnics," particularly for Christian groups? Although the prevailing model of spirituality separates religion and ethnicity, for many immigrants religious identity and traditions are an inextricable part of ethnic identity. Immigrant religious organizations often enshrine long-established religiocultural traditions, and scholars have shown that as in the case of earlier European immigrants, religious institutions play an important role in contemporary immigrant adaptation, since they become the means for parents to create community and transmit their homeland culture and values to their children. They also provide economic benefits through information sharing and networking among members and, for nonwhite immigrants, act as a buffer against racism and discrimination in the wider society (Hirschman 2004; Warner and Wittner 1998).

Despite the sociocultural benefits provided by immigrant religious institutions, several studies show that contemporary second-generation Christian Americans are attracted to forms of evangelical or charismatic Christianity through the influence of friends and coethnics. Most of the literature on this topic is dominated by studies of second-generation East Asian American Protestants (Alumkal 2003; Ecklund 2006; R. Kim 2006; S. Kim 2010). Although they grew up in immigrant churches, both Korean and Chinese American youth have generally attended separate, English-language services within these churches, using the worship style and music of American evangelical churches. As adults, many of them have prioritized religious identity over race or ethnic identity and disagreed with the ethnic practices of immigrant churches, resulting in their "silent exodus" from their parents' churches (Chai 1998; Lee 1996; Min 2010, 137). In the long run, however, they have preferred to join evangelical religious organizations catering to second-generation East Asian Americans rather than attend white or multiracial churches. This was due to their feelings of racialization within the wider society, their experience of marginality in predominantly white churches, their lack of familiarity with white evangelical families, and the comfort they obtained from continuing to worship with second-generation coethnics (Alumkal 2003; Jeung 2005; R. Kim 2006; S. Kim 2010; Min 2010).

Groups such as East Asian American Christians that are relatively homogeneous culturally and religiously, and have sizable numbers of second-generation members concentrated in a few areas, have the option of forming separate second-generation ethnic churches. However, such churches are the exception rather than the norm. Most ethnic churches remain intergenerational (Gornik and George 2015). Indian American Christians are a smaller and more diverse group than Korean Americans. Due to the historical differences and tensions among Syrian Christian denominations, most are not in "full communion" with each other, and there are no pan-Syrian Christian churches. Because of the big differences in language, culture, and caste between Christians in India, there are few nondenominational Indian American churches. Consequently, with some exceptions, the choice is generally between remaining in a multigenerational ethnic church and attending a nonethnic church. This case study of Indian American Christians illuminates some of the dynamics in multigenerational ethnic churches.

Those who stay in the immigrant church are challenging many of its traditions and practices and bringing about change, and they comprise the focus of this book. Those who attend nonethnic churches are also bringing about shifts and adjustments in these institutions, which are working to incorporate their nonwhite members. That will have to be the subject of another project.

Background to the Study

Kerala is a small state on the southwest coast of India with the highest rates of out-migration among all Indian states, both to other parts of India and internationally.[2] Despite being largely agrarian and rural, Kerala is one of the country's most densely populated regions, with very high unemployment rates. Kerala is also the most literate state in India, with a literacy rate of 93.91 percent in the 2011 census (compared to the national literacy level of 74 percent). The combination of high population density, scarcity of land, and high unemployment and education levels in Kerala have led to out-migration since the early decades of the twentieth century.

Kerala's religious composition is unique among Indian states, with large proportions of Muslims and Christians, in addition to Hindus. In the 2011 census, Muslims accounted for 26.56 percent (compared to 14.23 percent at the national level), Christians 18.38 percent (2.3 percent nationally), and Hindus 54.73 percent (79.79 percent nationally). Although Christianity in most parts of India is a product of Western missionary activity during the colonial or postcolonial period, as we have seen, Syrian Christians in Kerala are part of an ancient church from the Middle East, and they are very proud of their Saint Thomas heritage and upper-caste status. Consequently, they consider themselves to be a distinct ethnic group, maintain a separate identity from other Indian Christians, and have their own churches. Syrian Christians in Kerala, about half the Christian population in 2001 (Zachariah 2006, 10), follow the Syriac rite in their religious services, while Latin Christians follow the Latin rite. Both Syrian Christian and Latin Christian denominations follow episcopal traditions.

As noted above, the Saint Thomas Syrian Christian church split several times over the course of its history, and there are now over ten different denominations—Orthodox, Catholic, Eastern Reformed, and Protestant—that claim an upper-caste, Syrian Christian heritage. Since religious and even denominational affiliation is traditionally determined by birth (except in the case of women who join their husbands' denomination) and not by personal choice in India, the liturgical services and rituals of each denomination are not easily accessible to the uninitiated. In other words, until recently, traditional Indian Christian denominations have had a virtual monopoly over their membership. This is beginning to change as India has become the target of aggressive evangelical Christian proselytizing efforts, funded by American groups (Baldauf 2005). Concerned Hindu groups have mobilized against such proselytization, giving rise to state regulations on foreign evangelists, and against conversion with monetary inducements or coercion (Fernandes 2011).

The Mar Thoma Denomination

The Mar Thoma is the third largest Syrian Christian group (Zachariah 2006, 13). In 2015, the denomination had 1,223 parishes and congregations, and dioceses all over India and in many parts of the world, with around 1.5 million members.[3] Mar Thoma Christians are largely concentrated in the central Travancore Christian belt of Kerala, an area that was the center of Christian missionary activity and Christian educational institutions during the British colonial period. Their location and Anglican missionary connections gave them an educational advantage: Mar Thoma Christians are the most educated group in the state next to Brahmins, who constitute a very small group in Kerala (Zachariah 2006, 207).

Although the denomination has parishes around India and the world, its administration is centralized, with its headquarters in Tiruvalla, Kerala. The Metropolitan and the synod of Mar Thoma bishops based in Kerala maintain control over the global network of Mar Thoma parishes. However, the church also has a *Prathinidhi Mandalam* (representative assembly), currently numbering 1,459 members with three-year terms, of which 65 percent are from the laity (including representatives from every parish) and 35 percent from the clergy. The Mandalam meets annually in Kerala to approve the annual report and budget, and also "decides all spiritual and temporal affairs of the Church."[4] A consequence of this centralization is a remarkable uniformity among the ritual and organizational practices of Mar Thoma parishes in different countries, all of which maintain its ancient St. James liturgy (translated into Malayalam). As a concession to the children growing up outside Kerala who are often not fluent in Malayalam, parishes in other parts of the world and in many parts of India now offer services in English at least on alternate Sundays, with a translated liturgy.

Since the Mar Thoma church is a blend of Eastern traditions and Western Reformed theology, it often describes itself as a "bridge-church" between Eastern and Western ecclesiastical traditions. However, because of its complicated history, what exactly its "Eastern Reformed" identity means is not clearly understood by lay members or even most of the clergy, a problem exacerbated by the fact that the official Mar Thoma position is that "the liturgy is the theology." Since the theological assumptions of the Mar Thoma church tend to be unarticulated, this overview is based largely on the only Mar Thoma source I could find, a description of the difference between the "Western" and "Eastern" theological traditions offered by a Mar Thoma bishop, Geevarghese Mar Theodosius (2000), the bishop who was in charge of the North American diocese at the end of my study.

Perhaps the central theological concept of the Syrian church is that of "mystery," or the idea that God and the ultimate truth are beyond the ability of human reason to fully comprehend. This means that God is treated with awe, in contrast to the Western Christian conception that treats God as a person and an intimate friend (Mar Theodosius 2000, 98–99). In the Eastern tradition, God is believed to be within us, since we are created in the image of God. Consequently, "prayer is being in the presence of God. It is acknowledging and accepting God within us. It is an intimacy and communion with the Emmanuel in whom we live and move and have our being" (Mar Theodosius 2000, 102).

The Mar Thoma church maintains an Orthodox liturgical theology of worship based on an emphasis on a nonrational element in worship and uses music, color, and smell along with gestures and actions to express the mystery of Christ and to manifest the gospel. The liturgy is in ornate, ceremonial Malayalam with some Syriac and Aramaic words. It is sung in a sonorous chant, with congregational responses. The *achens* (priests) and bishops wear elaborate robes, the altar and sacristy are richly arrayed, censers are swung at several points during the service, and the liturgy includes several ritualized gestures (bowing, signing the cross). "The Mar Thoma community derives its identity and cohesiveness from the . . . liturgy it uses. The whole theology of the church is embedded in the liturgy" (Mar Theodosius 2000, 97).

Liturgical worship in turn is based on two interrelated concepts: that worship is a fundamental obligation of human beings and that worship should be corporate and participatory. The idea that worship is a fundamental obligation of human beings means that worship is an end in itself, and that any psychosocial benefits that the individual gets from worship are secondary and not the primary reason for worship. This is very different from the contemporary idea that worship is a "spiritual filling station" for individuals (Verghese 1967, 21). Corporate, participatory worship, and the idea of the co-creation of the transcendent through community worship is in contrast to many nondenominational services which only expect the passive participation of the congregation in the worship. By partaking in the liturgy, the biblical message is implanted in the believers' minds and hearts; this is considered a more effective way of imparting the scripture than through formal teaching, and it is through the liturgical calendar of the church that Christians are believed to "experience the mystery, mystically" (Mar Theodosius 2000, 98; see also Varghese 2004; Verghese 1967). The service is around two and a half hours long; the sermon or message is usually brief, generally only around fifteen to twenty minutes, and is based on the church lectionary.

The emphasis on corporate, participatory worship is based on the idea that *theosis* (divinization, defined as becoming aware of the di-

vine core inside humans) is worked out in the individual but is attained
through corporate worship and is granted to the church as a whole (Mar
Theodosius 2000, 99). Whereas nondenominational churches target religious seekers, the Syrian Christian church emphasizes communitarian
worship of the initiated, since "one can know the spiritual riches in worship only by full and repeated participation along with a community
nurtured in the same liturgical tradition" (Mar Theodosius 2000, 101),
and because "the Eucharist was never intended to be for the unbeliever
or the unbaptized" (Verghese 1967, 20). This also means that, as in other
Orthodox churches, the worship is not readily accessible to newcomers.

Since the biblical message is primarily transmitted through the liturgy, the central function of the achen in a Mar Thoma church is to
lead the liturgical service, to preach the sermon based on the lectionary,
and to follow the rules and regulations of the Mar Thoma church, not
to provide clear, moral guidelines based in scripture that are relevant to
the everyday lives and struggles of people in the contemporary world, as
in evangelical churches. In fact, dogma or doctrine is less important in
the Syrian traditions. As Mar Thoma bishop Mar Theodosius declared
(2000, 103), "Eastern spirituality is not to be derived from certain doctrines or systematic theology but from the very living and dynamic relationship the religious community has with God, with each other and
with nature." Consequently, the church is reluctant to take hard-line positions on many contemporary debates.

Religion and Migration from Kerala

In 2007, the overwhelming majority, 89 percent, of Kerala emigrants
went to the Middle East (on a strictly short-term basis, since there is
no possibility of permanent settlement in those countries), and 5.7 percent to the United States. The Kerala Migration Study conducted in 1998
estimated that there were 33 international migrants for every 100 households. By 2007, this proportion had declined to 24.5 per 100 households
(Zachariah and Rajan 2007, 8). About 17 percent of Kerala households
received money from abroad as remittances in 2003 (Zachariah 2006,
212). Based on 1998 figures, Muslims in Kerala had the highest proportion of international migrants (49 migrants per 100 households), with
the overwhelming majority going to the Middle East. Christians had the

second highest proportion of international migrants, 25 migrants per 100. A large proportion of emigrants from the Christian community, 28.4 percent, were women, compared to 16 percent among Hindus and 8 percent among Muslims. Around 15 percent of Christian emigrants from Kerala went to the United States, and Christians made up more than three-fourths of the Kerala emigrants to the United States.[5]

Probably as a result of their educational advantage and missionary connections, Mar Thomites had an early start in their migration and consequently had the highest migration rate (combining internal and external migration) of all groups in Kerala—148 migrants per 100 households in 2004 (Zachariah 2006, 211–212). Of Mar Thoma households, 31 percent received remittances (compared to 17 percent of Kerala households as a whole), with an average of Rs. 22,000 (about U.S. $450) in 2004, compared to Rs. 8,000 (about U.S. $160) for the average Kerala household.[6]

The large-scale migration of Mar Thoma Christians from the early decades of the twentieth century was initiated through their connections with British missionaries. Consequently, migrants generally went to regions of the world that were part of the British Empire: Malaysia, Singapore, and Sri Lanka, as well as countries in Africa and the Middle East. A distinctive feature of the migration, particularly to Africa and the Middle East, was that it included both male and female migrants and a large number of female nurses. The migration to the United States started after the passage of the 1965 Immigration Act that removed barriers to Asian immigration. Until around 1990, this migration was largely dominated by nurses and their families.

The globalization of the Mar Thoma church brought several dilemmas, including the question of whether Mar Thoma Christians should integrate into Protestant churches with which the Mar Thoma church was in communion, or remain distinct in separate parishes. The Mar Thoma leadership originally opposed the formal establishment of separate Mar Thoma parishes in regions such as Africa, the United Kingdom, and the United States, where there were established mainline churches belonging to Anglican, Episcopal, Methodist, or Presbyterian denominations. Immigrants in the United States, however, felt culturally, linguistically, and racially marginalized in mainstream American churches and wanted to form Mar Thoma parishes where they could maintain their community and their Malayalam liturgy. The leadership finally yielded, and Mar Thoma parishes in the United States were officially established in 1976. The North America and United Kingdom diocese (now the North America and Europe diocese) was formed in 1988. Several other Mar Thoma dioceses were also established around the world. In 2015, there were fifty-four parishes and four congregations in the United States, serving 6,677 residentially scattered Mar Thoma families, or around 27,000 individuals (data provided by the Mar Thoma diocesan office in Merrick, New York).

Gender, Religious Networks, and Mar Thoma Migration

An overwhelming majority of early Syrian Christian migrants in the United States comprised of female nurses and their families, the nurses being recruited to meet the U.S. nursing shortage which began in the late 1960s (Williams 1996). Even though Christians in Kerala composed only about one-fifth of the population of the state, female nurses hailed almost entirely from this group until at least the late 1990s (George 2005, 39). Religious networks played a critical role in this development and in their migration outside the country. Syrian Christians were strongly influenced by British Christian missionaries during the colonial period and joined missionary educational and medical institutions in record numbers. At that time, nursing was considered to be a low-status profession for women in Kerala (very few men went into nursing) since it challenged traditional gender norms of limited male-female interaction, as well as Hindu ideas of pollution stemming from contact with bodily fluids. However, the identification and alliance of Syrian Christians with British missionaries who promoted nursing as a "noble profession" gradually made the community more open to the idea. Still, in the colonial and early postcolonial period, largely lower-middle-class women went for nurse training to take advantage of the stipend that was provided at this time (see also George 2005). As a result, most of the older women who went into the profession, usually after a nursing diploma, and the men who married them, hailed from lower-middle-class families. As nurses came to be in big demand in the United States, Syrian Christian nurses became primary migrants from their communities and were able to sponsor family members and even friends (in the 1970s when immigration rules allowed for this possibility) and also sent remittances back to parents and relatives in Kerala. Their success prompted Kerala Christian women from a wider range of classes to turn to nursing and migrant religious networks continued to facilitate their out-migration.

A second group of early migrants to the United States between the late sixties and eighties comprised individuals (largely men) who had arrived in the United States to obtain professional or higher education and who then stayed on to work in the United States. Both groups of early migrants were able to bring over family members to the United States over time, through the family reunification provision of the 1965 Immigration Act. Beginning in the 1990s a new group of Mar Thoma immigrants arrived in the United States. These included both young men and women who had completed their education in India (some had been educated in Kerala but most had been educated outside Kerala) and had come to the United States as part of the information technology boom. There were also Syrian Christian immigrants who came to the United States after having lived in the Middle East or Africa.

To summarize, Kerala, a religiously diverse state that has had a tradition of international migration for about one hundred years, presents an excellent case study of how religion shapes out-migration, and how migration in turn reshapes religion in migrant communities. The Syrian Christian Church in Kerala is ancient and non-Western in origin. The Mar Thoma denomination has the largest out-migration rates of all Syrian Christian churches. Its denominational structure is more centralized than many of the other immigrant churches, and it emphasizes uniformity of practice in its parishes and also maintains full control over the placement of its achens in parishes around the world. Due to the East-West bridge character of the Mar Thoma, it is a denomination that maintains most of its traditional Eastern practices but also has a Western Christian legacy and consequently is "in communion" with many mainline American denominations. Preserving its traditional liturgy, rituals, and episcopal heritage, while also being open to Western influences in a postdenominational, seeker-oriented era presents a big challenge. Consequently, the Mar Thoma church represents a quintessential example of how the new paradigm of ethnicity and religion brings about religious change in traditional denominations that have been established in the United States.

The Research

This book is based on multisited research in the United States and India, including participant observation and 144 interviews, and focuses on the transnational dynamics of the Mar Thoma church. Between 1999 and 2003 and then between 2006 and 2009, I carried out field research and interviews (mostly in English but also in Malayalam as necessary) for this project in various parts of the United States. In 2015 and early 2016, I conducted some additional interviews and also did some secondary analysis of Mar Thoma websites to update the research. I started my study in 1999 by attending the Bethelville parish for one and a half years and conducting participant observation. I also interviewed thirty-four members of the congregation. Next, I attended a Mar Thoma parish in another region sporadically for six months between 2002 and 2003. As I am of Syrian Christian ancestry (from the Church of South India, which is in full communion with the Mar Thoma church), I was able to participate in and understand the Mar Thoma service. In addition, I have interview data from Mar Thoma members and achens in four more parishes in the Midwest and eastern regions conducted over the phone or with the help of a research assistant. I also attended three Mar Thoma U.S. conferences in 2001, 2007, and 2008, where I conducted interviews. Interviews conducted over the phone and at the annual conferences helped me to obtain a picture of the issues facing the Mar Thoma church on a national level. Since I worked through church contacts, the individuals I interviewed were largely drawn from members who attended services on a regular basis and were active in the church, or those who attended other churches but still maintained close relationships with Mar Thoma church members. Despite my best efforts, I was unable to talk to individuals who had stopped attending the Mar Thoma church and did not maintain connections with church members. Either I did not have their contact information or the persons I contacted were not interested in participating in the study. This is a limitation of the research, since such individuals seemed to constitute a significant proportion of Mar Thoma youth and could have provided an important perspective on the church. I noticed that two well-educated groups from both the first and the second generation tended to be underrepresented in the Mar Thoma church: those who were liberal, who usually attended nonethnic mainline churches, and those who were conservative and strongly evangelical, who usually preferred to attend nondenominational evangelical churches.

In total, this book draws on data from ninety-five interviews with first- and second-generation Mar Thoma Americans and Mar Thoma achens in the United States: forty-four with the immigrant generation,[7] and fifty-one with the second generation (including some who had come to the United States when young).[8] Twenty of the second-generation interviews were conducted by a graduate research assistant. Many were formal, taped interviews. Others were informal interviews conducted during the course of my fieldwork, which I incorporated into field notes. As there are few Mar Thoma churches in some regions of the country, with one exception (the new second-generation Mar Thoma church in Dallas), I have changed names and identifying information of individuals and parishes to protect the confidentiality of the interviewees. I have also omitted any incidents or characteristics that would make the parishes or the individuals easily identifiable.

I had conducted fieldwork for a prior project on Syrian Christian outmigration to the Middle East in a Mar Thoma–dominated rural region of Kerala, in 1990. This research provided me with a good understanding of Syrian Christian life in Kerala and the context from which Mar Thoma Christians were emigrating. To understand the functioning of the Mar Thoma church in India, I conducted three months of research in two other areas of central Travancore and in a metropolitan area in India (Bangalore) over the summer of 2006, attending worship services and interviewing lay members, as well as some achens and their wives. I conducted a total of forty-nine interviews in India in the summer of 2006, thirty-nine in Kerala and ten in Bangalore.[9] These interviews (which were largely not taped) were conducted in English or Malayalam and shed light on the similarities and differences between the functioning of Mar Thoma parishes in different contexts in India. In addition to the interviews, I also had many informal discussions with a variety of Mar Thomites in the United States and in India. I analyzed the interviews and field notes for themes, following the guidelines established by Glaser and Strauss (1967) and Strauss (1987).

This book contributes important insights to our understanding of post-1965 immigrant religiosity and its transmission to the second gen-

eration, and specifically to the profound impact that American evangelicalism is having on the religious life of recent immigrants. It also takes
a global approach to immigrant religion, examining the background to
the development of the church in India and to the migration, the impact
of migration on the home church in Kerala, and the many transnational
connections maintained with Mar Thoma groups in India and around
the world, by the laity and the clergy.

Plan of the Book

Chapter 1 presents the complex history of the Mar Thoma denomination, which is essential to understanding many of the contemporary
features of the church. As discussed above, early Syrian Christians considered themselves to be "Hindu in culture, Christian in religion, and
Oriental in worship." This chapter draws on archival and secondary
research to examine how Syrian Christians were viewed and treated very
differently by Portuguese Catholic and British Protestant missionaries
during the colonial period and how their self-understanding, practices,
and communities were fundamentally transformed by these encounters. It also examines the influence of Indian nationalism and the Indian
independence struggle on the church.

Chapter 2 provides information about the Mar Thoma church in contemporary India and its role in the lives of members. It then moves into a
detailed discussion of the migration of Mar Thoma members from Kerala
to the United States, their settlement in various parts of the country, and
their initial struggles. Issues dealing with gender relations and intergenerational relations are discussed, as well as the dilemmas and issues that
developed as Mar Thoma parishes were set up around the country. This
chapter also briefly discusses the experiences of the children growing up in
the United States at home, in school, and college, as well as in the church.

As illustrated at the beginning of this chapter, first- and second-
generation Mar Thoma Americans had very different understandings
about the meaning of being Christian. Religion and ethnicity also played
different roles in their lives. Chapter 3 focuses particularly on the intergenerational cleavages that developed due to the divergent models of
religion that the two generations espouse. The different models of religion meant that immigrants and their children had very different ideas

about the role of the church, Christian worship, and evangelism, with the result that the two groups were often at odds, both in the church and at home on the subject of religion. This chapter examines some of these differences and their implications for the Mar Thoma church.

Perhaps not surprisingly, gender norms were another source of tension. First- and second-generation Mar Thoma Americans had divergent ideas about the obligations and behavior of Christian men and women in church, and the gender norms and behavior of professionally educated immigrants also differed from those of less well-educated members. Changes in gender roles and class position as a result of migration and settlement often roused gender insecurities that were manifested within the arena of the church. Chapter 4 focuses on how three groups within the Mar Thoma church—immigrant nurses, who were often the primary income earners in their families, and their husbands; professionally educated immigrant men, who were generally the primary income earners, and their wives; and well-employed second-generation women and men influenced by American evangelicalism—performed gender and normative Christian identities in very different ways in church, leading to some tension between the groups.

Chapter 5 shows how negotiations and disagreements between generations shape the civic engagement of Mar Thoma American congregations in the United States and in India. Recent studies have demonstrated that participation in religious institutions facilitates the civic incorporation of contemporary immigrants. These studies have focused on either the immigrant generation or the second generation. In one way or another, these studies indicate that concepts of identity and of religious obligation play an important role in motivating civic participation. Not surprisingly, given the different models of religion of immigrants and their children, definitions of community and their perceived Christian obligations toward this community varied between first- and second-generation Mar Thomites. There have not yet been any studies examining how intergenerational differences in the understanding of religious and racial identity affect the civic engagement of multigenerational congregations. This is important to understand, however, since most religious institutions of contemporary immigrants are multigenerational.

There is currently little literature on how religious institutions are influenced by the international migration of its members, in other words, on how the transnationalization of a religious organization is felt and practiced on the ground. Chapter 6 examines how and why the international migration of Mar Thomites, particularly to the United States, has brought about multifaceted changes in the home church and the home communities in Kerala. Some of these impacts were due to the leadership's having to accommodate the needs of its international membership, whereas others were the unintended consequence of the church developing the infrastructure to manage and use the inflow of remittances. Yet other consequences were due to larger transformations in Kerala society caused by migration and rapid social change. The chapter also examines the theoretical and practical implications of these changes.

The Conclusion provides an overview of what the Mar Thoma case teaches us regarding the types of changes globalization is bringing about in Christian immigrant communities in the United States, and in Christian churches in the Global South. It examines the impact of transnationalism on the Mar Thoma American denomination and community, specifically, how the Kerala background of the community and the history of the church in Kerala impacts the immigrant church. It also examines how the contemporary shifts in the understanding and practice of religion and ethnicity in Western societies impact immigrant communities and churches in the United States, the incorporation of immigrants of Christian backgrounds into American society, and evangelical Christianity in America. Finally, it discusses how large-scale out-migration and the global networks facilitated by international migrants affect Christianity in the Global South. The book concludes with an overview of how religious traditions are changed through global movement.

1

Syrian Christian Encounters with Colonial Missionaries and Indian Nationalism

On May 20, 1498 the Portuguese explorer Vasco da Gama, leading an expedition of four small ships, landed in Calicut, a port city in Kerala. Although the aim of the Portuguese expedition was to discover a new sea route to spice centers in India, da Gama was also in search of Kerala Christians, whom the Portuguese had heard about (Subrahmanyam 1998). Dom Manuel, the Portuguese king who had sponsored da Gama, apparently had big plans for Christians to regain their position in the Middle East and wrest control over spice routes from Muslims, and wanted Christian allies to achieve these goals. The religious zeal of the Portuguese monarch and the welding together of commercial and religious goals meant that Portuguese explorers and traders viewed proselytization in areas where they settled to be a "governmental and national responsibility" Brown (1956, 12). Vasco da Gama met the zamorin (king) of Calicut during this trip, but it is unclear whether he actually met any Kerala Christians, since he seems to have mistaken a temple to a Hindu goddess for "primitive" Christian worship of the Virgin Mary (Subrahmanyam 1998, 131–132). By Vasco da Gama's second visit to Kerala in 1502, this time with twenty ships, Kerala Syrian Christians, locally known as Saint Thomas Christians, had heard about da Gama and his claim that his king "was one of the most . . . powerful kings of Christendom" (Schurhammer 1934, 9). Consequently they sent representatives to meet him, submitted themselves to the king of Portugal, and asked for his protection from the local Muslims and Hindus. As a token of their submission, they gave da Gama a "staff of authority . . . a red-coloured stick decorated with silver, with three silver bells on top" (Brown 1956, 13). They told him that the staff had belonged to a former Saint Thomas Christian king of Kerala.[1] The Portuguese were only too happy to take the local Christians under their charge, since all territory they conquered came under the control of the king of Portugal. This control also meant that the Portuguese expected that any Christians they encountered or converted would come under the dominion of the pope, something that the Kerala Syrian Christians did not understand when they submitted to the Portuguese (Williams 1996, 59).

In the early period, when the Portuguese were establishing themselves as an economic and political force in Kerala, the Saint Thomas Christians and the Portuguese saw themselves as Christian allies. A letter written in 1504 by some Kerala Syrian Christian bishops to their patriarch in Mesopotamia, describes the Portuguese as their Christian "brethren." This feeling was clearly not just one-sided, since the same letter describes how they were warmly welcomed by the Portuguese, given gold and beautiful vestments, and asked to celebrate mass according to Syrian Christian traditions after the Portuguese priest had finished his mass. The letter indicates that the Portuguese found the Syrian Christian religious rite "pleasing" (Schurhammer 1934, 7). Early Portuguese administrators of the two fort cities they had captured in Kerala made treaties with local monarchs that included favors for local Christians, such as rebuilding their Saint Thomas churches and restoring their ancient privileges (Brown 1956, 19).

However, religious developments in Europe soon affected the warm relationship between the Portuguese and the Saint Thomas Christians. The Reformation had begun in the early sixteenth century in Europe, and by the late 1520s the Protestants had broken away from the Catholic Church. The Counter-Reformation, or the reform of Catholicism in reaction to the Reformation, began with the Council of Trent, in 1545–1563. In 1560, the Portuguese launched the Inquisition in Goa, to the north of Kerala. The determination to eradicate heresy, which was the defining characteristic of the Council of Trent and of the Inquisition, also came to impact the Saint Thomas Christians as Portuguese missionaries and religious functionaries worked to rid the group of Hindu influences and Nestorian ideas, which they were believed to have imbibed from their East Syrian connection, and to bring them under the Church of Rome.[2]

A little over one hundred years after Vasco da Gama first landed in Kerala, the East India Company (EIC) was formed in Britain in 1600 to establish a trading base in India. However, religion and commercial interests were not intertwined with the EIC as in the case of the Portuguese traders. In fact, the view of Christian evangelicals in Britain was that the EIC was "hostile to Christian Missions" through the entire period of its history from 1600 until 1858, when it was dissolved and India came directly under the Crown (Stock 1899, 51). The only role for religion within the EIC was the appointment of chaplains to look after the spiritual needs of the employees of the East India Company in India. These chaplains were expressly instructed not to undertake missionary activity among the Indian people (Davidson 1990, 30). Apparently the Company was afraid that missionaries would alienate the natives and consequently hurt their trading prospects (Stock 1899; Buchanan 1819, 268–271).

In the meantime, England (together with Europe and North America) saw a religious revival in the eighteenth century. The Evangelical movement arose, characterized by a nondenominational, antiritualistic, gospel-oriented Christianity with an emphasis on a personal experience of Christ, inward piety, and evangelism (Bebbington 1989, 5–10; Shenk 2009). The British Evangelical view of ancient churches was diametrically different from that of the Portuguese Roman Catholics. The Evangelicals viewed as "pure and primitive" all the ancient episcopal churches that rejected the supremacy of the pope (P. Cheriyan 1935, 116). They looked back to the primitive church for guidance, since their view was that "the nearer we approach the ancient Church the better" (Stock 1899, 63). Consequently, their aim was to help to "revive" the Eastern Orthodox churches to their primitive purity and vitality, and purge them of all Roman Catholic influences. They believed that "the Greek, Armenian, Syrian, Coptic, and Abyssinian Churches, though in many points far gone from the simplicity and purity of the truth . . . possess within themselves the principle and the means of reformation" (Stock 1899, 227, citing the Church Missionary Society's Missionary Register 1829, 407). But the British Evangelicals realized that these churches did not even have printed copies of the Bible and that most people did not understand the ecclesiastical languages. Consequently, their efforts became focused on providing these ancient churches with translations of the Bible in the vernacular.

The British Evangelicals began a movement to change the charter of the EIC to establish an Anglican Church in India and to allow the church to conduct missionary work. An attempt by the evangelical forces to change the EIC charter in 1793 when it came up for renewal was defeated; William Wilberforce, the Christian leader, lamented, "all my clauses were struck out last night, and our territories in Hindostan, twenty millions of people included, are . . . committed to the providential protection, of—Brama [Brahma, a major Hindu deity]" (Stock 1899, 55). This attempt actually led the company to tighten its regulations against allowing missionaries into India (Stock 1899, 95–96). The Evangelicals of the Church of England thereupon formed the Church Missionary Society (CMS) in London in 1799. In 1812, when the charter again came up for renewal, they were finally successful, and "England prepared to pour into India the civilization, the Christianity, and the science of the West" (from *Expansion of England*, 310, quoted in Stock 1899, 104). In 1813 the British resident in Travancore, Kerala, Colonel John Munro, initiated the process to establish an Anglican seminary for Syrian Christians and in 1816 the CMS sent its first two missionaries to Kerala, Thomas Norton and Benjamin Bailey. Two more missionaries, Henry Baker and Joseph Fenn, followed in 1818. The missionaries were given strict instructions by the CMS Committee:

> [Not] to pull down the ancient Church and build another, but to remove the rubbish and repair the decaying places. The Syrians should be brought back to their own ancient and primitive worship and discipline rather than be induced to adopt the liturgy and discipline of the English Church, and should any considerations induce them to wish such a measure, it would be highly expedient to dissuade them from adopting it . . . for the preservation of their individuality and entireness, and greater consequent weight and usefulness as a Church." (cited in Stock 1899, 233)

In short, the Portuguese and the British Christians had very different understandings of Christianity, which in turn affected their interactions with the Syrian Christians in Kerala. Whereas the Portuguese "traced all the evils of the Syrians to their isolation from Rome . . . English Protestants, on the other hand, considered that if only the Roman elements which had been introduced by the Synod of Diamper could be eliminated, and the Syrian Church could return to her ancient canons, there would be a glorious exhibition of primitive purity in doctrine and worship" (Rae 1892, 283). Portuguese and British traders also differed in their views on how trade and missionary activity should be related.

Since the Portuguese traders were sponsored by the monarch, they were agents of the *padroado*. The East India Company on the other hand was a private company that was given monopoly privileges on all trade with the East and consequently viewed any actions that might interfere with its ability to make a profit to be a hindrance to its mission. Both groups of colonial missionaries would bring about profound changes in the Saint Thomas Christian church in Kerala.

Colonial Missionary Encounters and Their Impact

There is a large literature on colonial Christian missionary encounters between Western and non-Western groups, examining how these "extended conversations" shaped the self-understandings and practices of religion on both sides (Comaroff and Comaroff 1991, 1997; Keane 2007; Tomlinson 2009; Keller 2005; Robbins 2004).[3] As we will see, the two Western Christian groups encountered by Saint Thomas Syrians— the Portuguese and the British—operated with very different models of Christianity. The three Christian groups consequently disagreed with one another on what constituted the core elements of the faith that needed to be preserved. We see the workings of colonial power, as also some of the factors leading to conversion and to syncretism, or the borrowing or blending of ideas and practices from a variety of traditions, among Syrian Christians as a result of their encounters with the Portuguese and the British.

There is a vigorous debate regarding how and why the colonized adopt new religious ideas and practices. Some of this literature, especially studies that focus on group conversions, adopts a utilitarian perspective and emphasizes economic, social, or political motivations (Bayly 1989; Oddie 2000). Other literature uses Gramscian notions of hegemony or Foucauldian conceptions of micropower to discuss colonial conversion as the outcome of a process of internalizing dominant ideas, and to frame resistance and hybridity (Comaroff and Comaroff 1991, 1997; Copland 2007). As we will see, Syrian Christian conversions to various types of Christianity do not fit neatly into any of these perspectives.

Syncretism is a contentious and disputed term within the study of religion, since it either suggests that there was a "pure" essence that was then sullied, or is tautological since all religions are syncretic. Some of the literature discusses the importance of power in the study of syncretism, but even here there is a disagreement about whether syncretism is an outcome of an attempt to integrate with a dominant group or is a manifestation of resistance to assimilatory pressures (Apter 1991). Or is it antisyncretism that is an indicator of resistance and the attempt to protect religious boundaries (Shaw and Stewart 1994)? Charles Stewart (2005, 265) points out that European missionaries active during the process of colonialism used syncretism as a "term of abuse" against non-Western churches that indigenized Christianity. Both the Portuguese and the British missionaries tried to purify or purge Syrian Christianity in Kerala of what they considered to be "heretical" elements, in order to bring it back to the "true religion." In the case of the Portuguese, these elements were the "Nestorian" heresies they believed the church had imbibed from its contact with the East Syrian church, as well as the local Hindu practices that were integrated with Christianity. The British, on the other hand, considered both Roman Catholic and Hindu customs as the "rubbish" that needed to be removed to revive the ancient church.

Different lenses on Christianity can also be seen in the approaches of the various authors, religious functionaries of a variety of Christian traditions, to the early history of Syrian Christians, before the coming of the Portuguese. Many of the Roman Catholic writers view Syrian Christians as having always hewed to the Catholic Roman faith (e.g., Schurhammer 1934, 33; Podipara 1973, 108–109). Orthodox Christians, on the other hand, argue that Syrian Christians had practiced the original Orthodox faith without any Roman influence (C. V. Cheriyan 1973, 144; Verghese 1973). Anglican commentators (Geddes 1694; Hough 1839) saw the Syrian Christian church as being very similar to the early Christian church, which they themselves used as a model. Similarly, key events of colonial history are interpreted through the religious frames of the various authors. Each Syrian Christian denomination has a slightly different narrative of many of these events, presenting their own religious and social leaders in the most favorable light and casting aspersions on the actions of the leaders of rival denominations.

In this chapter, I examine Syrian Christians' understandings of Christianity and how these understandings were honed, but also readjusted, as they encountered new and powerful Christian groups, the Portuguese, and the British. I also focus on the encounter of Syrian Christians with Western evangelical doctrines which would lead the Mar Thoma group to break away and form a new Syrian Christian church, attempting to blend Orthodox and Reform elements together. Since there is no neutral perspective on the colonial and precolonial history of the Syrian Christians, I will endeavor to present this history largely from the perspective of the Mar Thoma tradition.

Syrian Christians in the Precolonial Period

The church in Kerala that traces its origins to Apostle Thomas is called the Malankara Syrian Christian church because Saint Thomas is believed to have landed in Malankara, in Kerala (Brown 1956, 52). Legend has it that he converted several Brahmin Malayali Hindus to Christianity. Although the historical evidence to support the visit of Apostle Thomas to Kerala is inconclusive, there are several local oral traditions as well as palm-leaf manuscripts in Kerala detailing the Apostle's life and work in Kerala that have been carefully preserved to the present (Frykenberg 2008, 99–101; Brown 1956, 49–51). Robert Frykenberg (2008, 245), who has examined the oral traditions of the Syrian Christians, indicates that at the time of the arrival of Westerners in Kerala, Syrian Christian lineages "claiming direct descent from Brahmin converts of the Apostle, could be recited from memory for as many as seventy or more generations." The upper-caste status of the converts is important to the identity and prestige of Syrian Christians. It is believed that Saint Thomas subsequently moved to the east coast, near present-day Chennai, and was martyred there on July 3, 72 C.E. According to the tradition, his body was moved from Mylapore, near Chennai, to be reburied in Edessa where Saint Thomas is believed to have founded a church (Moffett 1992, 46).

There is considerable evidence that Christians existed in the Kerala region in the early Christian centuries (Neill 1984, 36ff). Kerala's long western coastline and strategic position at the center of the Indian Ocean, together with its tremendous natural wealth of spices, teak, and ivory, brought traders from the Middle East as early as the third millennium B.C.E. if not earlier. There was regular trade between the Persian Empire and the coast of Kerala, and Christianity, along with Islam and an ancient Jewish community, arrived in Kerala through this route. The five old Syrian crosses with inscriptions in Pahlavi (ancient Persian) that can still be seen in south India (four in Kerala and one near Chennai) provide evidence of the Middle Eastern provenance of early south Indian Christianity (Williams 1996, 55).

The arrival of other Christian groups from the Middle East in Kerala in the early decades of the Christian era, through maritime trading routes, strengthened the early Saint Thomas Christian community (Neill 1984). Kerala sources provide accounts of a migration of East Syrian Christians to northern Kerala in 345 C.E. led by a merchant, Thomas of Cana. According to the traditional account, the Metropolitan of Edessa had a dream about the difficulties experienced by the Christians in Kerala and sent Thomas with four hundred East Syrian Christians to help. Thomas and the others landed at the Kerala port Cranganore, and the ruler of the region is believed to have welcomed them and given them gifts of land and also bestowed social honors on them so that they had a social status equal to the Brahmin Christian converts who were already in Kerala at the time. These gifts were documented on copper plates. The original copper plates apparently disappeared "mysteriously" shortly after being shown to Alexis de Menezes, the Portuguese archbishop of Goa in 1599. However, copies of these plates have survived (Frykenberg 2008, 108).

The early Malankara Syrian Christians were known as Nazranis or Saint Thomas Christians. The East Syrian Patriarch in Persia periodically sent them bishops, whom they revered highly and honored as saints. In practice, however, it was the local archdeacons who were the "social and political leaders" of the community (C. V. Cheriyan 1973, 138). The Nazranis used the Eastern Syrian liturgy in Syriac, a dialect of Aramaic. Since Aramaic was the native language of Jesus it was viewed as a "divine" language, and the Syriac liturgy was a source of great pride to the Saint Thomas Christians. Their Syriac liturgy may also have been a means of retaining a distinctive identity in a society where each of the major religious communities (Hindu, Muslim, Jewish, and Christian) had their own "sacred language" (Neill 1984, 38).

In the early centuries of the Christian era, the Christians increased in numbers through conversion and fresh migration. They were a prosperous group, and foreign trade was almost entirely in their hands. Historian Susan Bayly (1989, 249) also describes them as being an "elite warrior group." In addition to the honors bestowed on the community in the fourth century, Kerala rulers conferred several high privileges on them in the eighth and ninth centuries as well, in return for economic and political support provided by the Christians (Ayyar 1926, 53; Narayan 1972, x). Five copper plates inscribed with these privileges are still preserved in the Mar Thoma institutions in Kottayam and Tiruvalla in Kerala (Juhanon Mar Thoma 1968, 100).

The Anglican bishop Leslie Brown, who lived in Kerala for around fourteen years in the early decades of the twentieth century and became principal of the ecumenical Kerala United Theological Seminary, has written a detailed account of the Saint Thomas Christians and describes them as a group that "lived in two worlds at the same time, but with no consciousness of tension between them or disharmony within themselves. They were Christians of Mesopotamia in faith and worship and ethic; they were Indians in all else" (Brown 1956, 3–4). In the highly caste-stratified society of ancient Kerala, valued new groups were incorporated into the society by being accorded an honored position within the caste system. Even Christians and Muslims were assimilated into the system as quasi-castes. Susan Bayly (1989, 250–251) gives several examples of the way in which the Nazranis were integrated "within the wider 'Hindu' society of the region—the term 'integration' being used here to convey a position of high status and acceptance within the region's most prestigious social and religious institutions." She points out that many of the Christian churches were endowed and protected by Hindu kings. Christian churches looked just like Hindu temples except that they had a cross on the roof. Nazrani rituals and rites in this period were very similar to those of Nayars, a high-caste group, ranking just below the Brahmins. Nazranis dressed like Nayars, except that they added some praying beads or a cross to a ribbon on their heads (Gouvea [1606] 2003, 250), their houses were built like the Nayar houses, and they practiced many of the life cycle rituals and ceremonials of the Nayars. Like the Hindus, the Malankara Syrian Christians had hereditary priests (following a line of descent from maternal uncle to nephew like the Nayars). Consequently, they were "accorded the same position [as Nayars] within the region's elaborate gradations of caste rank and ritual purity" (Bayly 1989, 251). In several respects however, they had more privileges than the Nayars (Ayyar 1926, 55). For instance, Pothan (1963, 34) points out that the copper plates show that the Nazranis were given several princely privileges that included "the right to carry the curved sword, the right of proclamation, the privilege of forerunners, the litter, the royal umbrella, the ceremonial drum, the gateway with seats and ornamental arches." Again, the touch of a Nazrani was believed to purify articles defiled by the touch or approach of lower-caste people. Consequently local kings had Nazranis living near them to benefit from this service (Podipara 1971, 83). Susan Bayly (1989, 252) argues that it was by their punctilious observance of the Hindu rules of caste and untouchability that Saint Thomas Christians were granted high status in society, including "one of the most critical signs of ritual status within the society, the right of access to Hindu temples and sacred precincts." Not only did Nazrani Christians have the right of access to temples, but they were also important temple donors and sponsors of temples and temple festivals (Bayly 1989, 253).

At the same time, it is clear that Nazranis had a strong Christian identity and greatly valued their venerable apostolic tradition, sacred language, beautiful Syriac liturgy, and their Chaldean patriarch (Williams 1996, 59). Antony de Gouvea, a Portuguese monk who wrote a detailed account of how archbishop Menezes brought the Malankara Syrian Christian church under Roman Catholicism, printed the Nazrani Christian liturgy in 1606, "corrected" of its "Nestorian heresies" by Menezes. Based on an analysis, Bishop Leslie Brown identifies it as the East Syrian liturgy of the apostles Addai and Mari (Addai is believed to be a disciple of Saint Thomas and Mari was Addai's disciple), indicating that the Nazranis had been able to maintain it uncorrupted for many centuries (Brown 1956, 281). The Nazranis also abhorred image worship as idolatry (this was to become a point of dispute with the Portuguese Catholics), a characteristic of the East Syrian church that distinguished them from Hindu groups. Even though they practiced many of the same customs as other Hindu groups, they often had a different, Christianized interpretation of these customs (Gillman and Klimkeit 1999, 178–179). Gouvea ([1606] 2003, lxxxi) describes the Syrian Christians as the Portuguese found them: "although not well instructed for want of clear guidance and true doctrine, nevertheless they adored Christ Our Lord and venerated his Very Holy Cross. They called themselves Christians and believed perfectly in the Mystery of the Very Holy Trinity, the basis of the whole Christian Religion." Similarly, Francis Roz, S. J., the first Portuguese bishop in Kerala attested in a letter written in 1601, "These Christians are certainly the oldest in the Orient . . . although they have lived among the heathens, Jews, and Maumethans [Muslims], *they have till this time always stood very firm in the faith*" (cited in Podipara 1971,112, italics from Podipara).

Encounters with Portuguese Missionaries
Early Period

By the time of Vasco da Gama's landing, Syrian Christians had lost control of the spice trade (except pepper, which they still traded) on the Kerala coasts to the Muslims. When Portuguese traders arrived in Kerala in the early decades of the sixteenth century they established forts in two cities, Cochin and Cannanore. However, they were under constant threat of attack from Muslims in Calicut, the port city where Vasco da Gama had landed. Consequently they were interested in making local alliances and Christians seemed to be the obvious choice. Besides their common religious heritage, high status, and relative prosperity, Syrian Christian men were excellent marksmen. Gouvea (1606) writes that the monarch of Cochin had an army comprising fifty thousand Christian gunmen, trained so well that "they rarely miss" (cited in Brown 1956, 15). The Saint Thomas Christians had their own reasons to desire such an alliance, since they wanted to protect their trade and strengthen their position to make sure that the Kerala kings continued to uphold their ancient rights.

A letter from Mar Jacob, an East Syrian bishop working in Kerala, written to the Portuguese king in 1523, translated from the Portuguese and published by Jesuit scholar George Schurhammer (1934), makes the interests and concerns of both sides clear. Mar Jacob blames local Muslim traders for turning Kerala Christians against the Portuguese, but writes that he had taken Kerala Christian leaders many times to meet the Portuguese in their fort at Cochin, "until I had brought them [the Kerala Christians] to love thee, and then they agreed and swore to me, never more to sell the pepper to the Moors [Muslims] and to bring it clean and dry to thy factory. . . . And further I have won all these Christians of this country for thy service, so that when thou shalt be in need of them, thou shalt find in it over 25,000 warriors" (Schurhammer 1934, 11–13). In return for securing the allegiance of the Kerala Christians to the Portuguese king, Mar Jacob wanted the king to ask the Portuguese viceroy in India to see that land that had been granted to Christians as part of the copper plate charters (which had been usurped by local kings) was returned. "Only I ask thee, order that this land be restored to us, and to thy Viceroy, that he favour and guard us" (Schurhammer 1934, 14).

Some of the Portuguese missionaries of this period treated the Saint Thomas Christians as heretics in the belief that they had adopted the Nestorian doctrines of the Chaldean church. Due to the relative isolation of the Saint Thomas Christians, however, they seem to have been somewhat insulated from the theological disputes and controversies that affected churches in the Middle East in the fourth and fifth centuries, although some of their texts and hymns contained elements that were viewed as heretical (Williams 1996, 61). There were also other differences between the Latin Church and the Saint Thomas Syrian church that led to tensions between the two groups. The Saint Thomas church did not worship Mary as the mother of God. Their only sacraments were Baptism, Ordination, and the Eucharist (the Catholic Church had seven sacraments). They did not practice confession and were strongly averse to it. Unlike in the Catholic Church, the Saint Thomas priests were married and the wives of priests were honored and highly regarded. It was only the bishops who remained celibate (Gouvea 2003, 237). Priests received their income from fees and gifts from performing religious services—there was no concept of a "salary" or other steady income for them from the church. Consequently, the Portuguese accused the Syrians of "simony." The Syrians celebrated many holy days for the apostles and their East Syrian bishops (Gouvea 2003, 241). Again, unlike the Latins, the Saint Thomas church rejected the use of images, viewing it as Hindu idolatry. Gouvea (2003, 190) mentions that in the early days of the Portuguese, when an image of the Virgin was shown to the Saint Thomas Christians they closed their eyes, "saying he should remove that dirt, that they were Christians and did not adore idols nor temples, from where they felt came all the images." Although a bishop from Syria exercised spiritual authority, the main local power in the church was held by an archdeacon. The Portuguese did not approve of this structure (Williams 1996, 62–63).

With Mar Jacob's death, relationships between Portuguese and the Saint Thomas Christians in the Serra (the Portuguese term for the territory of the Saint Thomas Christians) changed (Neill 1984, 200). The Portuguese bishop of Goa was now considered to be the bishop of all of India (including Kerala), and the Portuguese passed an order forbidding any priest from Syria to come to India without their express permission. Some bishops tried to dress as sailors in order to get into India but they were not allowed in (Gouvea 2003, 49). Once the Portuguese had gained control over the southwestern coast of India, Jesuit missionaries such as Saint Francis Xavier arrived. They were primarily successful in converting many fisher folk communities and other lower-caste groups who suffered under the disabilities of the Hindu caste system. A Latin diocese was established in Cochin, Kerala, in 1558 (Williams 1996, 61). These Christian converts were called Latin Catholics. The Portuguese now wanted to bring the Saint Thomas Christians also under Portuguese *padroado*, and thereby under Rome, which the Saint Thomas Christians resisted. Gouvea comments several times on how attached the Saint Thomas Christians were to the "schismatic Patriarch of Babylonia" (e.g., 2003, 241) and to their customs and practices. Another reason for the resistance of the Saint Thomas Christians to coming under Rome was that they did not want to be lumped together with the lower-caste Latin Catholic converts.

In the meantime, the Portuguese had established a Roman Catholic seminary in Kerala. The Saint Thomas Christians were willing to let their sons study in the seminary but the newly ordained priests were not allowed to conduct services in the Saint Thomas churches. As a result they only worked in Latin churches. Even after the Roman Catholics allowed them to learn Syriac and to perform the Roman Catholic rite in that language, Gouvea (2003, 32) reports that the newly ordained priests did not "dare" to go against their traditions or their bishop. In 1595, a zealous thirty-five-year-old Portuguese Augustinian missionary, Alexis de Menezes, was appointed archbishop of Goa (Neill 1984, 208). The *Jornada* of Gouvea (1606), based on eyewitness accounts and journals (translated by Pius Malekandathil [2003] into English with extensive comments and notes) provides the primary account of how the Saint

Thomas Christians were brought under the church of Rome by Menezes. Although Gouvea was a fellow Augustinian and wrote his book to
"eulogize" the work of Menezes (Malekandathil 2003, lxi), it still gives
us a good idea of how the Syrians resisted the pressures to Latinize at
every step, as well as some of their perspectives on their Saint Thomas
Christian faith.

In 1597, on the death of Mar Abraham, the last East Syrian bishop to
be allowed into India, Menezes appointed Portuguese Jesuit missionary
Francis Roz as the bishop of the Serra. Before he died, however, Mar
Abraham had appointed a Kerala Christian man, his archdeacon George,
as the Vicar-General of the Serra, and many Saint Thomas Christian
churches were loyal to him. Archdeacon George took a stand against
Menezes, saying that he would not profess the Roman Catholic faith or
recognize the Church of Rome. The Saint Thomas Christians convened
a synod where they swore that they would not give up their traditions,
"nor would they allow the destruction of the law of Saint Thomas [their
religious practices] . . . nor would they receive any Prelate who did not
come by the order of their Patriarch of Babylonia, whence always the
Bishops had come to them. All of them offered to defend these with their
lives and estates" (Gouvea 2003, 57). The Saint Thomas Christians also
stopped allowing Catholic priests to visit and preach in their churches.
Archbishop Menezes kept trying to force archdeacon George to profess
the Roman Catholic faith, but the latter eluded him as long as he could.
George was finally forced to make a confession before a group of Roman
Catholics in a church. But the confession was in Portuguese, which archdeacon George did not understand. He went back and told his people
that he had agreed that the pope was the head of the church, but that
he meant the church of Saint Peter, not the church of Saint Thomas. He
had also agreed that archbishop Menezes was the prelate of India and of
the Latins of the Serra, but not of the Saint Thomas Christians, who had
their own (East Syrian) prelate (Gouvea 2003, 65).

Hearing how the archdeacon had twisted the confession, archbishop
Menezes went in person to the Serra on February 1, 1599, and sent word
to the archdeacon to come and meet him in Cochin, assuring him that
he would not be arrested. The archdeacon feared that "if he did not go,
the Christians of Saint Thomas would lose entirely the trade with the
Portuguese and the dealings with the Pepper Kingdom [the native king-

dom where the pepper was produced] . . . and in addition the kings and his friends would disfavour them" (Gouvea 2003, 122). So he went reluctantly to meet the archbishop, taking with him as precaution two skilled warriors as personal guards and an additional three thousand armed men (Brown 1956, 28).

That meeting was uneventful, but subsequently Menezes discovered that the priests who were being trained in the Jesuit seminary in Kerala continued to pray in public (in Syriac) for their Babylonian patriarch, calling him the "universal pastor of the Catholic Church" (Gouvea 2003, 123). This upset him greatly. So he called all the priests and the archdeacon and read out an excommunication notice ordering that no one should even mention the Babylonian patriarch in any prayers or rituals. Gouvea (2003, 124) writes that the archdeacon "felt this very much, and . . . almost lost his colors" when Menezes read out the notice. The archdeacon and the priests left and on arriving at the archdeacon's house, "all raised their voice and began to make a big and pitiful cry," at which everyone in the area gathered with their weapons outside the house (Gouvea 2003, 124). On hearing that the *cassanars* (priests) were crying since they saw the Portuguese "removing the law of Saint Thomas in which they been brought up" and that furthermore the Portuguese were insulting their patriarchs "who were governing them for more than one thousand and two hundred years," the people were ready to fight the Portuguese to avenge the archdeacon. But he asked them to be patient, and said that he was forced to sign since he was surrounded by Portuguese and was afraid of being arrested by them (Gouvea 2003, 124). He also pointed out that the king of Cochin was on friendly terms with the Portuguese, which meant that the Saint Thomas Christians would be risking their lives and property if they objected. Archdeacon George told the gathering that "he would die for the law of Saint Thomas" and would not allow the law of Saint Peter to be introduced in the Serra. He said that the Portuguese could live under the law of Saint Peter but that the Saint Thomas Christians would continue to live under the law of Saint Thomas. The people gathered there also vowed not to come under the law of Saint Peter or the patriarch of Rome (Gouvea 2003, 125–126).

Gouvea (2003, 125–126) writes that Menezes spent a long time explaining the Roman Catholic teachings to the Saint Thomas Christian priests of the college and also gave them some beautiful gifts, and managed to win them over to his side. Later, he continued his preaching in another town in Kerala, where he spoke against the concept that there were two laws—that of Saint Peter and of Saint Thomas—and emphasized instead that there was only one law of Christ, that of the Roman Catholic church (Gouvea 2003, 130). The crowd listened quietly but when the archbishop asked them to come to be confirmed, they got up, arms in hand, saying "that they would not allow the Confirmation, because their Bishops never did so . . . nor was that Sacrament instituted by Christ, but his [the archbishop's] invention, with which he wanted to make them captives, and vassals of the Portuguese by putting the seal of Portuguese [the sign of the cross] in their forehead" (Gouvea 2003, 130). Translator Malekandathil (2003, n. 124, 130–131) notes that the Saint Thomas Christians, along with the local kings and others in Kerala, first saw the confirmation as a ritual invented by the Portuguese to bring them under Portuguese control.

Archbishop Menezes challenged the angry Syrian Christians to kill him and said that he was willing to die for the sake of the truth, but no one moved. Realizing that his life was in danger, Menezes slept in a row boat that night protected by his people (this became a regular practice while on this trip). Gouvea (2003) repeatedly writes about how the archbishop "dissimulated" with the Syrians and told his people to similarly dissimulate—to get what they wanted at the end. He also writes that the Saint Thomas Christians believed that the archbishop was jealous of the love they had for their patriarch and that he was trying to turn people away from Babylon since his patriarch (the pope) was in competition with the patriarch of Babylon. Finally the archbishop was forced to respond, saying that it was not about competition but about the "pure truths of the Catholic faith," without which there was no salvation (Gouvea 2003, 138).

Realizing that the only way to persuade the Saint Thomas Christians was by going through archdeacon George, Menezes wrote to him again, this time a letter "full of much love" (Gouvea 2003, 141) promising that he did not want to do him any harm, but only wished to preach to them about the truths of the Catholic faith. The archdeacon yielded and the two met. Menezes brought up John's gospel, "The Word was made flesh and lived among us," and told George that the Babylonian patriarch challenged the gospel, since he said that God did not become man. Bypassing Menezes's reference to Nestorianism, the archdeacon replied, "Your Lordship is trying to persuade us that we cannot be saved without rendering obedience to the Pope of Rome, and this was not said by St. John, and we have a letter from St. Cayo who was also Pope of Rome and saint, in which he says and confesses that the Church of Babylonia has nothing to do with that of Rome, nor does it owe it obedience" (Gouvea 2003, 143). Finally archdeacon George and archbishop Menezes came to an agreement that these issues of theology would be discussed in more detail at a synod, and called a truce in the meantime. The archdeacon asked Menezes to stop trying to convert Syrians to Roman Catholicism and said that in return the Syrian Christians would cease their hostility and Menezes would be received as a bishop and as their guest, but not as their prelate (Gouvea 2003, 144).

But Menezes went to Diamper and ordained a large number of priests there (without charging them a fee, as the Syrian bishops did), with the goal of having his own supporters before the synod (Gouvea 2003, 158). On hearing of this, the archdeacon became angry because Menezes had gone against his promise of not exercising his jurisdiction before the synod had been held. Archdeacon George told Menezes that if he wanted to ordain priests, he should do so among the "Latins" and not the Syrians. Menezes replied that he wanted to remove this schism between the Latins and the Syrians and bring them both under Roman Catholicism and the pope (Gouvea 2003, 159). Realizing that Menezes would be able to bring over lots of supporters (priests and their relatives) through his free ordinations, archdeacon George sent out a notice indicating that anyone who received such an ordination would be excommunicated from the Saint Thomas Christian community. He also said that the Syrians should not allow Menezes into their churches to give a sermon or conduct any confirmations (Gouvea 2003, 161). Archdeacon George also got the kings and Nayars to support him. In addition, he contacted the "Pepper Queen" (the queen of the land where pepper was grown) and she issued an edict asking Menezes to leave her territory and to stop making her Christians the vassals of the Portuguese. Menezes replied, however, that he did not want to meddle with temporal issues and was only concerned with spiritual matters. He also emphasized to the queen that the Portuguese were powerful and that it was unwise to make them her enemies. Finally he also sent the queen's advisors several "heavy bribes" (Gouvea 2003, 178). The queen yielded to this pressure and withdrew her complaint (Gouvea 2003, 178–179). Menezes also dealt with the king of Cochin (who had been supportive of the Syrians) in a similar manner and the king's representative had to change his position and tell the Syrians to obey the archbishop (Gouvea 2003, 200–207). According to Leslie Brown (1956, 27), the local Kerala rulers were afraid of the Portuguese, since they were known to attack kingdoms in India which opposed their interests.

Menezes spent the Holy Week of 1599 in Kerala, conducting services with majesty and pomp, with the use of holy oils (which the Syrians knew about from the Bible but had not been using in their services). Consequently, the Saint Thomas Christians started feeling that the rituals of the Roman Catholics were better than theirs (Gouvea 2003, 181). Gouvea (2003, 181) writes about how Menezes conducted the ritual of the washing of the feet of the *cassanars* on Maundy Thursday, "kissing them and cleaning them with many gestures of humility, devotion, and tears," and the *cassanars* marveled at such a great person washing their feet. Gouvea (2003, 184) indicates that Menezes so impressed the *cassanars* that they began to say that it was the archdeacon who was preaching falsehood and that the elaborate rituals showed that the Roman Catholic Church was pure and holy and that they should go to Menezes and ask forgiveness and submit themselves to him. After the services during the Holy Week, a group of *cassanars* went to Menezes and said they renounced their errors and their patriarch and wanted to come under the Roman Catholic Church and the pope (Gouvea 2003, 186). Menezes was delighted to see that his efforts were finally yielding results. He was loving and tender with them and talked to them about his clashes with archdeacon George and his plan to appoint another person as archdeacon. The *cassanars* asked for twenty days to go and talk with the archdeacon to try to persuade him to renounce his errors and come under the Roman Catholic Church, which Menezes granted them (Gouvea 2003, 189).

Realizing that the tide had turned in his favor, Menezes wrote a strongly worded letter to the archdeacon, threatening to give an account, on Judgment Day, of how the archdeacon's work had condemned so many souls. The archdeacon felt threatened, wondering if Menezes was prognosticating his imminent death. He sent a reply saying that he had realized his error and now wanted to meet with him and come under the Roman Catholic Church (Gouvea 2003, 211–213). Menezes sent a stern reply listing ten conditions for the archdeacon and giving him twenty days to come and meet him, saying that if the archdeacon had an issue with even one of them he should not come. The ten conditions were that the archdeacon should 1) abjure errors of Nestorius; 2) confess that there was only one Christian law; 3) subscribe to and make the Roman confession of faith; 4) deliver all the books of the dioceses to be amended or burned; 5) swear obedience to the pope; 6) curse the patriarch of Babylon; 7) not receive any bishop except one sent by the pope; 8) acknowledge Menezes as the true prelate of India; 9) bear the cost of the synod and attend it himself; and 10) accompany the archbishop wherever he went without any personal guards (Gouvea 2003, 214–215).

Not wanting to meet these onerous conditions, the archdeacon tried to stall, saying that he could not come within twenty days since his king needed him. But Menezes sent a messenger to the king and asked him to release the archdeacon. He also complained to the king about the archdeacon and threatened to take the matter to the Portuguese. The king feared that his interests would be affected and asked the archdeacon to go and make the confession. So archdeacon George was forced to go and meet Menezes and confess that he was a sinner and ask for pardon. Menezes asked him to make a public confession of the Roman Catholic faith. The archdeacon said that if he made a public confession of the Roman Catholic faith, the Saint Thomas Christians would revolt, so he said he would do it privately, which he did, and also signed a document with the confession and the ten conditions (Gouvea 2003, 219–227).

Menezes continued his ministry, including baptizing a lot of children, without taking money. He also gave charity to the poor and infirm, apparently something the Saint Thomas Christian bishops were not in the habit of doing. All this earned him the goodwill of the people and more supporters. Gouvea (2003, 190) indicates that many Saint Thomas Christians now accepted an image of the Virgin Mary for their churches. Menezes started planning for the synod and was able to have it situated in Diamper, a place where he had a lot of supporters. He went about winning more supporters by organizing another large ordination (fifty men), showing attentiveness and concern, and showering people with valuable gifts (Gouvea 2003, 228–236).

The Synod of Diamper

A large and solemn gathering took place in the church at Diamper, near Cochin, from June 20 to 26, 1599. On the first day, over eight hundred Saint Thomas Christians came up to make the profession of the Roman Catholic faith. Menezes told the gathering that the others that did not attend should also make the profession and that no one could become ordained without doing so. There was some fighting outside on the first day and when Menezes inquired, he was told that since the Syrian Christians had come under the pope and the Portuguese, the king of Portugal should take them under his protection and relieve them of the taxes and other burdens imposed upon them by the local kings, particularly a very burdensome inheritance tax on the Christians, "invented by the King of Cochin, which other kings were already initiating, of claiming a share of the estate of the Christians on the death of the parents . . . on whose authority he used to deprive them of almost the entire estate which was left" (Gouvea 2003, 267). Menezes asked the synod to continue, promising to deal with the matter. On the second day, Menezes called the Portuguese Captain of Cochin and declared that all the Catholic Christians of Saint Thomas now came under the pope and the protection of the king of Portugal except for the secular obligations that they owed their local kings (Gouvea 2003, 269). This was to satisfy both the Saint Thomas Christians and the local kings who, according to Gouvea (2003, 269), had spies in the gathering. Gouvea (2003, 275–276) writes that a group entered the church intending to declare that they wanted to keep their law of Saint Thomas and their patriarch but they were so overwhelmed by the pomp and grandeur of the setting, the vestments of the archbishop, his mitre and crosier, and the large number of people in attendance that they did not speak up. According to Gouvea (2003, 275), archbishop Menezes was able to win people over in the first few days of the synod by conferring on them honors and privileges, and by promises of what they would get in heaven.

Gouvea (2003) does not present the actual decrees of the synod but only offers a discussion of the events of each day. The first English translation of the decrees of the Synod of Diamper was published by Michael Geddes, a Scottish clergyman of the Church of England in 1694 in a book on the impact of the Portuguese on the Saint Thomas Christians.[4] The decrees show that Menezes got the Syrians to swear to follow all the creeds of the Roman Church, celebrate its seven sacraments, swear allegiance to the Roman church, condemn and anathematize the Patriarch of Babylon, and reject the argument that there is a separate Law of Saint Thomas and another Law of Saint Peter (Geddes 1694, 114–116). Anyone writing, or speaking against the Church of Rome was to be reported to the bishop and punished. However, recognizing the strong attachment to Syriac, the Syrians were not forced to give up their sacred language. Instead, the synod gave them an approved Syro-Malabar liturgy. This liturgy also allowed the Syrians to separate themselves from lower-caste converts who had a Latin liturgy (Bayly 1989, 268).

One of the actions that Menezes took was to require priests who were bigamously married, or married to widows, and those who were married after the council in Goa (which had ruled that priests could not get married) to separate from their wives on pain of excommunication. He permitted older priests who had married one woman to remain married but they could not perform sacraments and their women had to give up their "badge of honor," the cross around their necks which signified that they were the wives of priests (Gouvea 2003, 279–280).

Menezes also brought about changes in the inheritance and adoption laws of the Saint Thomas Christians, forbade them to pierce their ears or wear ear jewelry so the Christians could be more easily distinguished from the Nayars, and forbade their practice of other "barbarous" local customs (Gouvea 2003, 282). Gouvea (2003, 282) writes that the one custom that archbishop Menezes was not able to change was the ban against touching lower castes, or the requirement of having to wash themselves if they touched the lower castes, that the Saint Thomas Christians observed. Menezes pointed out to the Saint Thomas Christians that the practice was a superstition but he also recognized that it was necessary for their social and economic survival, "because on the moment that they violate this style they will not be able to communicate with the Nairs [Nayars], nor to enter into the homes of the kings, nor to sell and to purchase, nor to have dealings and trade of any sort, nor will they be able to live comfortably, nor will they be allowed to continue to enjoy the honours they hold . . . for the above reasons it was not possible to solve the problem, which the archbishop felt very much" (Gouveau 2003, 283). Menezes told the Syrians that where none of this was at stake they should not observe untouchability.[5]

Decree XIV of the synod provided a long list of Syrian books to be burned and also corrected "errors" in other Syrian books and texts (Geddes 1694, 154–167). The listing shows a range of books with a variety of theological positions (including a book that indicated that there were three different faiths, the Nestorian, Jacobite, and Roman, that the Nestorian was the true faith that was taught by the apostle, and that the Roman faith was false and heretical [Geddes 1694, 157]). Paul Verghese (1973) indicates that the confused jumble of Syrian documents was probably collected over a long period of time, between the early centuries of the Christian church and up to the period between the first visit of Vasco da Gama and the synod, and that they reflect schisms and rivalries in Syria and their periodic tensions with Rome, with different groups (including West Syrians who were not clearly differentiated from the East Syrians in the early period) sending material to India. The synod ended with the burning of the Syrian documents considered heretical, while the gathering processed around the church a few times (Gouvea 2003, 288–289).

Jornada translator Malekandathil (2003, 260, note 201) challenges Gouvea's (1606) presentation of the synod, which seems to indicate that there was some discussion and that the views of the participants were incorporated into the decrees of the synod. Malekandathil (2003) cites the 1603 letter of Portuguese Bishop Francis Roz to the Jesuit General which indicated that the canons were read out in Portuguese which the Syrians listened to, without comprehension. Roz also wrote that Menezes added some canons after the synod was over (see also Neill 1984, 219).

After the synod, archbishop Menezes visited all the Syrian churches to make sure that the changes made by the synod were being implemented. He baptized, confirmed, and ordained large numbers, and absolved a lot of those who had been excommunicated. He also prayed for the sick and gave many gifts to children. People lined up, first men, and then women, to kneel and kiss his hand according to the traditional custom of Syrian Christians. Menezes also visited the local kings, gave them lavish gifts and then asked them to issue "*olas*" (edicts) in favor of the Syrian Christian churches (Gouvea 2003, 293–301). Commenting on

the synod, Stephen Neill, CMS Anglican Bishop from Scotland and author of the two-volume magnum opus, *A History of Christianity in India*,
writes, "Menezes believed that he had brought peace, order and unity to
the ancient church. But force has a way of rebounding on itself. What he
had actually done was to sow the seeds of dissensions and divisions—
divisions which up to the time of writing have not been healed" (Neill
1984, 219).

These dissensions were soon to manifest themselves. Many Syrians,
particularly the priests, resented the way they were tricked and forced
to abandon their cherished traditions and their Patriarch as well as their
local autonomy. They also disliked the control of the Portuguese bishop
and the loss of power of their archdeacon, to whom they continued to
remain loyal. They particularly objected to the authoritarian ways of the
Jesuit priests (Brown 1956, 99). Archdeacon George wrote to the papal
legate in Lisbon criticizing the actions of the Jesuits in the Serra and
asking that the next archbishop not be a Jesuit. When that yielded no
results, he also wrote to the king of Spain and Portugal, accusing the
Jesuits among other things, of not paying the *cattanars* (priests, referred
to as *cassanars* by Gouvea) their due (Neill 1984, 314). A letter from Fenicio S.J., a close associate to bishop Roz, makes it clear that the *cattanars*
also objected to the Jesuit policies. Fenicio writes, "The Thomas priests
do not want the Jesuits in their parishes . . . they have sworn they will
never again submit to a Jesuit bishop. . . . Let the most important matters
be still in the archbishop's hands, the rest in the archdeacon's" (cited in
Podipara 1971, 149).

Tensions between the Syrian Christians and the Portuguese came to
a head under archbishop Francis Garcia, S. J. who took office in 1633.
Thomas, nephew of archdeacon George was appointed archdeacon and
succeeded in 1640 when the latter died (Neill 1984, 314). Archdeacon
Thomas first sent a petition to Goa, signed by local kings and by the Syr-
ian Christians, protesting the actions of archbishop Garcia (Brown 1956,
99). Not receiving a satisfactory response, Thomas finally wrote to the
East Syrian and West Syrian patriarchs as well as the Coptic patriarch in
Alexandria asking them to send a bishop to the Serra (Brown 1956, 99;
Neill 1984, 316). In 1652, a Syrian bishop, Ahatallah, managed to bypass
the traps of the Portuguese by landing in Surat, a port in northwestern
India. He then made his way to Mylapore in Madras (current day Chen-

nai) on the southeastern coast of India (Neill 1984, 316–317). However, bishop Ahatallah was soon captured there by the Portuguese and sent to Goa to face interrogation by the Inquisition. En route to Goa, the ship docked in Cochin. Hearing of the arrival of the ship carrying bishop Ahatallah in Cochin, archdeacon Thomas and several thousand Syrian Christians came to the Cochin port to receive the bishop. Fearing a riot, the Portuguese hurriedly sent the ship to Goa. A rumor circulated that the bishop had drowned and the simmering discontent of the Syrians burst into an open revolt. On January 3, 1653 several thousand Syrians gathered at a church in nearby Mattancheri with an old Persian stone cross. Since they could not all touch the cross at the same time, they held onto ropes tied to the cross (the Coonen or Crooked Cross since the cross is said to have bent a little under the weight) in the courtyard and took an oath to sever their allegiance with the Jesuit missionaries and to remain under archdeacon Thomas until the Syrian Patriarch had sent them another bishop (Brown 1956, 100).

Hearing of this event, the pope sent Discalced Carmelite (a Catholic mendicant order) missionaries to Kerala who worked to placate the Syrians, with the political and economic support of local kings. Eventually most of those who had revolted (84 out of 116 congregations) agreed to continue under the Roman fold using their East Syrian liturgy with a Syrian Christian bishop, Chandy, cousin of archdeacon Thomas. At his consecration, Chandy was made to excommunicate his cousin Thomas (Brown 1956; Neill 1984). The 32 congregations that wanted to remain independent consecrated archdeacon Thomas as interim bishop (twelve of the *cattanars* laid their hands on him, following an ancient custom of the Eastern Orthodox Church of Alexandria when a bishop was not available to conduct an ordination) and appealed to the Eastern Church to send a bishop (Neill 1984, 320). In 1663, the Dutch captured the Kerala port of Cochin from the Portuguese, ending Portuguese control of Kerala. Since the Dutch were Protestants, this paved the way for non-Catholic bishops to reach Kerala. In 1665, Mar Gregorios, a West Syrian bishop who was under the Syrian Orthodox Jacobite Patriarch of Antioch arrived, so the breakaway group of Syrians came under the West Syrian (Syrian Orthodox) church. Archdeacon Thomas is believed to have been reconsecrated by Mar Gregorios as Mar Thoma I in 1665 (Juhanon 1968, 107).[6]

To summarize, the Saint Thomas Christians were respected and well-integrated in the largely Hindu society of Kerala. Their high caste status and honored position within Kerala society was symbolized by their participation in temple and purification rituals. They took pride in their venerable apostolic heritage, their traditional practices, their sacred language of Syriac, their ancient and long-standing connection to the Syrian Patriarch, and their local autonomy. Their ethnic identity as a distinct and unique Christian group began to develop under the Portuguese. The rationale for their identity formation was that they were a different type of Christian group—Syrian or Saint Thomas Christian. They considered themselves to be "Hindu [Indian] in culture, Christian in religion and Oriental in worship" (Podipara 1973, 107). Consequently they resisted pressures to Latinize and be subjugated to the Church of Rome. The Latinization of the Kerala church was finally accomplished through a combination of force and fraud by the archbishop Menezes of Goa through the Synod of Diamper in 1599. Under the decrees of the Synod, the Kerala church was brought under the Roman church, a revised Syro-Malabar liturgy which omitted the parts deemed heretical and included other elements translated from the Latin liturgy was introduced along with other Western Christian doctrines and practices, and many of the books of the old church were burned. Jesuit priests in Kerala were entrusted with the work of carrying out the decrees of Diamper. But the intransigence of the Jesuits and their lack of respect for the tradition of autonomy and the status of the archdeacon among the Syrian Christians roused great discontent and led to the Coonen Cross rebellion. Carmelite missionaries sent by the pope together with economic and political inducements eventually brought back most of the rebel groups under the pope with a Syrian Christian bishop. But a breakaway group led by archdeacon Thomas came under the Jacobite Patriarch of Antioch (Neill 1984, 324–328).

In the Malankara Syrian Christians we see a group that was able to integrate Hindu practices and culture with Eastern Christianity. Like the other religious groups in Kerala (Hindus, Muslims, and Jews), they had a sacred language unfamiliar to the masses (Syriac, comparable in this respect to Sanskrit, Arabic, and Hebrew), a religious institution that resembled Hindu temples, and many rituals and practices similar to those of the Hindu Nayars. The Portuguese missionaries viewed the syncretic practices of the Syrians as heresies to be expurgated, to bring them back to the "pure" religion, the Roman Catholicism of the day. Using the economic and political power at their disposal, Portuguese missionaries "converted" the Syrians to Roman Catholicism. Archbishop Menezes spent a lot of money to win over people with gifts, to travel around conducting ordinations and baptisms, and to produce pomp and ceremony at the services that he conducted. He also used the political power of the Portuguese to pressure local rulers to support his activities. However, despite all the resources at their disposal, the Portuguese were not able to make the Syrians into Latin Catholics. The Portuguese had to allow them to keep their Syriac liturgy and also to maintain some of their practices such as their caste observances, so that the Saint Thomas Christians could preserve their economic and social position within the society.[7]

In other words, rather than creating new adherents to the "pure religion," what the Portuguese did was to produce new types of syncretism. Susan Bayly (1989, 286) argues that many of the Portuguese Roman Catholic practices (elaborate processional rites and church rituals, the veneration of the Virgin and saints, and the use of images for worship) were familiar to the Syrian Christians since they were similar to Hindu practices; so the change to Roman Catholicism was probably not as radical as it might seem. The Portuguese encounter with the Syrian Christians also shows that hegemonic control and the deployment of political and economic resources alone may not be enough to result in long-term conversions. A lack of understanding and respect for the concerns of the Syrians, their *cattanars*, their archdeacon, and their reverence for their Eastern tradition, drove most of the Syrians away from the Portuguese missionaries. Leslie Brown (1956, 101, citing an eighteenth-century Roman Catholic author) indicates that only four hundred Christians out of two hundred thousand remained loyal to the archbishop Garcia at the time of the Coonen Cross revolt. Further political and economic incentives and threats certainly played an important part in persuading the majority to return to the Roman Catholic fold. Another important factor was the question of the legitimacy of the ordination of archdeacon Thomas by the *cattanars* (Neill 1984, 322). Because of their emphasis on their apostolic heritage, the Saint Thomas Christians traditionally had a very high regard for the sanctity of maintaining an unbroken apostolic chain of ordination.

Encounters with British Colonial Missionaries

Early Period

In 1795, the Kerala port of Cochin was taken over from the Dutch by the British. The Central Kerala area, which is the home base of the Mar Thoma church, was under the control of a native Hindu king even in the British period, but from 1800 a British Resident was located in Kerala, exercising considerable control over the region (Brown 1956, 125). Colonel Macaulay was the first British Resident in the native states of Travancore and Cochin.

In his 1694 book, Michael Geddes, clergyman of the Church of England, had written triumphantly, on the basis of his analysis of the decrees of the Synod of Diamper, that doctrinally the ancient church in Kerala was quite similar to the Church of England. He listed fifteen primary doctrines where the two churches agreed, including rejecting the supremacy of the pope, viewing the church of Rome as "fallen from the true faith," condemning the adoration of images, denying the necessity of confession, and allowing priests to marry (Geddes 1694, G3). The British had learned about the synod and the 1653 rebellion of the Syrian Christians through European sources such as Geddes's book but had not had much information about the Syrian Christians after that. Consequently, a British Anglican missionary, Rev. Dr. Kerr, was sent to visit the Syrian Christians in 1806. Like Geddes (1694), Kerr wrote that "in the creeds and doctrines . . . internal evidence exists of [the Syrians] being a primitive church . . . the service of their Church is performed very nearly after the manner of the Church of England; and when the Metropolitan was told that it was hoped that one day an union might take place between the two churches, he seemed pleased at the suggestion" (cited in Buchanan 1819, 145–146). Claudius Buchanan, another British Anglican missionary, made a longer visit to the Syrian Christians later in 1806. He was also interested in forging an alliance with the Saint Thomas Christians in Kerala. Buchanan's book, reporting on his study of Syrian Christians and other religious traditions in India, *Christian Researches in Asia*, first published in 1811, was widely read in England and went through many editions. In that book he cites his 1807 report on the Syrian Christians: "the Patriarchate of Antioch, being now nearly extinct . . . the Christian Church in Malay-ala looks henceforth to BRIT-

AIN, for the continuance of that light which has shone so long in this dark region of the world" (Buchanan 1819, 11th ed., 124). However, fellow Anglican Stephen Neill remarks that Buchanan, like his predecessors, "gravely underestimated the differences which in fact existed between the Church of England and the Thomas Christians" (Neill 1984, 239). Buchanan (1819, 146) estimated the breakaway Jacobite Christians to be around seventy or eighty thousand, and the Roman Catholics to be about ninety thousand—likely overestimating the numbers of Jacobite Christians, since they were a much smaller group to start with.

When Buchanan met with the Jacobite Syrian Christians in 1806, they described themselves as a church in decline, their decline being a consequence of the Portuguese. "About 300 years ago, an enemy came from the west, bearing the name of Christ, but armed with the inquisition; and compelled us to seek the protection of native Princes. And the native Princes have kept us in a state of depression ever since. . . . The glory of our Church has passed away; but we hope your nation will revive it again" (Buchanan 1819, 115). As noted earlier by Gouvea (2003, 267), the native princes had made excuses to take over the property of the Syrian Christians, leaving them impoverished. Consequently, the Jacobite Syrian Christians said that they did not get many converts because "it is not so creditable now to become Christian, in our low estate" (Buchanan 1819, 116). They complained about the learning of the Bible being also "in a low state amongst us" (Buchanan 1819, 116). Since each copy of the Syriac Bible had to be laboriously copied by hand, they did not have many copies among them. When Buchanan produced a printed copy of the New Testament in Syriac, they marveled at it and were delighted when he told them that he could get printed copies of the whole Syriac Bible for each of their churches, as well as printed copies of a Malayalam translation of the Bible (Buchanan 1819, 116–117). Their elderly bishop (Mar Thoma VI who had taken the name Dionysius), said he would get to work getting the Bible translated into Malayalam. Buchanan, who was favorably impressed with the bishop, goes on to report their subsequent conversation.

> "If I understand you right," said I, the greatest blessing the English Church can bestow upon you, is the Bible." "It is so," said he. "And what is the next greatest?" said I. "Some freedom and personal consequence as a people."

By which he meant political liberty. "We are here in bondage like Israel in Egypt." (Buchanan 1819, 117)

Buchanan remarked that the English would no doubt recognize them as fellow Christians and take an interest in their behalf, "as far as our political relation with the Prince of the country would permit" (since the Syrian Christians were under a native ruler and not directly under the British). Buchanan indicates that the priests who were gathered there then asked for an account of the "History of the English nation, and of our secession from their enemy the Church of Rome. And in return, I requested they would give me some account of their History" (Buchanan 1819, 118).[8]

Buchanan (1819, 128) indicates that he wanted to secure the support of the non-Catholic Syrian Christians and forge an alliance with them so as to "withstand [the] influence" of the Roman Catholic Church in India. When he broached the subject with Syrian Christian priests in a subsequent conversation, however, he learnt that the Syrian Christian leaders had "doubts as to English Ordination" (1819, 129). They explained,

"The English," said they, "may be a warlike and great people; but their Church, by your own account, is but of a recent origin. Whence do you derive your Ordination?" "From Rome." "You derive it from a Church which is our ancient enemy, and with which we would never unite." (Buchanan 1819, 129)

The Syrian Christian leaders then went on to elaborate on the importance they attached to their apostolic origin through ordination by the laying on of hands, in succession from the apostles. When Buchanan indicated that the same ordination had "descended from the Apostles to the Church of Rome," they responded, "It might be so: but that Church had departed from the faith." Buchanan responded that "the impurity of the channel had not corrupted the ordinance itself" (Buchanan 1819, 129). He told them that the Church of England "derived Apostolical Ordination *through* the Church of Rome, as she might have derived it *through* the Church of Antioch" (130, italics in the original). He comments that he was careful not to indicate that the ordination of the Church of England was more sacred than that of the Syrian Church (this was what the Portuguese had done, by stressing that the only legitimate ordination was through Peter and Rome) since he knew that he was being tested on this point (Buchanan 1819, 130).

On hearing of the conversation, the bishop asked Buchanan to indicate what the Syrian Church would gain from a union with the Church of England. Buchanan responded that missionaries of the Church of England would help the Syrian Church "in the promulgation of pure religion, against the pre-pondering and increasing influence of the Romish Church." He also suggested that Syrian Christian priests might be able to preach in the Church of England churches in India since the church only had a few preachers at that time and few of these Anglican preachers could preach in the native languages. The bishop agreed that such a union would be of benefit to the Syrian church provided they did not have to "compromise anything of the dignity and purity of their church." Buchanan reassured him that the Church of England "did not wish to degrade, we would rather protect and defend it. All must confess that it was Christ's Church in the midst of a heathen land." The bishop was agreeable to these conditions (Buchanan 1819, 130). The bishop gave Buchanan a Malayalam translation of the gospels in 1807 and in 1811 some printed copies were given to the Saint Thomas Christians by then British Resident Colonel Munro (Brown 1956, 126).

Middle Period: Further Splits in the Syrian Church

Colonel Munro, who followed Colonel Macauley as the British Resident in Kerala in 1810, was a fervent evangelical Christian and took a lot of interest in the Syrian Christians in Kerala. According to the account of a Metropolitan of the Mar Thoma church, Juhanon Mar Thoma (1968), Colonel Munro saw that

[T]here was no spiritual vitality and no missionary zeal [in the Syrian church]. The Church during the period was Christian only in name. The clergy were uneducated and there was no centre for their training. . . . Compulsory celibacy of the clergy, introduced by Rome, remained the rule. There was no facility for the reading of the Bible. Church services were conducted in Syriac, which the congregation did not understand and the celebrant priest understood only imperfectly. The clergy earned money by saying masses for the dead. Superstitious practices which prevailed among the non-Christian people affected the Christians also. Though doctrinally Rome was rejected, the Jacobites . . . believed in many of the practices like masses for the dead, invocation of saints and auricular confession. The lay people cared little for doctrines and practices. The Coonen Cross had resulted only in a formal change in the life of the church. (Juhanon Mar Thoma 1968, 110)

The CMS "Mission of Help" to the Jacobite Syrians of Kerala was started in the year 1816 by Colonel Munro to effect a renovation of the church and to provide native allies for the British. The instructions to the missionaries made it very clear that they should not try to bring the Syrians under the Anglican Church. The first Anglican missionary who arrived in Kerala was Thomas Norton. Missionary Thomas Norton's arrival was first viewed with apprehension by the Syrian Christians but he wrote that he reassured them, "that it was our sole desire to be instrumental, by the Divine assistance, in strengthening the Metran's [Metropolitan] hands for removing those evils which they had derived from the Church of Rome, and which he himself lamented, and to bring them back to their primitive state, according to the purity of the Gospel, that they might again become a holy and vigorous Church" (letter from Norton cited by Stock 1899, vol. 1, 233). Colonel Munro apparently hoped that the Romo-Syrians would also return to the Syrian church once it had been purged of its "superstitions" (Munro's letter of 23 September 1817 to the CMS secretary in Madras, reprinted in P. Cheriyan 1935, 344). A famous trio of CMS missionaries followed Thomas Norton—Benjamin Bailey, Joseph Fenn, and Henry Baker. Munro designated the missionary Reverend Bailey to be in charge of the task of translating the Syriac Bible into Malayalam. Bailey also set up a printing press and by the middle of the nineteenth century, vernacular copies of the Bible were available. Munro prevailed on the Rani (Queen) to gift property to the Syrians for the Syrian seminary (P. Cheriyan 1935, 182). Baker started village schools and Fenn worked in the seminary which was built in 1813 on land donated by the Rani of Travancore. Mrs. Bailey began a school for the education of girls (P. Cheriyan 1935, 190) followed by several others started by the wives of other missionaries.[9] Colonel Munro also encouraged the marriage of Jacobite Syrian priests and even provided monetary incentives to encourage the first group of priests to marry (Neill 1985, 267).

During my earlier research (in 1990) in a Mar Thoma area of Kerala, I had heard about the missionary trio Bailey, Baker, and Fenn and how their work in providing vernacular copies of the Bible had led to an interest in reading by the masses, the desire for education which the missionaries had encouraged, and that education and the reading of the Bible had triggered a religious revival and reform movement within the Syrian church (Kurien 2002, 134–135). According to Mar Thoma bishop Juhanon Mar Thoma (1968, 110), the three missionaries were successful because they kept to the instructions given them by the CMS. The missionaries were careful not to directly antagonize the Syrians but they wished to remove from the Church what they "considered to be superstitions such as the use of the prayers for the dead, to the saints, the veneration of Mary, and other similar 'excesses'"(Visvanathan 1993, 21), in other words, to "Reform" the church along Protestant lines. Their goal was to remove the "evils" that the church had imbibed from the Church of Rome. But the problem is that by this time, the switch to the West Syrian tradition and the periodic communion between Rome and this church meant that many of these practices were also supported by Antioch (P. Cheriyan 1935, 120). C. P. Mathew and M. M. Thomas, both prominent lay leaders and theologians of the Mar Thoma church, point out that the religious tradition of the Syrian Church with its liturgy and rituals was also "in striking contrast to the dogmatic intellectualism of Western Christianity, whether Catholic or Protestant, which put central emphasis on the intellectual formulations of particular doctrines. Moreover, the religious individualism of Evangelicalism, which the missionaries represented was especially alien to the prevailing concept of the Church as corporate communion based on the continuity of tradition" (Mathew and Thomas 2005, 53). Again, although the goal of the CMS was to prepare Syrians to evangelize to non-Christians, P. Cheriyan (1935, 223–224) comments that there is nothing to show that the Syrians actually wanted to do this. High-caste converts were almost impossible to obtain and the Syrians did not want low-caste converts since such converts would "jeopardise their social status" (P. Cheriyan 1935, 224).

The missionary trio of Bailey, Fenn, and Baker returned to England between 1826 and 1833, and two new missionaries, Reverends Joseph

Peet and W. J. Woodcock were sent to central Kerala. Their style was considerably different from the earlier group of missionaries. They were tired of the slow pace of progress and were more confrontational and critical of many of the traditional rituals and practices of the Syrian Christians. At the same time, a Syrian Metropolitan, Mar Thoma XII (Cheppattu Mar Dionysius), who was not friendly to missionaries, took over in 1830. This combination of aggressive missionaries and a hostile Metropolitan set the stage for another assertion of independence on the part of the Syrian church (Mathew and Thomas 2005, 61–66). In 1835 Anglican Bishop Wilson of Calcutta in Eastern India tried to mediate the tensions between the CMS and the Jacobite Syrians and made some suggestions for the reform of the church, including the following provisions: 1) only those who were trained in the seminary should be ordained, 2) the church should keep accounts of the church and submit it to the British resident, 3) there should be a permanent endowment so that clergy could be paid a fixed salary, 4) every parish church must have its school, 5) the gospel should be preached during the Sunday service, and 6) the Malayalam liturgy should be used instead of the Syriac (Mathew and Thomas 2005, 66–68).

In 1836 the Syrian Metropolitan, Mar Thoma XII, convened a synod to discuss these suggestions but they were rejected by the council. The Metropolitan subsequently sent a message to the clergy forbidding them to associate with the British missionaries. The synod of Jacobite Syrians affirmed the supremacy of the Patriarch of Antioch as well as their loyalty to him and the liturgies, ordinances, and prelates sanctioned by him. They argued that for this reason they could not follow any leader or teaching "other than the orthodox faith of the Jacobite Syrian Christians" (cited in Neill 1985, 247).

Consequently, the CMS missionaries' mission of help to the Jacobite church was rebuffed after just twenty years. The missionaries decided to move their efforts from the Syrian church to working with non-Christians, particularly the lower-caste groups (since higher castes were generally not receptive to conversion) whose living conditions and social disabilities had become a matter of concern to the missionaries. Mathew and Thomas (2005, 76–79) write about the missionaries' attempts to improve the lives of their lower-caste converts and the initial resistance they faced from some Syrians, including having some of their buildings burned down. The lower castes for their part started to complain about Syrian Christians dominating the church and also that the church was neglecting them. These tensions between the lower-caste converts and the Syrians led to the eventual split into Syrian *idavakas* (parishes) and lower-caste *puthusabhas* (new churches) (Juhanon Mar Thoma 1968, 112; Mathew and Thomas 2005, 107).

Even though the missionaries had stopped their work among the Syrians in 1836, the Anglican influence began to be slowly felt among the Syrians, and an Anglican community and subsequently a diocese were formed in Tranvancore in 1879 (Juhanon 1968, 112).[10] More and more missionaries came into the region under the British and became involved in social welfare programs, introducing schools, hospitals, and other charitable institutions. They also frequently interceded with the British government on behalf of the Christians in the population. The identification and alliance of the Syrian Christians with the British led to their large-scale participation in the wide range of mission-run institutions. Thus, Syrian Christians led the other groups in English education (Nossiter 1988, 50) and a large proportion of the community secured positions as teachers, lecturers, doctors, nurses, and administrators in the mission schools, colleges, and hospitals (as Christians, they were given preference in these institutions). Their English education and British contacts also helped them migrate to other parts of the British Empire (both within India and to other countries like Ceylon [Sri Lanka], Malaya [Malaysia], Singapore, and the Middle East) for well-paying white collar positions.

Reformation of the Syrian Church and the Formation of the Mar Thoma Denomination

Abraham Malpan has been described as the Martin Luther of the Mar Thoma church since he was the person who initiated the reformation of the church (Juhanon Mar Thoma 1968, 114). Malpan was born in 1796 in Maramon in central Travancore. His father died before he was born and his mother died before he was three years old, so he was brought up by his father's brother, a priest. He was sent to study Syriac and the Bible, was ordained as a priest in 1815 by Mar Thoma VIII, and became the vicar of the Maramon church. Since there was some question about the legitimacy of the ordination of Mar Thoma VIII, Abraham Malpan had himself reordained by a visiting Jacobite bishop from Syria. Hearing about this, Mar Thoma VIII lodged a complaint with the government and Abraham Malpan was charged with defying the authority of the Saint Thomas Christian bishop and sent to prison for a short sentence (Juhanon Mar Thoma 1968, 114).

Some years later, Abraham Malpan was appointed as a professor of Syriac (locally called Malpan) at the Syrian seminary in Kottayam. Here he was able to interact closely with some of the Anglican missionaries who taught at the seminary. Abraham Malpan and a fellow Syrian priest, Kaithayil Geervarghese Malpan, who was also working at the seminary, came under the influence of the missionaries and became interested in trying to reform the Syrian church (Juhanon Mar Thoma 1968, 113–114). In 1836, after the Jacobite church under Mar Thoma XII had decided to separate from the Anglican church, Abraham Malpan and eleven other priests wrote a petition to the British Resident listing twenty-four practices of the Jacobite church which they alleged were not part of the Saint Thomas tradition and which needed to be reformed, requesting his help to make the reforms. The British did not respond to the memorial (Tovey 1995, 52). Abraham Malpan and Kaithayil Geevarghese Malpan's attempts at reformation angered the Syrian Metropolitan, Mar Thoma XII, and he forbade the Jacobite clergy from having any relationship with them. This put the Malpans in a difficult position as they did not want to leave the Syrian church and join the Anglicans. Abraham Malpan decided to make the reforms himself. He revised the liturgy of the Jacobite church and began using it in the seminary later that year. In 1837 he held the first Malayalam Holy Communion service at his home church in Maramon. He also did away with a church festival to a local saint during which the image of the saint would be taken around in procession and people would offer prayers and offerings to it. The Syrian Metropolitan was offended by Malpan's use of a revised liturgy and the changes he had made in Jacobite practices, so he excommunicated Abraham Malpan and denied the priesthood in the Jacobite church to the deacons Malpan had trained in the Syrian seminary. But some of the clergy supported Malpan; this group came to be known as the Reformists (Juhanon Mar Thoma 1968, 114; Neill 1985, 251).

The Reformists revised the liturgy to drop references to the mediation of the saints and the adoration of the Virgin Mary as also the burning of candles before images and the sounding of gongs and cymbals during the Eucharistic service. They also translated the liturgy into Malayalam and emphasized the importance of sermons with biblical messages and of hymns. The practice of auricular confession was discontinued as also some other practices absorbed from the local culture, which were deemed to be superstitious. Simony was discouraged and the clergy were organized and paid salaries. Priests were ordained only after a seminary education. Their marriage was encouraged but bishops remained celibate (Visvanathan 1993, 21–22; Williams 1996, 77–78). According to Mathew and Thomas (2005, 98), the reformers "were inspired by the vision of an Eastern Evangelical Church seeking to comprehend the Evangelical faith and experience within the corporate life and liturgical devotion of an Eastern Church." Mar Thomites contend that the reformation was actually a return to the original doctrines and practices of the earlier independent Saint Thomas Syrian church with the purging of "errors which were forced upon the church in the Middle Centuries by the Roman and Jacobite ecclesiastics" (Juhanon Mar Thoma 1968, 119).

According to the account of bishop Juhanon Mar Thoma, Abraham Malpan realized that he needed to have the support of a Metropolitan since "he was not prepared to give up an apostolic tradition and a valid episcopacy" (Juhanon Mar Thoma 1968, 114). He therefore sent a nephew, deacon Mathew, to Mardin, where the Patriarch of Antioch resided. Deacon Mathew was well received by the Patriarch who permitted him to stay in Mardin for over a year and then sent him back to Kerala as Metropolitan Mathews Mar Athanasius in 1843. However, Cheppattu Mar Dionysius (Mar Thoma XII) was still the Syrian Metropolitan in Kerala and he had the support of the Conservatives. Mar Athanasius went to Trivandrum to get the Travancore government (under a Native ruler) to proclaim him the Metropolitan of Malankara (the Kerala Syrian church) but this was opposed by Cheppattu Mar Dionysius.

The struggle between the two Metropolitans continued for almost ten years. In 1852, Mathews Mar Athanasius was confirmed by royal proclamation as the Metropolitan of Malankara (Mar Thoma XIII). The government also declared that the existing Syrian Christian churches and properties were to be under the control of Mar Athanasius. Once he was confirmed, he began to work to reform the church. He also worked to exempt Christians from their participation in Hindu temple rituals (Juhanon Mar Thoma 1968, 115). As early as 1815, Colonel Munro had a Royal Proclamation passed exempting Christians from all "menial jobs" connected with Hindu temples since the British viewed such involvements as an abomination and assumed that Hindus were forcing them to do it (Bayly 1989, 289). However, this was not always implemented (Philip 1991, 42).[11] By the middle of the century, such participation which had been perceived as a "social honor" earlier came to be viewed as a "social disability" (Juhanon Mar Thoma 1968, 115, uses the latter term).

The conflict in the Malankara church continued between supporters of the Conservative and Reformist factions. Taking the side of the Conservatives, the Patriarch of Antioch excommunicated Mathews Mar Athanasius in 1875 and arrived in Kerala to protect his authority (Juhanon Mar Thoma 1968, 115). In 1876 the royal proclamation recognizing Mathews Mar Athanasius as Metropolitan was withdrawn and the two sides were asked to take their dispute to a court of law. In 1868 Mathews Mar Athanasius had consecrated his cousin, Abraham Malpan's son, as Thomas Mar Athanasius and the latter continued the legal struggle after the death of Mathews Mar Athanasius. He argued that Malankara church was an independent church and was therefore not under the control of the Patriarch of Antioch (Juhanon Mar Thoma 1968, 115). In 1889, the courts recognized Joseph Mar Dionysius of the Conservative party as the rightful Metropolitan of the Malankara church and ruled that the Syrian Church in Kerala was under the Patriarch of Antioch. The Reform party therefore lost most of their property and churches. It was a blow to them but they persevered since they felt that "there were spiritual values at stake" (Juhanon Mar Thoma 1968, 115). At this point (1889), the Reformers had to organize themselves into a separate church. This was when the Mar Thoma Syrian Church was born. The Mar Thoma church was the first Indian church to become autonomous (Juhanon Mar Thoma 1968, 121).

To summarize, Syrian Christian experiences under the Portuguese made the Syrian Christians wary of any attempt by the British Anglican missionaries to criticize their Eastern traditions or to compromise the autonomy of the Syrian Christian church. Even though the British started out with very different premises than the Portuguese and had the goal of the "preservation of [the] individuality" of the Syrian Christian Church (Stock 1899, 233), Bayly (1989, 286) argues that they actually had "much more profound consequences for the St. Thomas Christians" than the Portuguese because the low church, individualistic evangelical Protestantism of the CMS missionaries was very different in terms of ideology and practice from the religious traditions that Syrian Christians were familiar with.

Although only a minority of Syrian Christians were directly impacted by Anglican doctrines (according to the 1901 Travancore census there were 10,000 Syrian Anglicans and 37,200 Mar Thomites, compared with 182,000 Jacobites and 256,000 Syrian Catholics [figures cited in Bayly 1989, 300–301]), many of the evangelical ideas regarding the equality of believers, the importance of evangelism, worship in the vernacular, anti-ritualism and individual pietism would begin to gradually gain ground in Kerala. For instance, Mathew and Thomas (2005, 79) assert that despite the opposition from Syrians to opening the church to lower castes, as a result of the activities of the Anglican missionaries "the traditional [Syrian Christian] understanding of the Church as an exclusive social caste or ethnic community which looked after their own interests and conformed to the caste hierarchy of Hindu society, began to give place to a new idea of the nature of the Church and its obligation for mission and service to those outside." The CMS missionaries were followed by other Western missionaries from England and from the United States (from the Church of God and Pentecost churches) and south-central Kerala became the base for many Christian denominations. At the time of my fieldwork in the region in 1990, I counted twelve denominations and nineteen subdenominations in the small village where I was located, although the majority of the villagers were Mar Thomites.

Cynical Mar Thomites told me that the Western missionaries were able to woo people away from the Mar Thoma church because the locals believed that they would obtain "soap [material goods], soup [food], and salvation" if they converted (Kurien 2002, 135). However, the discussion of the impact of Anglican missionary activities shows that economic or social gain is not always the motive for converts. Sometimes people convert even at great personal and economic cost. Abraham Malpan and the other leaders of the Mar Thoma church continued their reform movement even without the support of the British and of most Syrian Christian leaders and had to suffer ostracism and the loss of their church properties. However, not all those who joined the Mar Thoma movement did so as individuals. Sometimes church communities (e.g., the Maramon church members) converted en masse because of the influence of community leaders.

The Early Mar Thoma Church

The early Mar Thoma church emphasized the importance of preaching, Bible reading, and prayers in church and at home. Sunday schools were formed and a Sunday school association was formed in 1905 (Juhanon Mar Thoma 1968, 116). The Evangelistic Association was constituted in 1888 to preach the gospel in the church and to those outside. The church set up a few ashram centers with workers in the ashram living in a community with a common purse and devoting time for evangelistic work among non-Christians. Under the leadership of Metropolitan Abraham Mar Thoma, the Voluntary Evangelist Association was started in 1925 with the Edavaka mission in each parish as a unit of this organization. The Edavaka mission supported missionaries and also met for prayer and Bible study every week. The Sevika Sangham, the women's wing, was developed in 1919. It started a Bible school for women, a women's occupational training institute, as well as orphanages and hostels for working women. The Sevika Sangham also had a branch in each parish that met on a regular basis. Many of the reforms introduced by the Mar Thoma church such as worship in the vernacular, missionary work, ashrams, the women's association, and Sunday schools were subsequently adopted by the Syrian Christian Orthodox Church (Mathew and Thomas 2005, 138–141). The famous annual Mar Thoma Maramon convention was started in 1896. It is held every year, in February or March, on the banks of the river Pampa in Maramon. Tens of thousands of people from a variety of denominations and backgrounds, including from other countries, attend the convention, which is billed as Asia's largest Christian convention. The Mar Thoma church also began to establish many educational institutions—high schools and colleges. The Mar Thoma Theological seminary was established in 1926 in Kottayam.

Because of its unique heritage as a blend of Eastern and Western Christian traditions, the Mar Thoma considers itself a "bridge church preserving . . . the best features of Eastern traditional forms of worship and the Reformation principles of Luther and the Western Protestant

Churches" (Juhanon Mar Thoma 1968, 120). It follows Eastern churches in not codifying articles of faith. As mentioned, for the Mar Thoma church the liturgy is the basis of its doctrines. Consequently, the church does not make any major theological declarations, except to say that "the Bible consisting of 66 books is accepted as the basis for all subjects relating to faith and doctrine" (ibid.).

The Mar Thoma leadership describe the church as having a "progressive social outlook" particularly with respect to the "rights and equality of women" (Juhanon Mar Thoma 1968, 130), and its interest in uniting a "concern for social and economic justice to the Christian commitment" (Juhanon Mar Thoma 1968, 122). Since the church believes in corporate worship, the leadership is against individualistic evangelism. Mathew and Thomas (2005) write that the Mar Thoma church from the early days to the present has fought against the growing influence of conservative evangelists who "exalt the concepts of 'pure spirituality' and 'individual pietism'" and who have been gaining many converts in Kerala, and that it has done this through a "Church-centered evangelism" led by its Evangelistic Association (Mathew and Thomas 2005, 103). In his discussion of the missionary approach of the Mar Thoma church, Joseph Thomas (1997) indicates that the mission of the church came to be "understood as the redemption of the whole person, not one's spiritual welfare alone" (Thomas 1997, 46–47), which led the church to get involved in a variety of service projects to provide for the social, educational, and economic needs of the communities with which it engaged. "Thus evangelism, education and social service went hand in hand" (Thomas 1997, 47). Consequently, the Evangelistic Association ran educational institutions (from primary schools to colleges), hospitals, and homes for the destitute, and a few Christian ashrams in several parts of India. Mission outreach activities of the church have been carried out among underprivileged, lower-caste communities where new parishes were formed (Thomas 1997, 48). However, the separation into lower-caste *puthusabhas*, and Syrian Christian *idavakas* only reinforced the gulf between non-Syrians and Syrians, as "[t]he *puthusabhas* continue to nurture a non-Syrian caste-consciousness, just as the exclusively *idavakas* have for ages nurtured that of the Syrians" (Mathew and Thomas 2005, 108).

As a church that stresses its autonomy and indigenous nature, it should not be surprising that many Mar Thoma leaders became in-

volved in the Indian independence movement in Kerala in the twentieth century. It is likely that the emphasis on social justice and activism
of the Mar Thoma church came out of this involvement. Two of the
important Metropolitans of the church in the twentieth century, Abraham Mar Thoma and Juhanon Mar Thoma, were nationalists from their
younger days and leaders in the freedom struggle in Kerala (Mathew
and Thomas 2005, 160–161; Alexander Mar Thoma 1986, 94). Metropolitan Juhanon Mar Thoma was involved in a variety of other types of
social justice activism around issues such as caste, dowry, poverty, and
land rights and started a project to provide land for the landless and
houses for the homeless. He was also the only church leader in India
who wrote a personal letter to Prime Minister Indira Gandhi asking for
the Indian Emergency (a period when civil rights were suspended) to be
lifted (Alexander Mar Thoma 1986, 27–28, 162–163).

Perhaps inevitably in a church that blends Orthodox worship with
a Protestant theology and which does not make doctrinal pronounce-
ments, tensions between Conservatives who wanted to maintain its
Eastern traditions and Reformers who wanted to push it further toward
Protestant Evangelicalism continued even after its formation (Mathew
and Thomas 2005, 114–118). In the middle of the twentieth century,
another reform group which alleged that the Mar Thoma church had
slipped back into many elements of the Jacobite theology and practices
emerged. They were excommunicated from the church and took some of
the leaders of the Mar Thoma church to court in 1955. Like the original
Mar Thoma leaders, this reform group lost in court and so formed a new
church in 1961, the St. Thomas Evangelical Church of India (Mathew
and Thomas 2005, 120). Juhanon Mar Thoma, then Mar Thoma Metropolitan, issued orders forbidding members of the Mar Thoma church
from marrying anyone in the St. Thomas Evangelical Church and from
attending any of its services on pain of losing their membership in the
Mar Thoma church.[12]

Conclusion

This overview of the history of the Mar Thoma church shows the
diverse elements of its heritage and some of the tensions between its
different components. The encounters of the Portuguese and Anglican

missionaries with Syrian Christians led each group to articulate their own model of Christianity and forced them to make decisions about the elements they considered to be central and what they could relinquish. For the Portuguese, the most important aspects of Christianity were adopting Roman Catholic practices, abandoning heresy, and coming under the pope. They were able to compromise on the language of worship (Syrian instead of Latin) and Syrian practices of untouchability. The British Anglicans, on the other hand, did not want to bring Syrian Christians under the Church of England. Instead, they intended to maintain the independence and uniqueness of the Syrian Christian church but rid it of Roman Catholic influences. Converting the language of worship to the vernacular and abandoning practices of untouchability and other Hindu superstitions were important to them. Syrian Christians on their part wanted to preserve their high-caste status, apostolic heritage, episcopal tradition, the legitimate ordination of their bishops, and their Eastern liturgy. Under both the Portuguese and the British, Syrian Christians internalized many elements of the dominant Christian ideology of each group, but also wanted to maintain their autonomy and individuality.

The history and heritage of the Mar Thoma church has had a profound impact on its relationships with other Christian groups in the present. Although Mar Thoma church leaders distinguish themselves from Syrian Christian Orthodox and Catholic groups (the dominant Christian groups in Kerala) by stressing their Protestant doctrines, traditional Syrian Christian theologies of worship are an unarticulated but deeply internalized and institutionalized part of the Mar Thoma tradition. From its inception until the present there have been internal tensions in the church between bishops, priests, and lay members who lean more to the Orthodox strand of the church and those who are more supportive of the Reformed strand. Again, there is frequent intermarriage between Mar Thomites and Syrian Orthodox members (women are expected to switch to their husband's denomination on marriage), and many members of the Mar Thoma church are exposed to Syrian Orthodox doctrines and worship. Since the Mar Thoma church wants to maintain its tradition of Eastern corporate worship, Mar Thoma church leaders also distance themselves from individualistic evangelical and charismatic forms of Christianity (nondenominational evangelicalism, Pentecostalism) in India and the United States.

Despite the CMS-inspired outreach and evangelical mandate of the church, in practice Hindu influences prevail. Mar Thoma parishes largely maintain their ascribed, upper-caste ethos and are not open to outsiders. Membership is generally accorded only to members who are born and baptized in the church and to women who have married into the church.[13] While evangelists belonging to the Mar Thoma church do work among the lower castes in Kerala and in other parts of India, such convert communities are formed into separate parishes and are not integrated into the Syrian Christian community or parish. Ideas of female impurity during menstruation imbibed from Hindu society (and possibly also from Eastern Orthodox or ancient rabbinical Judaism) mean that Mar Thoma women are usually not allowed to go into the altar area. Consequently, women are not permitted to be pastors or (with a few exceptions) even lay deacons in the Mar Thoma church. However, the church maintains that there is no theological reason that women cannot become pastors and that it is only disallowed due to the cultural traditions of Syrian Christians.

As a consequence of the Anglican evangelical emphasis on the democratization of the church, the Mar Thoma church has institutionalized greater lay participation when compared to the Syrian Orthodox and Jacobite churches. Lay Mar Thoma members have a role in the decision making of the church through their participation in the diocesan level and denominational level assemblies. The position of women in the Mar Thoma church is also better than in the Orthodox Syrian Christian church where women do not have any independent membership but are only accepted as the wife or daughter of a male member. Mar Thoma women are involved in the decision-making assemblies and the church now has mandated quotas for women members. The church also plays a much more active role in social service and humanitarian projects than the Orthodox Church on account of its "social gospel" orientation. As noted, key Metropolitans of the church were ardent nationalists, active during the Indian independence movement, and progressive political involvement has continued to be a tradition of the church.

Mar Thoma bishop Juhanan Mar Thoma (Mar Thoma XVIII) indicated that for Mar Thomites, reformation of the Syrian Christian church meant an emphasis on a "personal religion" (1968, 112), "the freedom of the individual to approach God, to enter into the spirit of worship by intelligently following the service, to read the Scriptures and understand the ways of God" (1968, 115). We will see that, ironically the criticism of second-generation Mar Thoma Americans against the Mar Thoma church is that they lack such freedom. They feel that the Mar Thoma church's emphasis on retaining the liturgy and Malayalam worship detracts from their ability to fully "enter into the spirit of worship." We will also see that encounters with American Protestantism in the United States have resulted in a replaying of the tensions between the Eastern and Western elements that have dogged its history, with the leadership and older generation wanting to maintain their traditional and denominational identity, while the second generation is working to refashion the church in the Protestant evangelical nondenominational mould.

2

The Role of the Church in Migration and Settlement

Mr. Thomas Mathews was a middle-aged migrant from Kerala in the Bethelville church who had arrived in the United States in the 1980s and was a friendly and active member of the congregation. When I asked him how he had located the church (which was far away from where he lived), he told me, "The first thing Mar Thoma Christians do even before getting to a new place is to find out where the nearest Mar Thoma church is!" A second-generation member of another Mar Thoma parish, Reeni, talked about how the Mar Thoma church became "a translator" of American society to her parents when they arrived from India. "And like people who had been here for thirty years could explain to them oh . . . that's just how they do it . . . I mean, just the basics of everyday living, they picked up [from people in church]." Religion and religious institutions generally play an important role in shaping the out-migration and settlement patterns of immigrants (Ebaugh and Chafetz 2002; Kurien 2014a; Levitt 2003). This is true of the Mar Thoma case as well, where church networks have enabled the global migration of Mar Thomites, helped them to find jobs, and get acclimatized in their new contexts. The influence of Mar Thoma congregations also permeated the intimate lives of its members, shaping gender and intergenerational relations within households.

The church networks of the Mar Thoma denomination were an outgrowth of its ecumenical engagement. To continue the story of the history of the Mar Thoma church from the previous chapter, one consequence of its reformed heritage is that the church has been an active member of several ecumenical Christian bodies at the national and international levels. When India obtained independence from British rule in August 1947, the Anglican dioceses in south India merged with the other major Protestant churches in India (Presbyterian, Methodist, and Congregational) and a Church of South India (CSI) came into being in September 1947 (a Church of North India, CNI, was subsequently formed in 1970). Because of its Anglican heritage, the Mar Thoma church has been in full communion with the CSI. At the time of the formation of the CSI, there were some discussions about the desirability of forming a pan-Indian church. Although such a church did not come into being, the Mar Thoma Metropolitan, Juhanon Mar Thoma, had indicated in 1952 that should such a union take place, the Mar Thoma church "must be willing to lose itself" in the interest of creating an Indian Church of Christ (letter appended in Juhanon Mar Thoma 1968, 130). As we will see, this idea that the Mar Thoma church must be willing to lose itself in the interest of larger ecumenical relations also came up in the U.S. context, when the leadership initially wanted its members to join mainline American Protestant denominations.

The Mar Thoma church was a founding member when the World Council of Churches (WCC) was formed in 1948. Mar Thoma Metropolitan Juhanon Mar Thoma (1947–1976) was one of the presidents of the WCC in the 1950s, and many other Mar Thoma leaders, both lay members and bishops, have been involved in a variety of WCC committees. This involvement continues to the present. Due to its historical Anglican connection, the Malankara Mar Thoma Church entered into a full communion relationship with the Anglican Church in 1961.

These global ecumenical connections with Protestant missionaries and institutions facilitated the early migration of Mar Thomites (including Mar Thoma achens) to the United States for higher education, and later, after the passage of the 1965 Immigration Act, for work. However, they have also given rise to questions about the church's distinctive identity and central values, particularly as it set up parishes and a diocese in the West, questions that Mar Thoma achens struggle to address due to the nature of the theological education that they receive in India.

The Theological Training of Mar Thoma Achens

The complicated and multistranded history of the Mar Thoma church is one that many achens do not fully understand. This is because, although the Mar Thoma denomination has its own theological seminary in Kottayam, Kerala, Mar Thoma achens are not required to obtain their theological education there but only have to attend a six-month training in the Mar Thoma liturgy at the Kottayam seminary at the end of their theological education. Achens serving in Mar Thoma parishes receive their theological education at a variety of mainstream Protestant seminaries in India (although they are required to have an affiliation with a local Mar Thoma congregation during their seminary training period). Recently, several mainline American Protestant seminaries were also approved by the Mar Thoma synod as institutions where Mar Thoma achens of American background may obtain their theological education. After this theological education, they spend at least six months to a year at the Mar Thoma seminary in Kerala. During this time they are located in a Mar Thoma parish in the area and are mentored by a senior achen.

Even the Mar Thoma seminary in Kerala[1] is constrained in the degree to which it can offer course content that fits in with the theology and orientation of the Mar Thoma denomination. It is affiliated with the interdenominational theological Serampore University in eastern India, and has to follow its curriculum and examinations. The theological college at Serampore (which later achieved the status of a university) was founded in 1818 by three British Baptist missionaries to provide seminary training for individuals working in Protestant and Orthodox denominations in India. Amanda Mathew,[2] a second-generation Mar Thoma American theological student who had recently returned to the United States after spending time at the Mar Thoma seminary, commented that the course offerings in the seminary were very varied and that students there were "studying things I would never have imagined." For instance, she said that the seminary offered a class in feminist theology with readings from many radical Western feminist theologians. However, Amanda remarked that many of the seminarians seemed to see the course content as just something to study (i.e., memorize) in order to pass the exams, not something that could or should be used to inform their practice once they were ordained in the Mar Thoma church.

Due to the confluence of influences on the Mar Thoma denomination and the relative freedom of choice of seminary training, the theological orientation of individual Mar Thoma achens tends to vary from liberal, to conservative evangelical, to reformed orthodox, with the conservative evangelical apparently being the most common orientation now, due to the mushrooming of evangelical churches around India and their appeal to religiously oriented youth. However, many of the intellectual leaders of the church are theologically progressive and pluralist: several of the

Mar Thoma bishops have done their Ph.D. research on facets of Hinduism or on Dalit (the term for castes formerly considered "untouchable") theology. The theologically liberal intellectual leaders of the church maintain that the Mar Thoma denomination is not upper caste, Syrian Christian, or even Kerala based. One such leader comments, in response to an article of mine, that the Mar Thoma Church "has consciously been struggling to overcome 'the upper-caste connotation'" of its identity. He continues, "the very principle of Reformation that led to the formation of the Church involved a commitment to mission and outreach which were understood by the Church as transcending the barriers of caste, race and language" (Athyal 2015a, 4). However, despite the theoretical commitment to a nonethnic and noncasteist church, in practice the Malayali, upper-caste identity of the Mar Thoma denomination continues to be reinforced in numerous ways, not just by lay members but also by the leadership, many of the achens, and the structure of the Mar Thoma seminary. On its website, the denomination is labeled the "Malankara [Kerala] Mar Thoma Syrian Church" (in English and in Malayalam).[3] Within the denomination, there is generally a sharp differentiation between Syrian Christian congregations and Dalit congregations (as mentioned, Dalit converts are almost always located in separate parishes led by Syrian Christian achens). Although the liturgy used by the convert communities outside Kerala is translated into the local language, this only reinforces the divide between the core Malayali Syrian Christian congregations and those of the Dalits.

The Mar Thoma seminary classes are conducted in English but the seminary education also provides training in the Malayalam liturgy, giving sermons in (formal) Malayalam, and reading the Bible in Malayalam. This training is provided even for students brought up outside Kerala (including the American students) who are not fluent in Malayalam. I asked an older achen in Kerala why Malayalam was still required of all seminary candidates if the Mar Thoma was viewed as a "global church." He replied, "This is still a Malayalam church. Except for the mission fields [the Dalit churches outside Kerala], all other churches around the world hold services in Malayalam. Mar Thoma achens are trained to be available to serve anywhere." A second-generation American achen (one of nine current second-generation American achens) explained that even though achens like him were generally allowed to stay and serve in the United States, they still had to minister to multi-generational congregations, which made the knowledge of Malayalam important for them. Another American theology student of Mar Thoma background, however, was critical about the fact that part of the education at the seminary was "to learn how to be Malayali," and lamented, "It is a shame, because we are increasingly a global church, but the way our formation system for achens goes, it is still only Malayaliness that is embraced." The inability of Mar Thoma clergy to articulate the distinctiveness of the Mar Thoma theology and to make clear that at least theoretically the church transcends race and language, has become a problem for the contemporary Mar Thoma church, particularly in the United States.

In the past, this was not an issue in Kerala or even in the larger Indian context where inherited religion was the general norm and youngsters did not usually raise questions about the "meaning" of their religious identity. Lay Mar Thomites who had grown up in Kerala had their own ways of assessing the distinguishing characteristics of their denominational background. My conversations with Mar Thoma members, both during my earlier research in 1990 in south-central Kerala and for this book, made clear that older immigrant Mar Thomites were proud of their denominational identity. They saw the Mar Thoma church as a denomination that was able to be a path-breaker and progressive religious leader (due to its reform movement), while maintaining its heritage. This was in contrast to Anglican (now CSI) Syrian Christians who, as I overheard a Mar Thoma achen in the United States explaining to an immigrant church member, were viewed by Mar Thomites as people who had abandoned their traditions and culture to "go after the white man." Consequently, Mar Thomites in Kerala perceived their denomination as being located in the ideal middle ground between conservative Jacobites and Westernized Syrian Christian CSI members. The Maramon convention and the huge crowds that it drew every year was a particular matter of pride for Mar Thomites.[4]

Mar Thomites also had a high regard for Mar Thoma achens and bishops, who were known for their humility, simplicity, and "down to earth" qualities as well as their warm relationships with members, which often contrasted with the more formal and distant style of the leadership of the Orthodox Church. In many cases, Mar Thoma achens had guided members to choose the vocations they were in. They had also played a big role in the educational choices of Mar Thoma children, since many of the schools and colleges in Kerala were tied to Christian churches. In addition, Mar Thomites were proud of the economic and educational achievements of prominent church members (many of the early international migrants from central Travancore were from the Mar Thoma church). Consequently, Mar Thoma immigrants carried with them a great attachment to the Mar Thoma church and liturgy and tried to form Mar Thoma congregations as soon as they were able to find enough Mar Thomites in the region to be able to do so.

Religion and Migration

Recall that Mar Thoma members migrated to Malaysia, Singapore, and Sri Lanka in the early decades of the twentieth century, followed by migration to countries in Africa and the Middle East after World War II, facilitated by contacts with Anglican missionaries. In 1936, the Mar Thoma church sent its first achen overseas to serve a diasporic Mar Thoma church in Malaysia. Subsequently, achens were sent to Singapore and the Middle East. Mar Thoma members in Africa did not form Mar Thoma congregations but instead, as instructed by the Mar Thoma leadership, obtained temporary membership (since the migration was generally only for a short term) in the Anglican churches in the region.

In 1990, when I was doing my fieldwork in a predominantly Mar Thoma Christian area in Kerala, the migration to the Middle East had been in full swing for two decades. I learned that although Syrian Christians considered the Middle East to be a desirable destination for temporary residence, the United States was viewed as the "promised land" due to its high standards of living, outstanding educational system, the possibility of permanent residence and citizenship, and because it was a "Christian country" where Syrian Christians could practice their religion freely, unlike in the Middle East (Kurien 2002, 146). Some Mar Thomites, including Mar Thoma achens, had arrived in the United States beginning in the early decades of the twentieth century for higher education, including Christian theological education (assisted by the ecumenical connections between the Mar Thoma leadership and Protestant institutions in the United States), but at that time, due to the immigration laws in place, U.S. settlement was not an option. Consequently, these individuals returned to Kerala after their education and many provided leadership in the Mar Thoma church (Thomas 2008a, 27–28). Large-scale Mar Thoma American immigration and settlement began in the late 1960s after the passage of the 1965 Immigration Act.

There were two different groups of early Mar Thoma immigrants (Thomas 2008b, 32). The arrival of Mar Thomites in the United States for higher education continued after the 1965 Act, but now they were able to obtain jobs and stay on in the country. Most of these migrants were men (there were also a small number of women) who had arrived in this country between the late sixties and the late seventies, seeking professional education. They had either come with their wives or had gone back later and had married Syrian Christian women. However, those who came to the United States for higher education and subsequently obtained managerial or professional jobs were a relatively small group within Mar Thoma American parishes. Since many in this group were fluent in English and had studied in cosmopolitan urban areas in India, they attended local American churches in the early period of their migration (Thomas 2008b, 31–32). Some of them became members in Mar Thoma churches after such parishes were formed in various parts of the country, but their choice to do so depended in part on the distance they had to travel and the social class composition of the particular Mar Thoma congregation. At the time of my fieldwork in the Bethelville church, for instance, very few from this highly educated group attended on a regular basis, most preferring to go to a local mainline Protestant church. The majority of those who did attend came just once every few months. In the Bethelville church, another subgroup who had come to the United States for education comprised several men who had arrived in the region in the 1970s through church contacts, to study at a local Christian university that had an affiliation with a Bible college in south India (according to calculations, there were originally eleven such men in that parish). Some of these men married Syrian Christian nurses.

A second category of immigrants was composed of nurses. Beginning from the late 1960s there was a large migration of female nurses (and some male nurses who were almost always married to female nurses) recruited to meet a shortage in the United States (George 2005, 50). Nurses and their families soon came to constitute the largest group of immigrants in Mar Thoma churches. Some of the early nurse migrants mentioned that their migration had been aided by the Western missionaries they had got to know through their jobs in India, from whom they had received information and help. Female friendships and networks had also been critical to the large out-migration of Kerala nurses to the United States, as sponsorship rules were easy in the 1960s and 1970s. Several Mar Thoma nurses told me that coworkers and friends from nursing school in India were able to help obtain immigration visas (see also George 2005, 54–57; J. Mattackal 2008, 98). Many nurses had young children when they migrated, whom they had to leave in the care of their parents or their husbands (with live-in servants and relatives providing additional help). They told me how hard the initial period had been for both spouses. For instance, the Cherian family talked about how it had taken a month for the first letter from Mariamma to reach her husband in India (telephone calls were very expensive and few families in Kerala had phones at home). Sunny, her husband, said that he had been very anxious since he was not even sure if Mariamma had reached the United States safely until he received her letter. The nurses usually found accommodation in metropolitan areas with several hospitals, sharing an apartment with other Kerala nurses.

Beginning in the early 1970s, many states started requiring foreign nurses to pass state exams to work as registered nurses (George 2005, 57). Consequently, Syrian Christian immigrant women had to work long hours, often as nurses' aides, and take review classes in addition to their work in order to pass the exam. Their families joined them a few years later when the women had obtained the necessary sponsorship papers and had saved enough money to pay for their passage and for their support when they arrived in the United States. Their husbands, even those with a college degree from India, did not have a job waiting for them and many started out in "menial" jobs. They took night and weekend classes and obtained another degree in the United States (as their Indian degrees were not recognized in the United States), and many were able to obtain professional positions. Other men who did not have more than a high school education worked in blue-collar jobs at factories, airports, public transportation systems, or drove taxis. Some subsequently obtained the qualifications necessary for better positions and secured clerical jobs, or worked as postal service employees. A few men started their own businesses in the United States, some of which became quite successful.

Family and friends played a big part in helping with the adjustment process in the early period, often hosting families in their houses for several months. One young woman, Betty, emphasized the important role her mother's family had played when she and her brother arrived from India, along with their dad. "My mom's family here *definitely* helped. Um, the first couple months we lived with them, and then they helped us to get an apartment. They also helped my dad to get a job and my mom to get a job. And then, um, they helped me and my brother get adjusted to school." Miriam mentioned the difficulties her parents experienced in the early days. "I haven't really asked my parents, but they've always said it was a struggle in the beginning. You, you're in an environment very different from India. You're in an environment where you're the minority, you're unaccepted by everyone, you don't know anything, you don't know the language at first." Many of the early migrants said that they had only planned to stay for around five years, save enough money to live comfortably in India and fund their children's college education, and then return to India. However, they gave up that plan once their children started getting incorporated into the American educational system and society, because they realized that it would be difficult for the American-raised youngsters to relocate back in India.

Establishing the Mar Thoma Church in the United States

Since Malayali, usually Syrian Christian, networks were crucial in facilitating the migration of nurses to the United States, nurses and their families often arrived in areas where they had family or friends, and lived near them. The early migrants talked about how they would get together for at least occasional interdenominational Sunday services, led by lay leaders as they "felt like fish out of water without any Malayalee [Malayali] fellowship" (J. Mattackal 2008, 99). In areas where there was no public transportation, the community would arrange for the nurses who did not have families with them to be picked up, taken to the service, and then dropped back home. Visiting Syrian Christian bishops or achens would stop over in Malayali communities in the United States and hold Holy Communion services in local churches. People would drive long distances to attend such services. Other Syrian Christian achens who were in North America for education would hold services at their seminary chapel or in another church, and all the local Malayali Christians, irrespective of their denominational background, would attend. These "student achens" would also travel to locations around the country to hold periodic Sunday services. In a 2008 book discussing the early Mar Thoma community in the United States, Joseph Mattackal, a Mar Thomite, writes about how he and his wife were able to attend a small Malayalam Jacobite service at the Union Seminary chapel in Manhattan for the first time after arriving in the United States. Getting there involved taking a bus and three trains, but "once we got there, it was like an oasis in a desert" (J. Mattackal 2008, 97).

New York City was an important port of entry for those who arrived by ship or plane from India. It became an important hub for Mar Thomites, as many of them lived and worked in or near the New York City boroughs. The first Mar Thoma congregation that met weekly in the United States was formed in Queens, New York, in 1972, but soon congregations began to form in other major gateway cities in the United States such as Philadelphia, Los Angeles, Dallas, Houston, and Chicago. In the early 1970s, Mar Thomites in New York wrote to the Metropolitan asking for the synod's permission to form an official Mar Thoma parish in the city (Thomas and Mattackal 2008). However, the Mar Thoma leadership at the time opposed the formal development of Mar Thoma parishes in regions where there were Protestant churches with which the church was in communion, and wanted Mar Thoma members to become members of an Episcopal church (the American branch of the Anglican church) or to join Methodist or Presbyterian churches and to just meet once a month with CSI members for Malayali fellowship and worship, to be led by Mar Thoma achens studying in the United States. Mar Thoma American congregations were also asked to bear the travel (including the trip from India and back) and monthly expenses of these achens. The 1973 letter of the Metropolitan, Dr. Juhanon Mar Thoma, written in English, conveyed this decision to U.S. Mar Thomites:

We appreciate your loyalty to the mother church, and the desire to take part in our Liturgy which only brings us complete satisfaction. [But] [w]e felt that it would be a very undesirable thing to organize ourselves as a parish. To establish ourselves as a separate worshipping community in such centres where there are a few communions with which we are in contact, would be developing divisive tendencies. Where we are, we should identify ourselves with local communions. Because of racial difference there would be some difficulties. Yet we should not be victims of race conflict. (Thomas and Mattackal 2008, 232)

Mar Thomites around the country protested this decision strongly. In the meantime, internal tensions developed between Mar Thoma and CSI members in the Mar Thoma-CSI congregation in New York City due to fundamental differences in the orientation and liturgy of the two groups, causing the joint congregation to disband (Thomas and Mattackal 2008, 42, 120). The Mar Thoma leadership finally yielded to the demand of their American members, and U.S. Mar Thoma parishes were officially established in 1976. The Mar Thoma church developed a partnership agreement with the Episcopal church in 1979 through which the Episcopal church issued the documents to obtain a visa for Mar Thoma achens who were sent to take charge of parishes in the United States and also to rent or purchase buildings for worship (Thomas and Mattackal 2008, 47). In the early period the achens, who were usually also full-time seminary students, often served several parishes, commuting between them so that Holy Communion services could be held once or twice a month in each parish (Thomas and Mattackal 2008). From the mid- to late 1980s, many congregations that grew large were able to purchase or build their own churches and have a full-time achen conducting Holy Communion services every Sunday. The North America and United Kingdom diocese (now the North America and Europe diocese) was formed in 1988. In 1998, the Mar Thoma Church was recognized as an independent American entity, able to sponsor achens to the United States on its own.

The formation of parishes and dioceses around the world meant that the Mar Thoma church had to develop a formal system of assigning and rotating achens across the globe, each serving, at present, three-year terms. The church and the achens also had to meet the needs of Mar Thoma emigrants who were living in cultural and social contexts that were very different from central Travancore in Kerala. The Mar Thoma achens, posted abroad for relatively short terms, faced several demands for which they were poorly prepared. These included living and work-ing in a new environment, driving long distances, coping with different accents, dealing with the hectic schedules of their members, and un-derstanding the problems of immigrants. Due to the stresses of reloca-tion and settlement in a new country and the status struggles within the church, church events and general body meetings often tended to be emotional and conflict-ridden, requiring the skillful mediation of the achen. In the diaspora, families were also more likely to turn to the achen and his wife with problems (which they did not do in Kerala as they had families and friends nearby), and achens and their wives found themselves having to provide counseling services for which they were not prepared. Some of the achens who were serving or had served in North American parishes confessed to me that their training to cater to "sacramental questions" had not equipped them to deal with the many challenges they faced during their foreign posting.

These challenges were made the more difficult for them by changes in the way members, both in India and the United States, perceived and treated achens, and in the way they in turn wanted to be treated by the clergy. In the past, achens in Kerala had commanded a great deal of reverence and authority because they were seen as "men of God" and because they were also more educated than most members of society. The increase in the educational levels of Mar Thomites, their interna-tional exposure and enrichment, and the spread of egalitarian ideals in Kerala due to the communist influence (Kerala has a strong Communist Party which is often elected to power in the state), had led this attitude to change, and achens and even bishops were often viewed as "employ-ees of the church" (not the "owners of the church," as in the past), ac-countable to the membership. Mar Thoma members in Kerala and in the diaspora were also calling for more democracy and egalitarianism in the church, and were pushing back strongly against many of the clergy's and bishops' traditional hierarchical and autocratic style of functioning, demanding to be treated with "respect."

Mar Thomites in the United States also emphasized that it was im-portant for the church and the achens to recognize the distinctiveness of the American context and how their lives and those of their children were different from those of their coethnics in Kerala. Susan Skariah, an immigrant and the mother of a teenager, summed it up this way:

The Mar Thoma church in the U.S. is trying to be like the Mar Thoma church in India and that won't work here. The generation gap is very different. Many families have a lot of problems and I don't think that the Mar Thoma church has awoken to that situation. The achens are not really prepared. They come here and try to run the church like they do in India but this is a totally different environment, and they are not really equipped.

Consequently, one of the major issues the Mar Thoma church faced was how to make the church, its practices, and its administrative structure relevant to Mar Thoma members living and growing up in other countries.

Mar Thoma churches in the United States also presented lay Mar Thomites with many new challenges. First, unlike in Kerala where the Mar Thoma church was generally only a short distance away, in the United States Mar Thoma churches were often in outlying localities where members were able to find a building with meeting space and also a parsonage at a reasonable cost. Consequently, most members had a long drive to church. In addition to the lengthy service and lunch (which apparently was provided almost every Sunday in the early days), all the activities—choir practice, Sunday school (generally held before the service), General Body, and committee meetings—had to take place on Sunday, which made it a full-day commitment for the whole family. As a result, Mar Thomites who were comfortable attending local, non-ethnic churches often opted to do this at least a few weeks of the month. The long distance also made youth programs difficult to organize, since the young people were not able to get to the church easily on weekday evenings or Saturdays.

Forming Mar Thoma parishes in the United States was also a big financial burden for American Mar Thomites. In addition to the expense of renting a church or purchasing property and constructing one, the achen and his family are fully supported by the local parish, which pays for their travel from and to India, housing (often by purchasing a parsonage), utilities, car and gas, and medical insurance, as well as a monthly salary. At the time of my fieldwork in the Bethelville church in 1999, the pastor's salary was about $1,400 a month. In addition, the Bethelville congregation supported several projects in India and also had to contribute to the mother church in Kerala. At the time of the departure of the achen and family after the three-year term, the congregation was expected to contribute to raise a generous financial "going-away gift" for the achen. Thus, the financial demands on parishes, particularly smaller ones like that of the church at Bethelville, were quite high. At the Bethelville church, each family was expected to contribute a minimum of $35.00 a month, in addition to the special collections during the year. In 1999, the church had a membership of over a hundred families and the annual income of the church, raised entirely from member contributions, was almost $100,000. Most of this money came from about 60 percent of the membership, and thus the average annual contribution of these families was around $1,500, though many contributed significantly more. At the second church that I attended in 2002–2003, the minimum family "subscription" was $50 a month (in 2015 it was $100), and the achen asked all registered members to contribute an additional $1,000 every year (later increased to $2,000) toward the church building fund so that this congregation, which was renting a church, could construct its own building. Contributions to the church were published and being a major donor was an important source of prestige for congregants. Church contributions were also a way to manifest support or demonstrate dissatisfaction with the current achen. Due to both these factors, finances were often a source of conflict. Several of the general body meetings that I attended at the Bethelville church featured emotional arguments around the subject of funds for the church.

Whereas congregational religious institutions in the homeland often serve "solely as sites for religious practice" (Ebaugh and Chafetz 1999, 599), in the diaspora they become community centers. Many immigrants turn to ethnic religious institutions to obtain the emotional, social, and economic resources to deal with the displacement and alienation produced by migration, and for the moral and cultural socialization of their children (Hirschman 2004, 1228; Yang and Ebaugh 2001). As immigrants, the Mar Thoma church became more important to its members, and many first- and second-generation Mar Thoma Americans described the church community as "an extended family." As the primary community center in the diaspora, the Mar Thoma church often became a refuge from the downward mobility, racism, and cultural misunderstandings that they faced in their work lives. Since men were more likely than women to face downward mobility in the United States, Mar Thoma American parishes also emerged as an arena where the "wounded male pride expresses itself" (in the words of a Mar Thoma achen who had served a term in a U.S. parish). At the same time, divisions based on class and education were deeply entrenched, and the "status consciousness" of people from Kerala was brought up by several members during our conversations. Consequently, the church also became a site for status displays and community conflicts.

A central division within Mar Thoma American parishes, largely carried over from the Kerala context, was between the highly educated, fluent English speakers, working in professional and managerial positions, who often hailed from well-known, upper- and upper-middle-class families in Kerala on the one hand, and those who had immigrated with a high school education or a technical diploma, who were not very fluent in English, and hailed from families in Kerala that had financial struggles, on the other. This social class division often overlapped with a status division between "high-status families" where men (and women who participated in paid employment) worked in professional positions and saw themselves as the "natural" leaders of the church on the one hand, and the "nurse families" on the other (since nursing was traditionally viewed as a 'low status' profession in Kerala). In his essay about the early Mar Thoma community in the United States, Joseph Mattackal, who was married to a nurse, writes about how some of the "old-timers" in the larger New York area resented the initiative taken by three recent immigrants to start a separate Mar Thoma congregation in Queens, and put out the word that "'nurses and their husbands' were not qualified [and] . . . did not have the social status to undertake such a venture" (J. Mattackal 2008, 100). George's 2005 book on female nurses and their families in an Orthodox Syrian Christian church in the United States focuses on how the downward mobility of many of the men and the stigma against nurses and "nurse-husbands" (the husbands of nurses) by the professional families and church leadership shaped the central dynamics in the home and church.

Often congregations were divided into several factions for other reasons as well. In the Bethelville church, I learned that there were divisions based on the region where members had lived and worked before coming to the United States, that is, between the "Madras [now Chennai] group," the Bombay [now Mumbai] group, and the Kerala group, with some members taking an opposing position just to go against the proposals of their rivals. All these dynamics led to tensions within and between congregations, particularly in the first few decades of the formation of the Mar Thoma church.

Another indicator of status carried over from the Kerala context also had important impacts on the Mar Thoma congregations: connections with the Mar Thoma leadership hierarchy. A Mar Thoma achen I met in Kerala, Mathai Kuruvilla, who had returned after a term in the United States, talked about the obsession of Mar Thoma immigrants who had grown up in Kerala with church politics. He told me that it was a matter of pride for Mar Thoma Americans to show that they were in close touch with what was going on in Kerala; their conversations and stories when they got together as a group were all about the different achens (who had been posted where, what their children were doing, which of their children was pregnant) and about the activities of the thirumenis (bishops). He also mentioned that access to Mar Thoma thirumenis became an important resource in the status struggles within the church.

Achen Mathai Kuruvilla indicated that members visiting Kerala would always call the *Poolatheen* (the residence of the Mar Thoma Metropolitan in Tiruvalla) office and try to meet with the Metropolitan so that they could return and boast about how they had close connections with him. Several times during the course of my fieldwork I also heard about how Mar Thoma American members had "called Tiruvalla" from the United States to complain about perceived infractions in the behavior of Mar Thoma members, achens, and achen's wives. Achen Mathai Kuruvilla also remarked that he perceived a sort of "competition" between Mar Thoma American parishes regarding which choir would be the first to sing the songs featured at the Maramon convention that year. According to him, even in the days before satellite TV channels from Kerala were available, when audio tapes of the songs had to be sent from India to the United States, it would take just two weeks for the songs to be picked up by congregations in the United States.

The Syrian Christian tradition of women adopting the denomination and parish of their husbands is another factor that shapes church dynamics. There is a great deal of intermarriage among Syrian Christian denominations, and traditionally women become members of their husbands' denomination and home church upon marriage. Leaving the religious tradition in which they were brought up can often be hard for women, and some mentioned this to me. Mrs. Idicula, who had grown up in the Syrian Orthodox Jacobite church, told me that although she now attended the Mar Thoma church, her "spirit is still with the Jacobite church." She said that she still attended a Jacobite church for Good Friday since she liked their service, an all-day fasting service that involved a lot of kneeling. Abraham Verghese, whose wife had been a CSI member before marriage, told me laughingly that the Mar Thoma service had given his wife a headache for months, until she got used to the antiphonal and sometimes off-key singing (the CSI liturgy is read, not sung). Since marriages within the same parish were rare, another way Mar Thoma marriage patterns impacted the church community was that girls and unmarried women in Mar Thoma church often did not feel the same sense of ownership and responsibility toward the church as the boys and young men.

Mar Thoma Families: Struggles of Settlement

Immigration can also create challenges in the home, since it often upends traditional patterns of gendered work both outside and within the household (George 2005; Hondagneu-Sotelo 1994, 2003; Parrado and Flippen 2005). Mar Thoma immigrant nurses were often the primary income earners in their homes. To manage child care and to maximize their income from overtime pay, most nurses worked at night for several nights a week as well as every other weekend, while their husbands worked during the day. Running a home and taking care of children in the absence of domestic help (earlier available even for lower-middle-class households in India) and extended family support was a difficult adjustment for many of these families. In Kerala, Syrian Christian men, irrespective of class, rarely got involved in household chores—"They don't lift a finger to do anything," as one of the immigrant women commented. However, based on the conversations I had with immigrants and particularly their children (who were more willing to speak candidly about these matters), it was clear that in the homes of nurses, men did quite a bit of housework and child care, reluctantly or otherwise.

There is now a large body of literature on the way the relative economic contribution of husbands and wives to their households can shape how they "do gender" (West and Zimmerman 1987). This research seems to indicate that when wives earn more than their husbands, they may attempt to "compensate" for their "gender deviance" by doing more housework than women whose economic contribution to the household is equal to or smaller than their husbands' (Bittman et al. 2003; Brines 1994; Greenstein 2000). Other research indicates, however, that social class is more important in shaping the division of household labor than beliefs about normative gender behavior. Due largely to financial constraints, working-class couples (particularly shift workers) with more traditional gender ideologies tend in practice to be more egalitarian than men and women in professional or managerial positions who espouse gender-egalitarian ideologies (Usdansky 2011). As we see below, the Mar Thoma case shows that while nurses and their husbands generally upheld a traditional gendered division of labor, the practical necessities of juggling child care, household chores, and paid work often trumped gender ideology. Professional immigrants and their spouses, on the other hand, espoused more liberal gender ideologies but tended to be more traditional in their practice.

Mrs. Philipose, a nurse who worked long hours, was one of the few immigrant women who was forthright about how women like her struggled to manage both home and work. She told me that she got her husband to help with household chores, despite his protests.

> You know Kerala men in India—they won't do a thing in the house. Here men have to do more in the house because the women are working and they have no choice. If you are working, just like him, then they have no choice but to do some housework. In India men don't help even if their wife works because the men's mothers support them. Here they don't have that and have to listen to the wife.

Mrs. Philipose pointed to two factors that led men to do more housework in the United States: the fact that women were working (and though she does not mention it, were also the primary income earners at home), and the isolation of the nuclear immigrant family. Mrs. Thomas, who also worked as a nurse, indicated that her husband had not done any work when they were in Kerala because their family had domestic help. She continued, "But now of course, he does much more. I do the cooking, but he frequently cuts things up for me, he cleans the house—he is the one who polished the floor [I had admired their glossy red floor that reminded me of the traditional red oxide floors in Kerala] and does the yard work. In fact, now when we go back to India, we feel strange if we can't do things for ourselves."

There were, of course, some households where men did not do much— here the children did many of the chores—but this seemed exceptional, and was of course only possible after the children were old enough to do the chores. Although the husbands of nurses usually did not do much cooking, particularly of Indian food, many helped with the chopping of vegetables and meat, and participated to some extent in all other aspects of housework. In shift-work households, men had primary care of their children and the house while their wives were at work. This might include getting their children ready for school, making breakfast for them, heating up their dinner (usually precooked by the mother), bathing them, and getting them ready for bed. However, men and women in these households still "did gender." In the conversations about housework, there was a lot of discussion of "men's jobs" (yard work and car maintenance) and "women's jobs" (housework), and it was clear that women did the bulk of the work inside the house and most of the cooking.

With respect to decision making at home, most of the second generation described it as "shared" by their parents, and it appeared that immigrant nurses had a big say in the home. A few of the younger generation mentioned that even though their mothers made more money, their father was the head of the household and made all the decisions. But even here, they added phrases like "but my mother would strongly sway him one way or the other." I heard of two cases where women appeared to be trying to "compensate" at home for making more money. Jacob stated,

My mother always submitted to my father when it comes to those types of issues. She . . . she knew it was already an issue that she made more money than my father did, so she never overplayed that, like, I make more money, I am going to make this decision . . . she definitely went out of her way to make sure that it seemed as though he was basically heading the household.

On the basis of reports by the second generation regarding their parents' behavior, however, this type of "compensatory" behavior at home seemed to be unusual. The general way Mar Thoma Americans tended to "do gender" and the difference between the behavior of immigrants (mainly referring to nurses and their husbands) at home and within Syrian Christian community spaces was summarized nicely by a young, second-generation couple, Alex and Sarah, in a joint interview.

> ALEX: In our parents' generation, socially it was like the wife should do everything [housework]. But really, behind closed doors, guys, even our dads, did a lot of things.
> SARAH: I mean it is like, our moms made 90 percent of the decisions in the household.
> ALEX AND SARAH TOGETHER, LAUGHING: But on the outside . . .
> ALEX: The dad actually vocalized the decision.
> SARAH: Yeah!

In the households of immigrant professionals, the husband was the primary income earner or both spouses earned about similar amounts (judging by the types of jobs they mentioned). Men in these households did some of the housework, particularly if the women had full-time jobs. But often the women in these families withdrew from the labor force, at least while their children were young. If they did not give up their jobs, they tried to work shorter hours and relied on day care to look after their preschool children. Since immigrant professional families did not do shift work like nurses and their husbands, the professionally educated men did not have to learn to take care of all the household details by themselves the way that the husbands of nurses did. They only had to occasionally "help" their wives.

Even though the husbands of nurses did more work at home than their professionally employed counterparts, the primary burden in nurse families was still on the women. I heard many accounts from the children of nurses about the incredible hours their mothers would keep, both at work and at home. Their mothers would come home in the morning after overnight work at the hospital, cook for the family, and then take care of the children during the day. It seemed as though they barely got any sleep. Jacob talked about how his mother worked from 7 a.m. to 3 p.m. in one hospital and from 3.30 p.m. to 11 p.m. in another hospital and would get up at 5 a.m. to cook for the family. Describing the punishing hours her mother maintained, Susan laughed and said, "Yeah, my mom's phenomenal. I don't even know like what planet she's from, like seriously because I'm a stay-at-home mom, and I have no idea how she even kept her sanity with the four of us [Susan had three siblings]." Mary described how her mother would take her Indian clothes to work on Saturday nights, change in the hospital, go to church with the family, come home, have lunch, and only then be able to rest. Later in the conversation, Mary remarked on her mother's ability to come home after her twelve-hour night shift and then cook a full meal in thirty minutes, describing her as a "super mom" who did "everything at home" even though she worked long hours at the hospital.

Sadly, despite the fact that the Mar Thoma parishes in the United States were composed largely of nurses and their families, and were built largely "on the backs" of nurses, this labor remains largely invisible to the Mar Thoma church leadership, both lay leaders and clergy.[5] Only one of the chapters of the book on the formation of Mar Thoma parishes in the United States refers even briefly to the contributions of nurses. Abraham Mattackal (2008, 222) recalls:

> Mothers of the Nursing profession were doing night shifts while taking care of their babies or little children during the day time. Hardly three hours' sleep did they get in a 24 hour period. Church life was part of their very existence. After coming from the night shift, they often had to prepare a dish to take . . . to the Church for lunch together after the service on Sundays.

Again, instead of lauding the additional household contributions of the husbands of nurses, "nurse-husbands" were often the subject of derision among the professional group within Mar Thoma congregations for being emasculated and under the thumbs of their wives.

Raising children in the American environment was another challenge for immigrants that came up frequently in my conversations, particularly with the women. I noticed an interesting difference between women who worked as nurses and the women in immigrant professional households. Nurses usually emphasized how strict they had been with their children and how they had brought them up within the traditions of Indian culture (that is, Indian culture as it had been when they were growing up), while the women in immigrant professional households (whether or not they themselves were working as professionals), usually underscored that they had followed a more liberal approach to child rearing and had given their children a measure of independence and freedom.

As an example, here are the contrasting accounts of Mrs. Philipose, a nurse, and Mrs. Ninan, the wife of a doctor. Mrs. Philipose, who was the mother of two teenage girls, told me,

> I was really strict with my daughters, bringing them up in the real Indian culture. I would keep telling them about my culture and how I was brought up. They have heard those stories so often that now they say, enough, we don't want to hear them anymore! Whenever they ask me if they can do something that their schoolmates are doing, I tell them, "No, we don't do that in our culture."

Mrs. Philipose told me that essentially her daughters were only allowed to go to school and come back. They could meet their friends in school and call them over the phone, but she and her husband did not permit them to go anywhere else with their school friends "because their culture and our culture are very different." The only exceptions were for school groups accompanied by a teacher. Mrs. Philipose and her husband also arranged their schedules so that one of them was always home with the girls. A little later in the conversation, she remarked that she "always tells the girls that they should marry from our people. Here marriages are not long lasting, people just get into one marriage after another." She said her daughter (talking about her older one) was agreeable to having an arranged marriage with a boy from India, as long as he was [a Malayali] from one of the metropolitan areas outside Kerala.

Like Mrs. Philipose, Mrs. Ninan had two girls; one was married and working, the other was in college. However, in contrast to Mrs. Philipose, Mrs. Ninan said that instead of imposing rules, she would have discussions with her daughters. "I would tell them that you don't have to do what your friends are doing if it is not right." Since I had heard by then, both from immigrants but particularly from the second generation, about Mar Thoma parents telling their children not to do what their friends were doing because "it is not Indian culture," I pressed her on this issue. Mrs. Ninan responded that she never brought up India in those discussions with her daughters. "I always said, this is how I feel. To me, this is not right." Her daughter's friends were mostly white Americans and she would let her children go to their friends' houses even for sleepovers (which most other church families would not permit). But Mrs. Ninan said she would make sure that the mother of the house was at home. She also encouraged her daughters to bring their friends to their home. She said that the only condition she insisted on when they went out was that they tell her where they were going. "But I never made them feel that it was because I was checking on them. I told them, it is not because I don't trust you, but it is for your safety." She went on to tell me that she believed "when in Rome, do as the Romans do," though within limits, "not the bad things." I asked explicitly about dating, again something that was taboo in most Mar Thoma households, and Mrs. Ninan said that when her older daughter (she too only talked about her older daughter) was in high school she would go out in a group with a couple of girls and a couple of boys, and she had been comfortable with that. She also told me that she had told her girls that they could marry whoever they wanted, "as long as they are educated." Her older daughter had married a white American man.

For a variety of complicated reasons to be discussed later, immigrant nurses and their husbands put a lot of pressure on their children to marry other Syrian Christians. However, several of the children of some of the pioneering Mar Thoma American nurses and husbands had married non-Indians, mostly white Americans, probably because there were hardly any second-generation Indian Americans in their age group at the time. The first few such marriages had apparently caused a huge uproar, both within the families and the church congregation, with parents threatening to cut off their relationships with their children, and church members "calling Tiruvalla" to ask the Mar Thoma leadership to excommunicate the parents. By the time of my fieldwork, although marriages outside the community were more accepted, the dominant pattern was that marriages of second-generation Mar Thoma Americans were with other Syrian Christians. The exception seemed to be children of the professional families, who continued to marry non-Indians. Due to the fact that it is hard for a non-Malayali to be comfortable in the Mar Thoma church, and because of the Mar Thoma church's own policies regarding men who were not Mar Thomites (see below), one of the consequences of these differences in marriage patterns was that children of professional families were much more likely to leave the Mar Thoma church. They were also far more likely to attend liberal American denominations even if they married a Mar Thomite.

The Second Generation: Growing Up Mar Thoma Christian in the United States

A common theme in the accounts of most second-generation Mar Thoma Americans, particularly the women, had to do with how "strict" their parents had been. Here is Sarah's narrative, which was quite typical of the experiences described by many second-generation women:

> My parents were very strict, they didn't like dances at school, they didn't let me go to any, whereas my friends would go. I felt really bad. I couldn't go to slumber parties with my girlfriends. In high school, there were times when . . . my friends were all involved and going to the dances, getting together and all that. And once they said, why don't you ever come and I never thought about it and I said well, maybe I'll come. I asked my parents and my dad especially was very adamant that it is not our culture. So I never asked again. He was very strict about it, didn't let me go. Even my prom. Here it is a big deal and I wasn't allowed to go.

Leela, who had a fairly similar account, provided the explanation her parents gave her for not letting her to go to her friends' houses for sleepovers. She said that they had told her, "There is no point in living in someone else's house when you have a home here. We have a house, we've established a home here." Leela commented, "It is more about honor and pride." Unlike Sarah, Leela said she did not have conflicts with her parents over their rules because, "I saw other Indian parents and they were the same exact way so I knew that everybody was going through what I was going through."

Although boys had more freedom than girls, George complained about the restrictions he had faced when he was young. He said his friends would go to the park, but "I was hardly allowed to go out. My father was very strict about this. The constant refrain was, 'in our culture, we don't do that. It is not right. In our culture, children stay at home with parents and study.'" Regarding school dances, his father had said, "Only crazy American kids do things like that. Indians don't do that." George told me that he had hated the restrictions and thought the constant emphasis on Indian culture as a reason was "all crock" and just an excuse to prevent him from going out and having fun. He said that he started rebelling in junior high and chose friends who were also rebellious.

Many of the Mar Thoma second-generation children were sent to parochial primary and secondary schools—either Catholic or Protestant—following the Indian pattern where there was a great deal of emphasis on sending children to Catholic, English-medium, private schools because such schools were expected to provide a better education, better discipline, and also to inculcate more Christian values and morals in children than the government (public) schools. Consequently, several second-generation members told me that they had first begun to develop an understanding of what it meant to be a Christian from the Christian programming in their schools. But this was usually a different type of Christianity from what they learned in the Mar Thoma church. High school was also the place where they first became part of interracial Christian youth groups.

Only a few of the second generation mentioned experiencing racial problems in school, but they tended to dismiss them as just a matter of a few prejudiced individuals. For instance, Leela explained,

> Growing up, I am the kind of person that if somebody treats me a certain way, for no reason at all, I just basically say it is their problem. I just brush it off. So I never took everything to heart. But I've seen a lot of prejudicial comments and . . . like, why is she in the United States, why didn't she do this in her country. . . . Like if I say anything about being proud that I am Indian, they would say, then why are you here in this country. And it is not anything about missing my country because I've basically lived here all my life so there is not a lot to miss. But that would be their comments. And taking up United States' money. . . . They felt that I was being like a freebie. But I've worked since I was almost 15 years old and I have paid my taxes.

George talked about feeling "inferior" as an Indian American when he was young "because I was dark. I wished I was white and not Indian. I developed a positive conception of Indian identity in high school but then it was for the wrong reasons." He said that Indians in his school were rich so he would boast that he was Indian and acted rich (he came from a middle-class family). But now, he said, "I am not being Indian to be cool but because it is who I am."

Particularly because their parents had not permitted them to spend much time with their school friends outside school, the friendships they formed in the Mar Thoma church were very important to the second-generation members. Sheila recalls, "I *loved* going to church actually because it was fun. It was a place that my parents felt comfortable to go and be open with our friends because it was church and nothing could go wrong." Similarly others remembered a close-knit community where the elders would get involved in their lives, to check in on how they were doing. When their parents needed something, they called their church friends, "and they were always there." In many areas where Mar Thomites lived close to each other, parents would organize "group baby-sitting" where an adult or older daughter of one of the families would take care of several of the younger children, so that the parents could attend to their shopping or other work. Even Shirley, who had since left the church, admitted, "Growing up, like my spiritual life I guess does stem from that [the Mar Thoma church]. Like I've made some awesome friends . . . we all grew up as like brothers and sisters. Literally."

Although members of the older second-generation cohort grew up attending the Mar Thoma church and its Sunday school, I discovered that because of the inability of parents and clergy to articulate the Mar Thoma theology, most of the older second generation absorbed their ideas about Christianity when they were in college through their exposure to evangelical college campus groups like InterVarsity, evangelical Bible groups like the Bible Study Fellowship, or nondenominational churches. The college years have been described as a religious "turning point" for many second-generation Americans (Min 2010, 143) and this was the case for American-born Mar Thomites as well. Their narratives indicated that it was during this period that they had searched for and developed a larger Christian identity. For instance, Reeba talked about how she had turned to Christianity and had started going to a local Calvary chapel:

Because everything was gone, all my support systems were gone. My college was less than 10 percent minorities. There was one other Indian person in my entire school. . . . I think that is where it started, when I knew I was a Christian. You look into my room [in college]—I had posters . . . [that] declared my faith—to show that I am not the kind of person you want to ask to go out drinking. I stuck out because I was brown, I stuck out because I was from New York and everybody else talked different, so being Christian was just another thing that added to that. . . . I really didn't mind that I stood out because I was a Christian.

Reeba seemed to be saying indirectly that she emphasized her Christianity in her largely white college because she preferred to "stick out" as a Christian rather than as a racial minority. She also used her religion rather than her ethnicity to declare her personal morality. Both these are themes that several other second-generation Mar Thomites echoed. Many who attended American evangelical churches during their college years did not return to the church even after they had moved back into the area.

Marriage was another topic that came up for a lot of discussion in the second-generation interviews. Several Mar Thomites admitted that they had dated in college without their parents' knowledge. Finding a spouse had been quite difficult for some of them. Here is Mary describing her struggle:

My dad was open if I was interested in anybody here in the U.S. . . . but [he] already said they have to be Christian, they have to be Malayali. . . . But, it's like I met a lot of nice people but there wasn't anybody that was, you know, in my age group here that was wanting to be settled. And I had very high morals, and [I wanted] someone who had those same values about marriage, and life, and their faith, and things like that.[6]

Some Mar Thomites had met their future spouses at regional or national Mar Thoma conferences, particularly the youth conferences, which were often known to be "marriage fairs." Immigrants who frequented Mar Thoma conferences also traded information about prospective brides and grooms they knew. I attended a national Sevika Sangham (women's) conference in 2007 where I roomed with an older woman, Mrs.

Valsa Thampu, whom I had met during the course of my fieldwork. Mrs. Thampu had come with pictures of two girls, daughters of two friends, and was going to show them to two immigrant women she knew who had unmarried sons in the appropriate age group. I had a meal with Valsa Thampu and her friends at the conference, and another immigrant woman at the table whose son had moved to Mrs. Thampu's region asked her for help to find a match for him. The young man had apparently told his mother that he did not want to go through newspaper advertisements or Indian Internet marriage websites like Shaadi.com (other common ways that Mar Thomites found spouses) but instead wanted to be introduced to prospective young women by "a church aunty."

Some second-generation American Mar Thomites had married spouses from India, which meant they had committed to marry someone they had only met briefly a few times. Mary, quoted above, ended up marrying a man from Kerala when she was twenty-four years old (she had been under pressure from her parents because she was close to being twenty-five years old "and it is like, that is the shelf life for a Malayali girl"). When advertisements in American papers had not produced anyone that Mary liked, her father put an advertisement in a Malayalam paper in Kerala. They culled the responses to come up with a list of five men who fit the profile they were interested in. Mary and her dad went to Kerala and Aniyan, the man who would become her husband, was the second man they met there. Mary liked him but was unsure whether he was the right person for her. "And usually in India, you know, they give you a week and then you gotta decide." She describes how she had anguished over her decision and "kept praying to God. I was like God, I hope that you show me the guy and he's got a green arrow on top of his head." She met with Aniyan two more times, and her family also met him. In the last meeting with Aniyan, Mary confirmed that he had "accepted Jesus Christ," an important criterion for her. She describes what happened next: "They [her family] kept on like oh, what do you think? What's your answer? Do you like him? And finally I felt you know, I had to give an answer. And so—I just looked at them and I said yes. And they all were just like, stunned, and then everybody, even my dad, just started crying."

Women who married Malayali men from India would generally only marry someone who could find a job easily in the United States, had been educated in metropolitan areas and was consequently fluent in English, and was also relatively cosmopolitan in their outlook. Men, on the other hand, were less particular and I was told that a larger proportion of Mar Thoma men than women married spouses from India. I heard about the "unmarried girls phenomenon" in several parishes around the country, that is, young women who were in their late twenties or thirties who were still single. Many of these women were also highly educated, and Mr. Lal Thomas, an older Mar Thoma immigrant who often helped to counsel Mar Thoma youth, told me that these young women wanted to have careers and it was difficult for them to find a supportive man. Additionally, more recently men from India had been having trouble finding jobs when they came to the United States, and Lal Thomas said that the women did not want to marry them and be "stuck [working long hours and being the primary income earner] like their mothers."

Shirley was an example of a Mar Thomite in her late twenties who was still single. She said that her mother had brought her up to be independent and self-sufficient. But this was proving to be a problem in her dating life. She had primarily dated non-Indian men in the past (but always men who were committed Christians, since this was important for her).

I have been dating and what not, but I just really enjoy being single. And every time I meet a guy, I feel like, God, do I have to relegate myself to going, "Honey, I have to go here" . . . you know. I've always been independent and I always date guys that are like—they've done their own thing. I've done my own thing. But now that I'm settling down, I tend to date more Indian [American] guys. But, past the first date, it doesn't go anywhere 'cause I'm so irritated. 'Cause it's like they want their wives to be submissive and what not, and I'm like, you know, it's one thing to be submissive, but, they want their wives to be like agreeing with everything they say. And I'm sorry, I have my own opinions, I am my own person. I'm not gonna be like "oh yes, Honey" for everything. No! And like, Indian [American] men, are very threatened by that. And the other thing is, I have a lot of guy friends, like I hang out with a lot of guys. That's the other thing with Indians. Indian [American] guys are like, oh, you should only be hanging out with me, and I'm like no. But yeah, I am looking.

In this discussion about why she was having a hard time dating Indian men, Shirley, despite being free-spirited and feisty, still seemed to agree with the concept that women needed to be submissive to their husbands. It was only the extent and manifestation of this submissiveness that she challenged. We will see that many of the Mar Thoma second-generation evangelicals shared this view, apparently a consequence of evangelical ideas reinforcing the conservative Kerala culture of the dominant immigrant group in the church. Shirley had left the Mar Thoma church for a large nondenominational church in the neighborhood. She now only attended a Mar Thoma service once every two or three months. She talked about the pressure that she and other unmarried women of her age faced in a Mar Thoma gathering.

> It's like, oh, welcome back! And I'm like, I'm not back. It's like oh, good to see you and then, since I'm like twenty-eight and not married, it's like, oh, any good news? And I'm like, no. And now I sometimes go, yes, I'm now pregnant. That's the good news [laughs]—I'm very sarcastic. And they just look at me like "oh." 'Cause you know with Indians, it's like, you know, I should have been married by now and had three kids.

Like Shirley, many second-generation Mar Thoma Americans (both women and men) who had dated people from other racial and ethnic backgrounds in the past said that over time they were gravitating toward preferring Indian Americans as it came time to "settle down."

Shelby, a young man in his early thirties, said he was dating a non-Indian, "but I am no longer completely against the idea of marrying an Indian girl." I asked him when his ideas had started changing. "I would probably say, within the last two years. More so after I've seen people who have married from India and seen the women and seeing that they are not backward, and they are very smart and educated and fit in just great, and look normal, and wear the right clothes." Shelby went on to explain that this change in his perspective had also come about because he had begun to see that when he was with his Indian American friends,

> The conversation is very smooth, and everything is just easy. Everybody knows where everybody is coming from, you can make kind of the Indian snide remarks and everybody gets it and you feel an immediate bond.

And I don't get that when I am anywhere else. So, there are times that I feel, maybe if this relationship didn't work, I wouldn't necessarily be objecting if they wanted to set me up with somebody.

He clarified that he would prefer a woman who had been raised in the United States, as he had.

The close community forged by the church also made some of the young women insist that they would only marry a Mar Thomite so they could remain in the denomination. Vinita spoke about how her cousins who were in a different denomination envied the vibrant youth group that she had in the Mar Thoma church. "And this church is amazing. I told my mother, I would never marry someone who isin't a Mar Thomite. This is the only church I know." However, even women who married Mar Thomite men and who remained in the same locality in which they grew up were not considered "members" of their home parish. Instead, they became members of their husbands' home parish upon marriage. Remani was an outspoken young woman who had married a man from India (she told me it had been "arranged through the Internet"). He had come to join her and she lived near her parents' home. Remani said that she had been outraged to learn that her membership with the local Mar Thoma church had lapsed the day after she was married and that she had automatically become a member of her husband's church in Kerala, even though she had not "set foot inside that church" and had been an active member of her own parish for a long time. The couple eventually started attending a liberal mainline American church.

Thanki was a young woman who had been very active in her home parish. She had dated, and then become engaged to a young white man whose father was a pastor. She and her fiancé had attended the Mar Thoma church a few times a month for English services during the period of their engagement and had been involved with several youth activities in the church. After their marriage they moved to another area of the United States. Thanki and her husband had wanted to become members of the Mar Thoma church there, but the Mar Thoma leadership, after deliberation, told them that the young man would need to renounce his home church and "become a Mar Thomite" in order for the couple to be officially considered members of the church. Thanki and her husband refused to do this and so they left the Mar Thoma church.

As in the examples above, the policies of the Mar Thoma church that insisted on church membership through the male line were additional factors leading many second-generation women to feel a lack of belonging and to leave the church.

Turning to gender issues within second-generation Mar Thoma households, the division of household labor did not seem to be too different from that of the immigrant generation, and in fact was probably more traditional than that of their parents. Among the married second-generation group, both men and women worked as pharmacists, software or computer professionals, laboratory technicians, accountants, and physiotherapists. One woman was a nurse and another was a medical resident. In all the cases, the man seemed to be the primary income earner or the men and women had roughly similar types of jobs. Many of the women who had young children were not working outside the home at the time of the interview. Although most of these second-generation members were children of nurses, they seemed to follow the pattern of the professional immigrants in their own households, with men "helping" with housework by doing the laundry, the dishes, and sometimes bathing the children. Some of the second-generation women admitted wryly that their household division of labor was a "work in progress" and that they were trying to get their husbands to do more.

In cases where the couples were living with their immigrant parents, some of the women expressed their frustration about how the older generation would not let their husbands do any of the work. For instance, Betty, who lived with her husband and his mother, said her husband refused to even learn how to do household chores and that he was supported by his mother on this issue. Betty wanted him to learn to do them so that he could take over when she was busy or when she was away. She said with feeling, "He is my husband and I am his wife so let me serve him as my husband and let him *be* a husband."

Although generally the unmarried women said that they would prefer to marry a man who would share in the housework, most of the unmarried men said that they would like to stick to "traditional pattern" at home where men did the "manly chores" ("the husband's job is doing the lawn, the girl's job is in the kitchen"). They were either opposed to cooking or said that they had not learned how to cook. For instance, Shelby admitted to conflicts with his non-Indian girl friend around these issues and said in his defense, "It was kind of something that I have grown up with. I just figured that once the cooking starts, guys sit outside [the kitchen] and wait for the food to show up."

The Mar Thoma Church and the Second Generation

Probably the biggest challenge that the achens who had been brought up in Kerala faced related to American children and youth who had grown up in a very different cultural and religious context. A Mar Thoma achen who had worked with the youth in the United States writes that "[T]here is always trepidation when one is asked to work among the youth . . . in the Diaspora" (Kuruvilla 2014, 97). Unlike Kerala, and even the Middle East and Malaysia, where the Mar Thoma church existed in a non-Christian environment in which it was relatively insulated (although this is changing with the spread of evangelical churches in these regions of the world), the U.S. church had to confront the issue of how to retain the allegiance of the second and later generations in the face of intense competition from local American churches. Mar Thoma American youth were attracted to large nondenominational evangelical churches, and many left for such churches. Even those who stayed in the Mar Thoma church imbibed many evangelical ideas: for example, they were against the long liturgical services of the Mar Thoma church and preferred nonliturgical praise and worship. While the church tradition is that the intergenerational Mar Thoma community worships together, the second generation was asking for separate youth services. They also tended to be quite critical about how "India-focused" the church was and the fact that Mar Thoma achens from India did not have the strong English-language skills and knowledge of the American context they needed to understand the lives of the younger generations (Kurien 2012).

Another topic of complaint had to do with the amorphousness of Mar Thoma doctrines. At the opening presentation to a conference of Indian Christian American theologians in New Jersey in August 2015, Amanda Mathew, a student of theology, spoke about her experiences growing up in the Mar Thoma church.

When I thought back to my church upbringing, I could not truly recall a consistency [in the theology]. I remembered what Christianity meant

during Holy Qurbana [communion] service, and how different that was
from what it was at our youth meetings, or in Sunday school, or at conferences. I would go to one Mar Thoma conference in which the speaker explained how evolution is in line with our understanding of God, and then
attend church the next Sunday and hear how the biblical creation story
is the only possible truth. The plurality was always present, but never
acknowledged. Each iteration of the faith was presented as the one truth
by whoever spoke it. (Mathew 2015)

The amorphousness of the Mar Thoma theology came up several
times during my conversations with the second generation. At a national
Mar Thoma family conference, I was sitting around the dinner table
with several second-generation members who were in their late twenties
and early thirties, the cohort that had seen a large number of their peers
leave the Mar Thoma church. We were comparing second-generation
Mar Thoma American youth with the second generation in Syrian
Christian Orthodox churches. The young men and women told me that
they had several friends who were Syrian Christian Orthodox and that
these friends were "loyal" to the church and had "an unshakeable Orthodox identity." In this context, I mentioned that I had seen that the Syrian Christian Orthodox Church in the United States had a FAQ section
on their website explaining their doctrines and how they were different
from that of evangelicals.[7] The Mar Thoma church would never have
this kind of discussion on their website, the second-generation members
declared. Bijoy, a young man who had been theologically trained, indicated that a characteristic of the Mar Thoma church is that it does not
have many clear doctrines and that it is consequently a fluid faith. Anju,
a woman in her early thirties, remarked, "If you talk to ten [Mar Thoma]
achens, you will get ten different responses." Another young man at the
table joked, "No, you will get twenty responses!" While Bijoy seemed to
see the openness of the Mar Thoma as a positive, Anju disagreed. She
replied, "You know, if you grow up in the Western culture, black is black
and white is white. You need a clear statement of doctrine and this is
what the Mar Thoma church lacks."

The Mar Thoma church has tried to be responsive to the needs of its
foreign-born generations and has made several changes in its functioning in the United States. This included requiring two services a month

in English with a translated and shortened liturgy. More recently, even the Malayalam services have been shortened. In addition, many parishes had a praise and worship session led by the youth before the service and also had a youth praise and worship service on the fifth Sunday of a month. The church developed booklets in English about the history of the Mar Thoma church and its liturgy. They split the youth fellowship into two: one for the English-speaking group and another for the Malayalam speakers (mostly newer immigrants from Kerala), and launched a young family fellowship for older second-generation Mar Thomites. They organized annual national and regional youth conferences (more recently also a Young Family Fellowship conference) and, from the early 2000s, sent "youth achens" (immigrant Mar Thoma achens who had good English skills and showed a special expertise in working with youth) to regions of the United States that had large numbers of Mar Thoma parishes. The U.S. church also developed its own Sunday school curriculum with input from second-generation members (earlier they had used one of the Sunday school series of David C. Cook, an American Christian publishing company offering several types of Sunday school curricula, including an Anglican edition). Following complaints from the second generation and some of their parents that the church should support projects in North America, in 2002 the diocese initiated a mission to fishing communities in Mexico and a Native American mission; some parishes also began local outreach efforts spearheaded by the second generation.

Recognizing the need to provide more theological education to its members and to get them more involved in the parishes, in 2008 the Mar Thoma church developed a Layperson Education and Development Program (LEAD) to provide theological education for church members both for personal spiritual growth and so they could be leaders in the church. Based on the titles of the topics, it appears that this two-phase program (with participants meeting once a month for six months) provides members with an understanding of Mar Thoma church doctrines but also explains some of the differences between Christian denominations in the United States. In 2013 the Mar Thoma church also started an "Altar Boys and Covenant Girls" program for teenagers so they could be educated about the practices of the church and help the achen with the worship services.

Several of these measures appear to be working. Many second-generation Mar Thoma Americans mentioned in conversations with me or in published articles that they were very touched by the passion of the Mar Thoma bishops posted in the United States, including the latest diocesan bishop, Geevarghese Mar Theodosius (affectionately referred to as "Mar Theo" by the second generation), "to make the [Mar Thoma] church more relevant for the second generation" (Jacob 2014; see also Vattakunnel 2014). Bishop Geevarghese Mar Theodosius encouraged more English services and initiated the publication of educational books and DVDs on the Mar Thoma church to serve as resources for the second generation. The bishop was also supportive of the desire of second-generation Mar Thomites to form their own English congregations in large metropolitan areas where there are enough numbers for them to do so. The first such second-generation Mar Thoma congregation in the United States, consisting of thirty-two families in Dallas, was given official approval in September 2015 to become a congregation after they had been meeting together in a local Mar Thoma church for three years for English-only evangelical services. A Mar Thoma achen had been assigned to the church in July 2015 to conduct liturgical Mar Thoma communion services in English. Recognizing the need to better prepare new achens arriving in the United States, the church has also been providing an orientation for them in the United States (this is in addition to a short training session conducted in Kerala before they leave) since at least 2009, with the involvement of the second generation, to help them get adjusted to the American context and the expectations of the second generation (Jacob 2014, 255–256). From a 2015 conversation with a second-generation achen, I learned that this session is now conducted over a two-day period around one month after the achens arrive in the United States, and that the new achens find it very helpful.

Conclusion

As we have seen, the Mar Thoma church has been a central presence in the lives of its members in the United States. Church networks played an important role in the migration of Mar Thomites to the United States. Settlement patterns were shaped by the availability of jobs, but also by the presence of Syrian Christians in the area. Relatives and friends helped sponsor migrants so newcomers settled near them. The Mar Thoma church community helped socialize newcomers to the American environment and provided family and child care support, forging a close-knit fellowship but also giving rise to class and status tensions. The church community functioned as an "extended family" even for the second generation, providing friends and marriage partners (from within the United States or from India), but it has also created a stifling atmosphere for older unmarried women, consequently pushing many of them out of the church. The Mar Thoma church leadership has been trying to be supportive of the needs of its American-born generation, particularly through the bishops posted in the United States, and has been bringing about changes in the North American and Europe diocese.

3

Coupling versus Decoupling Religion and Ethnicity in the First and Second Generations

Dissatisfied with the way the church was meeting their needs, some of the younger generation members of the Bethelville Mar Thoma church formed a youth focus group in 1998 to analyze the church's problems and come up with suggestions for reform, which they then planned to present before the congregation.[1]

> We met in the classroom behind the church every month. We started with the basics, What is our church about, what is the purpose of a church? We also went on field trips to a few churches. I kept the achen closely informed about everything. But the adults in the church kept asking, "What are they doing, what are they doing?" Then all of a sudden the rumors started flying, it is a secret group, Johnny is a cult leader. They couldn't wait and wanted us to present immediately. We said, fine, we will present what we have up to that point. I had all these transparencies prepared and rather than just saying this is what we want, I tried to give some background. I said, "We need to have a vision for the church." As I am trying to water the soil before planting the seeds, people are saying, "Get to the point, get to the point." People are interrupting . . .

Johnny, who had been the leader of the focus group, laughed as he narrated what happened that day early in 1999, the same episode (described at the beginning of the Introduction) that George had recounted to me in a separate interview. Since the congregation was getting impatient, Johnny said that he asked Sam, one of the youth leaders, to summarize their plan for youth ministry. Sam emphasized the importance of evangelism to the youth who no longer came to the church, and to those who came to church only because of parental pressure and spent most of their time outside during services. According to Johnny, it was at that point that one of the uncles jumped up shouting, "We don't need any evangelism. My father is a Christian, I am a Christian, and my son is a Christian." Johnny commented drily, "You see, some of them don't have the real knowledge of what Christianity is all about."

Johnny had started his interview with me by speaking at length about his "religious experience" as a young adult, when he had turned to the Bible during a time of personal crisis. "His word started to work in me," Johnny said, leading him to develop a personal experience with Christ. He and most of the other youth leaders believed that being a Christian meant having a personal relationship with Christ, often initiated through a "born again" experience of the kind that he himself had. Consequently, Johnny's critique of the uncle in the church (and of most of the immigrant generation) was that they were not true Christians because they viewed being Christian as primarily a matter of being born and raised in a Christian family and church community.

We have seen that the traditional version of assimilation theory had been based on the assumption of individualistic adaptation, with immigrants and their children expected to shed their ethnic identities to become Americans. In the sphere of religion, however, earlier European immigrants were able to maintain their communitarian traditions through American denominations. In contemporary society, multiculturalism, spiritual seeking, and post-denominationalism have reversed this paradigm. Consequently, contemporary first- and second-generation immigrants integrate by remaining ethnic- and group-identified, but religion is viewed as a personal quest. It is useful to examine how the paradigm shift creates intergenerational tensions within immigrant denominations like the Mar Thoma church. Second-generation Mar Thoma American understandings of religion diverged greatly from that of their parents. Religion and ethnicity played different roles in the lives of the two generations. Consequently, immigrants and their children had distinct ideas about the meaning of being Christian, the role of the church, Christian worship, and evangelism, which sometimes led to misunderstandings and disagreements.

The topic of generational cleavages within the church emerged right at the beginning of my fieldwork in the Bethelville parish and continued over the course of the rest of my research. "There is a split in the church between the older and younger generation," Chandy, a younger immigrant man, announced as we walked to the Bethelville Mar Thoma parish from the parking lot on one of my early visits to the church in the summer of 1999. Shortly after that, I went to the achen's house one weekday morning to meet him. He was out, but Kochamma (the term of respect for an achen's wife) welcomed me in and brought me some juice and a snack and sat down to talk to me until the achen returned. One of the first things she told me was that the youth in the Bethelville church kept demanding an English service every Sunday, while the older generation wanted a Malayalam service every week. She indicated that the current system (two English services and two Malayalam services every month) was a compromise. The church had tried having a Malayalam and an English service every Sunday (under the previous achen) but that had not worked, as people would attend the first service (whether Malayalam or English) and then leave.

That not having an English service every week continued to be a sore issue for the younger church members became clear when I met the youth representative, Philip, an undergraduate student, the following Sunday before the Malayalam service. With a short, bitter laugh he told me that in general the second generation "just sit and stand [along with the congregation] for the Malayalam service since they don't understand what is going on." As the mother of an active toddler, I found myself having to go out periodically during the service and I noticed that many of the youth, particularly the young men, spent a lot of time on the porch during the Malayalam service, several of them going in only for communion.

Due to its belief in corporate worship and its liturgy, children and parents are expected to participate in the worship together in the Mar Thoma church. Most second-generation American members, however, had imbibed the antitradition, antiliturgical, and individual worship orientation of nondenominational evangelical churches (Miller 1997). Unlike East Asian American churches that have a separate, evangelical English service for the second generation, the request of the youth focus group for a separate, "seeker-sensitive" English worship service in a room behind the church during the Malayalam service was denied by the achen and the church elders.

Of course, not all immigrant and second-generation Mar Thoma members embraced different models of religion or were at odds with each other, either in Bethelville or in other Mar Thoma American churches. For instance, some of the older members of the Bethelville church who had lived in urban India were influenced by Billy Graham and other American television evangelists, and did acknowledge the importance of having a "conversion" experience and a personal relationship with God. Similarly, some members of the more recent group of Internet technology workers had participated in American evangelical churches in urban India. In addition, because Mar Thoma parishes are also divided into several factions, some members always take an opposing position, just to go against the proposals of their rivals. Thus, during the above confrontation in the Bethelville parish, some of the first-generation members did stand up to support the youth, whatever might have been their motivation. Several second-generation members were apathetic about religion and only came to church because of parental pressure and so may not have been able to articulate what it meant to them to be Christian.

Despite all these qualifications, it is fair to say that most members of the immigrant generation (with the possible exception of some of the younger immigrants) to a lesser or greater extent had a shared understanding about the meaning of being Christian and the role of the ethnic church, one that differed in fundamental ways from the perspective of the majority of the second generation. The youth leaders of the Bethelville church (all male at the time I conducted my study) shared the American evangelical model of Christianity. Since these were the youth who were in charge of teaching high school and college students and organizing the youth Bible studies, cottage meetings, and retreats, their model was very influential and dominant among the second generation youth who were active in the church.

In my subsequent research on other Mar Thoma churches around the country, I found that fundamental differences between the generations were pervasive, though they were sometimes softened by the increasing presence of an intermediate group, new immigrants in their twenties and thirties who had grown up or had studied in urban areas outside Kerala where they had encountered American evangelical Christianity. Since both generations worshiped together, intergenerational divisions and frictions were often quite pronounced within Mar Thoma congregations.

Generational Differences in the Meaning of Being Christian

Immigrant Perspectives: Religious and Ethnic Identity Are Intertwined

For the immigrant generation, being Christian was inextricably intertwined with being Syrian Christian Malayalis. Except for those women who had become a part of the Mar Thoma denomination by marriage, it also meant being a Mar Thoma Christian. In other words, for most of this group, heritage, faith, and denomination were bound together and were all conferred by birth, as was the case of most other social groups in India. As Sam noted, "I did some reading about the Syrian Christian church—it was just another caste in the Hindu system instead of being about the worship of God." He meant this as a criticism, but for the immigrant generation, being part of the honored, successful, upper-caste Syrian Christian group was a matter of pride. In India, and particularly in Kerala, Syrian Christians had a clear subcultural identity as Christians belonging to an ancient, Middle Eastern church. Besides preserving their religious heritage, Syrian Christians maintained their distinct identity through the practice of prescriptive endogamy within the larger community, and through their characteristic names, cuisine, clothing, and jewelry as well as their inheritance, marriage, and death customs, all of which differentiated them from the groups around them.

The older generation told me that they had been taught about Christianity by their families and the Mar Thoma community: their parents, grandparents, other members of their extended family, and the local church. For the immigrant generation, being a good Christian (in India and the United States) meant attending the local Mar Thoma church every Sunday and participating in its activities, reading the Bible and praying every day, and being a "moral" person. Parents were expected to send their children to Sunday school, make them read the Bible, memorize verses from it, and to pray. Parents, particularly mothers, also periodically exhorted their children to live good Christian lives, a practice that they said they continued with their American-born children. "My mom would always tell me that I should be religious and follow the 'right way.' That was her big thing. 'Follow the right way.' I don't know what that means to this day," said Biju, a member of the second generation who rarely attended the church anymore. Members of the first and 1.5 generation indicated that in India being Christian meant in part that their parents had often been stricter than those of their friends outside the community. Several mentioned that they had not been allowed to watch movies at all or had been heavily restricted regarding which movies they could watch. Parties and dances (in the case of individuals who grew up in metropolitan areas in India where dance parties were sometimes organized) had also not been permitted.

Second-Generation Perspectives: Decoupling Religion and Ethnicity

Although second-generation American Mar Thomites grew up in the church and attended the services regularly in their childhood and teenage years, they had a very different understanding of the relationship between ethnicity and religion from the immigrant generation. Like many other religiously oriented second-generation Asian Americans (S. Kim 2010; Kibria 2008; Yang and Ebaugh 2001), almost all the second-generation members who were regular churchgoers—whether they currently attended the Mar Thoma church or a nonethnic church— separated their religious identity from their ethnic or sectarian identity, and said that their Christian identity was primary. In Sheila's words: "Being a Christian is more important than being a Mar Thomite. Mar Thoma is a secondary part of who I am. Being Christian is first and foremost—to know that Jesus Christ is our Lord and Savior. And only after that am I a Mar Thomite."

This decoupling of religion and ethnicity was partly a consequence of how they had learned about Christianity. Unlike East Asian American youth, for whom the family remains the most important influence on religiosity (Park and Ecklund 2007), all the young people I talked to who said that religion played an important role in their lives indicated that their primary sources of information about Christianity were not their parents or the achen, or even the Sunday school, as had been the case for their parents. As mentioned, many had attended private Christian schools and so had first learned about Christianity through the classes and speakers at the school. School and college friends and campus Christian groups were an even more important source of knowledge and support. A few had done a lot of reading on their own. They also mentioned television programs and websites. Most of the older cohorts of Mar Thoma second-generation members indicated that when they left home for college they "became Christian" through their involvement in evangelical churches and groups.

Although this qualitative study cannot provide numbers regarding the proportion of dropouts from the Mar Thoma church, every one of the older, postcollege young people that I talked to indicated that large numbers of their cohorts had left. This exodus began when they went away to college, but many did not return to the church even after they had moved back for jobs in the area. Many became unchurched, but those who were religiously oriented attended large, predominantly white or multiracial evangelical churches that were within commuting distance. In the words of Anu, a young woman in her late twenties who had grown up in the Mar Thoma church but now attended a large, multiracial evangelical church,

> As I got older, I started going to different churches to see what it's like . . . and I feel, once you attend another church besides the Mar Thoma church, most people tend to walk away from the Mar Thoma church. . . . Like our generation . . . the majority of them do not go. Yeah, they've all like pretty much started going to local churches and being involved.

My research on this phenomenon within the Mar Thoma church has also been corroborated by others. According to a 2013 study conducted by Mar Thomite Thomas Thazhayil, only about 20 percent of the second and third generation Mar Thomites continued to attend the Mar Thoma church on a regular basis.[2] An older Mar Thomite man I interviewed shared an unpublished essay on the Mar Thoma church that he had written in the mid-2000s. In the essay, he noted that out of the twenty-five children of the early Mar Thoma immigrants that he knew, only four still remained in the Mar Thoma church.

In the early 2000s, however, some activist, evangelically influenced Mar Thoma youth began to return with the goal of trying to minister to the second generation and to challenge and transform the church. Since then, younger members have been picking up evangelical ideas from within the Mar Thoma church. The youth leaders who teach in the Sunday school and who lead youth and young families classes are those who have attended (and in some cases continue to attend) evangelical campus groups like InterVarsity, evangelical Bible groups like the Bible Study Fellowship, or nondenominational churches. All the English oriented classes and organizations in the Mar Thoma church draw on resources provided by evangelical groups. For instance, the praise and worship songs sung in the Mar Thoma church are from large evangelical publishing houses like Indelible Grace and Hillsong, as well as contemporary Christian music singers; the young families groups use the resources provided by the Family Life series, Our Daily Bread ministries, and Charles Stanley's In Touch Ministries. One of the churches that I studied was using leaders from the Child Evangelism Fellowship and its curriculum for its Vacation Bible School session, at least for that particular year. As Elligson (2007) notes in his study of Lutheran churches encountering evangelicalism, the theological assumptions embedded in these organizations, forms of worship, and education are very different from those of the Mar Thoma church.

Although I am aware that there are several types of evangelical Christianity, following Ellingson (2007), Miller (1997), and others, in this study I use nondenominational evangelicalism as a generic term, since I heard remarkably similar ideas (with a few small variations) from second-generation members of parishes that were located in different parts of the United States, and from individuals who had attended a wide variety of churches and Bible groups. Some of these similarities might have been due to internal Mar Thoma networks where such beliefs were shared and discussed, but they were also articulated by individuals who were not hooked into these networks.

While there were differences in some of the specifics, being a committed Christian as opposed to a "nominal" Christian, according to the second generation, seemed to involve three primary components. The first was a personal relationship with Christ that was sometimes initiated as a result of a fairly dramatic "conversion experience." Often this happened as the result of a Christian revival meeting where a particular speaker had seemed to be "speaking to me directly." Many could give me the exact date on which they were "born again in Christ," "accepted Christ," or "gave my life to Christ." Having such a personal relationship with Christ in turn meant that "Jesus is the center of my life and the one that directs me in all that I do, in all areas of my life," in the words of one of the youth leaders. It meant knowing the Bible well and knowing how to apply it to everyday life decisions and problems. For some of the youth it meant that God was controlling every aspect of their life. "For instance, I believe that if my car didn't break down on my way to church, it is not because of mechanical reasons but because God is watching over me," said Joshua, a young man in his early twenties.

A second component, which was stressed particularly by some of the youth leaders, was the importance of having an intellectual understanding of Christianity. At a youth cottage meeting of the Bethelville church, the discussion was about a video they had just watched in which the speaker emphasized that Christians should eschew the relativism of many American youngsters and believe without any hesitation that Jesus was the only God. One of the teenage girls asked, "But people of other faiths believe with equal certainty that their religions are true. So how can we know which is the true religion?" She answered the question herself saying, "Well, I guess beyond a point, it has to be a matter of faith." Another of the girls followed up by saying that it was largely because of her upbringing as a Christian that she believed in the religion. Maybe if she had been born into another religion, she would not have believed in Christianity.

But Philip, the youth leader replied, "It is not just a matter of irrational and blind faith or upbringing. Faith should be belief based on logic and evidence. For instance, take George Washington. We were not there, we never met him, but we know and believe that he existed because of all the evidence we have." He talked about how there was all this evidence "proving" that the Bible was true and concluded by exhorting the group: "So, we should not just inherit our beliefs but actively study and educate ourselves about Christianity and make the personal commitment on this basis." In one way or another, all the youth leaders of the Bethelville church expressed this point of view.

The third component was the importance of evangelism, "spreading the word of God and bringing others to Christ." Some of the youth members argued that this was the central mission of a committed Christian. Many of the youth leaders told me that they felt a calling to particularly focus on the youth of the church—those still in church and those who had "fallen out." Johnny, who had become the Sunday school principal of the Bethelville church and the teacher of the most senior class (high school students), told his group after a particularly gruesome account of the horrors of hell, "This is why I am doing this, to save as many of the youth of the church as possible. I know I am headed for heaven. Hope to see you there too."

Generational Differences in the Role of the Church

The differences in the meaning of being Christian also meant that immigrants and their children had very different conceptions about the church, its mission, and structure as well as the role of the pastor, the types of sermons they wanted to hear, the language that should be used for worship services, the importance of liturgy, and even the type of worship songs sung in church.

Immigrant Perspectives: The Church Becomes Our Extended Family

Since the church that Mar Thoma Christians traditionally attended was the one that they were "born into," there was no question about which church to go to when they came to the United States (provided, of course, that there was a church of the denomination in the area). Although, as we will see, many of the second-generation members seemed to view the social and cultural function of the church as a distraction from its primary spiritual mission, most of the immigrants I interviewed emphasized that what they valued about the Mar Thoma church, particularly in the United States, was that it was not only their faith community but also their social and cultural community. As Nimmi Verghese told me, "Since our families are around in India, we are not so close to friends or members of the church. The church community here substitutes for the family we had in India." Thus the social lives of the members of the immigrant generation were closely tied in with the church. Most of them indicated that their close friends were other church members. Although many of the first generation were critical about the "groupism and in-fighting" as well as some of the achens, they said that they attended because it was a "comfort zone" where they felt at home.

A few members had previously been members of local American churches but although the congregations had been friendly, they had never felt part of the community. They had left and started driving a great distance to attend the Mar Thoma church. For instance, the Vergheses said,

> The members [of the local church] were nice—they said "hi" when you went into church and "bye" when we left—but that was about it. We didn't feel a sense of fellowship. If you fell ill there was no attempt to find out what was wrong. We also felt segregated there since we were not involved in any of the church activities.

Similarly, Gracy Mathai, who had been a member of a local Presbyterian church when she had lived in a part of the country where there was no Mar Thoma church, also contrasted the Mar Thoma church with the local church she had attended.

> One of the strengths of the Mar Thoma church is the strong sense of fellowship. For instance, my mom passed away in India. Within three hours of my hearing the news everybody came. I didn't even know anything about it—I was in a daze. They called my brother in India and found out when the funeral was and asked me if I wanted to go. They got the ticket for me and arranged to take me to the airport [in a city that was two hours away]. They picked me up when I came back. They arranged everything.

Another member mentioned that an important reason that people drove so far was that they knew that they could have a say in church matters. "People can speak their minds, which you can't do if you were part of an American church."

However, many immigrants said that the main reason that they had decided to join the Mar Thoma church (and drive the long distance there and back every Sunday) was for the sake of the children. "We wanted them to know our culture and to grow up in it." For instance, when I asked Priya Ittycheria, a woman in her late thirties who had immigrated to the United States when she was twelve years old, spoke with an American accent, and was very comfortable with American culture, why she attended the Mar Thoma church instead of a local church, she told me: "I like the traditions, I feel comfortable with my people and with Indian culture. I want my children to grow up with the Indian culture. This is the primary reason I attend the Mar Thoma church instead of a local church." Thomas Chacko told me, "It is important to maintain one's identity and culture. Maintaining the church language and traditions is an important part of this." He said this emotionally, after narrating a story about a Punjabi Indian man they had known in Canada who, on his deathbed, had asked his sons to promise that they would teach Punjabi to their children.

Another reason, usually unspoken, for immigrants to continue to attend the Mar Thoma church, also had to do with the children. Several people, both immigrants and second-generation members (usually those who were rather critical of the church and had left or were planning to leave), alluded to the fact that many who remained in the church did so to ensure that their children would marry Syrian Christians. For example, after saying that many of the older generation stay in the Mar Thoma church not because they liked it but because they had "no choice" [because they knew they would not fit into a nonethnic church], Lena Pothen, a woman in her forties, added that many others stay in the church "because they are afraid that if they attend an American church, their children will end up marrying Americans." Parents wanted to make sure that their children married within the Syrian Christian community. Besides wanting to maintain their language and traditions and to transmit them to their grandchildren, they also feared that they would not be able to form the close relationships with in-laws and grandchildren that is typical in the community (and perhaps not even be able to communicate with them); they might not be welcome to spend any length of time in their child's home after the marriage. Shelby, who was dating a non-Indian but who, as mentioned, had begun to lean toward marrying an Indian American, talked about how his mother felt uneasy even during short visits to her older son's house because of her white daughter-in-law. This was another factor that made him think that his marrying an Indian would make things much easier for her.

> The relationship between my mother and her daughter-in-law are a little strained . . . it is not a normal [Indian] in-law relationship. Because my mom goes in and starts cooking and she [daughter-in-law] immediately takes that as being, why, you think I can't provide for your son? She thinks that whenever my mom gets together with us, all she does is baby us. And

she doesn't like that. She thinks that my mom should treat us like an adult and like a lot of American families, should be friends with us, and not baby us. But there is nothing really coming from our side, to have that kind of relationship with her.

The Vergheses had a fairly similar explanation regarding why it was important for their children to marry Malayali Christians. One of Mr. Verghese's nephews had married a white girl and they described how she behaved "like a guest" when they all got together. Whereas another nephew had married a Malayali Christian woman "and they both just join in and help like part of the family" during get-togethers. Given the high divorce rates in the United States, parents were also afraid that their child would end up getting divorced if they married "an American."

In addition, there were racial fears. Another younger immigrant woman, Elsie, who had left the Mar Thoma church to attend a large Bible church, told me rather contemptuously, "People don't leave the [Mar Thoma] church because they are afraid that their children will marry from another culture." Here "culture" was probably a code word for race. It was only Roy, an immigrant man in his fifties, who spoke about intermarriage and the potential racial implications it might have in the future, as one of the factors keeping him and his wife in the church:

India is a "melted pot." We have people from all races there. . . . There are all shades of colors there. But we are afraid that if we attend an American church, the children will marry whites. Then our grandchildren will differ genetically from us. In the end, they may be too ashamed to put up pictures of the darker side of the family. You know this is what happened to Jefferson's descendants—they didn't want to acknowledge the black side of the family.

Although in this quote, Roy mentioned his fears about his children marrying white Americans, the fear of their children marrying black Americans was far greater. In the informal discussions that I was privy to during the course of my fieldwork, the marriage of their children to African Americans was always discussed as the worst case scenario a family could ever face. Like other Indian immigrants, Mar Thomites had a lot of negative stereotypes about black Americans and their culture.

But the loyalty of the older generation to the church was not just because of the community they were able to form or because it was part of their cultural heritage. Many spoke about how they appreciated the spiritual benefits of the liturgical service and the qurbana, which they had been used to from their youth. They found the liturgy comforting and it also put them in the "mood" to pray their personal prayers. For instance, despite the warmth with which Gracy Mathai described the fellowship and support she had obtained in the Mar Thoma church when her mother died, it was the liturgy that she said she had missed the most. The same was the case with the traditional Malayalam hymns, sung to the accompaniment of the organ. For example, Sosamma Mathew said she went to the English service for the sake of her children but that she did not like it. "It is not religious for me. I just go and come but don't feel spiritual at all." Like Mrs. Mathew, several others said that although they did come for the English service for their children or because it was the only Sunday they were free, they did "not get anything out of it." Because of the schedule of the nurses (most of whom had to work on alternate weekends), many families could not attend every Sunday and thus chose to attend on the Sundays that there was a Malayalam service. Perhaps because of this, many Mar Thoma churches had a much lower attendance for the English service, as Mr. Thampu noted:

> The very fact that there is a lower attendance for the English service shows that a lot of people don't enjoy the service. The Malayalam service is what we are used to. It is a cultural thing, like food. You can like rice and curry, or you can like hamburgers. . . . The liturgy puts me in the spiritual mode. It is like chanting, or singing the national anthem. You don't always think of the meaning but you still get a lot from it.

Since achens are rotated every three years, the older generation also recognized that attending church and participating in the qurbana was a spiritual good in itself, irrespective of whether they liked the particular pastor in charge and whether or not he delivered a good sermon. Their loyalty was to the Mar Thoma church, not to a particular pastor or bishop.

Mathew Alexander, an immigrant in his fifties, probably summed up the feelings of many in the immigrant generation when he articulated the reason he continued to attend the Mar Thoma church:

> I grew up in the Mar Thoma church. It was ingrained in me. I feel lost and left out [in the United States] and it is the Mar Thoma church that gives me a sense of proportion. We can go to a white man's church but our community is in the Mar Thoma. How much can we integrate into the local church? Do they accept us from their heart—for instance, if we want to conduct a funeral or baptism our way, will they accept it? I don't think so.

Despite being a highly successfully executive, Mr. Alexander spoke poignantly about his sense of alienation within American society and his need for the Mar Thoma church to provide him with a moral and personal compass as well as his community life.

Second-Generation Perspectives: Intertwining a Faith Community with a Socioethnic Community Compromises Spirituality

The perspectives of the second generation were virtually antithetical to that of the immigrant generation. In general, the American-born members did not seem to believe in the concept of an ascribed, inherited denomination but instead felt that it was important to "shop around" until they found a church that fit their requirements. The purpose of going to church was not to form social bonds but to develop a closer relationship with God; "worship isn't about anyone else but you and God" was a theme I heard often. Thus the community-oriented nature of the Mar Thoma church was seen as diluting its spiritual goal. Many of the youth seemed to feel that the Mar Thoma church was "just a social gathering" and not a faith community united in worship. They were critical of friends who they believed only attended the church for social reasons. For instance, Anu, who had left the Mar Thoma church, said dismissively, "I have a lot of friends who still attend Indian churches 'cause they want their kids to grow up with other kids that are their size and color and what not. And I feel—I don't feel that's necessary."

All the individuals who articulated these criticisms contrasted the Mar Thoma church with nondenominational evangelical churches. For instance, Manju said, "You go to church to learn about God, to be closer to him, to feel his presence, and to be renewed. Not for the politics and the social stuff." What she appreciated about Millbury, the large nondenominational church that she and her family now attended, was that she could "just focus on God," since "I don't have to think about anyone else, I don't have to worry about what anyone else might think about me or is going to say to me." In short, the second generation viewed ethnicity and social bonds as being distractions from achieving their spiritual goals.

The language barrier was another obstacle to spiritual growth that several youth mentioned. Even second-generation members like Mary, who knew Malayalam fairly well, mentioned the language barrier they faced during the Malayalam services:

> I know Malayalam, but when I pray from deep down in my heart, it's like in English. . . . You know, the parents always argue, well the kids should learn Malayalam. But you wanna ask them, it's like, Mom, would you be able to really feel, you know, the Holy Spirit moving in you if you sang a song in English versus Malayalam?

Several of the youth indicated that even the English service was not meaningful for them. Biju told me that the English service at the Mar Thoma church "really didn't do much for me at all. To me it was like reading a script when we were there. One person reads, and another person says something else and then I know, okay three more pages and I get to sit down!"

Other ethnic features of the church also came in for a great deal of criticism. Several focused particularly on the liturgy, which they thought should be "done away with." "Right now, no one focuses on the meaning. They just sing it from habit. I feel we should at least rewrite it so it is shorter and more meaningful," said Sam. Most of the American-born generation compared the Mar Thoma liturgical worship negatively to the worship in the evangelical churches they had attended, saying that it was "repetitive," "boring," "regimented," and "dead," in contrast to the worship in the nondenominational churches, which they described as being "on fire for Christ," "uplifting," "amazing," and "passionate." Several others also compared the restrained style of the Mar Thoma church to what they described as "free worship" (where people clap and raise their hands during worship). Reeba, a twenty-nine-year-old mother of two, said: "I feel that being in an Indian church inhibits me because if I raise my hands, someone is going to tell my mom and it is like, oh, is she Pentecostal now? So being able to worship free is a big deal, you know."

Rather than the traditional hymns sung to the accompaniment of an electric organ, the younger generation indicated that they preferred singing "praise songs" with a guitar, since they found singing that way to be "a very spiritual experience." About a year before I started my research in the Bethelville church, a few of the youth had done this regularly before the English worship service. But there had been a lot of criticism from the older generation. Joshua, one of those who had been involved in the singing, said:

> I would look out into the congregation and the expressions on people's faces alone told me that they did not like it. Some of the uncles even came up to us and told us that. They said that they did not want to add to the length of the service with the singing. And there was one uncle who asked the achen sarcastically, "Did the Thirumeni appoint them to sing before the service?" This kind of criticism really tore me up since we had to put in so much effort to keep the singing going. I had to get there early, before the Sunday school, to practice and set up the mikes.

Many in the second generation also seemed to feel that their parents' generation viewed religion as an ethnic ritual or a magical rite, and questioned whether they had a personal relationship with Jesus. For instance, in the words of Ravi, a young man in his late twenties:

> It's like we have a generation of parents, you know, and . . . I don't know if they've accepted Jesus as their savior, you know? But [they just do] the ritualistic things like coming to church, sending your kids to Sunday school, singing in the choir. Those are all great things, but do you have a personal relationship?

Like several others in church, Ravi saw his parents' religion as merely a superficial "Sunday Christianity" instead of being something deeper and more personal.

Second-Generation Perspectives: We Attend Church for Spiritual Food

Another common complaint the youth had about the Mar Thoma church was about not being "spiritually fed" and not experiencing "spiritual growth." This criticism primarily focused on the nature of the sermons given by Mar Thoma achens and the fact that achens from India did not have the English-language skills and the knowledge of the American context to preach sermons that were relevant to their lives and that addressed "the concerns of the second generation such as the pressures they face growing up here—dating, drugs, drink." For instance Chris, who attended a nondenominational church in addition to the Mar Thoma church, explained that although he liked attending the Mar Thoma church because of the community there, he attended the nondenominational church to address his spiritual needs. "You go to church for two and a half hours but the message is only for fifteen minutes. So I felt I was not getting fed. I wanted to be convicted by the message. I want a gospel message from the Bible." Alex explained the exodus of the youth from his church this way: "They were looking for more, in terms of being fed spiritually. Because every Sunday they'd come and hear a sermon that doesn't touch them, doesn't teach them anything, and it just makes them feel bad."

Several second-generation youth felt that the achens did not understand them, and were not really interested in getting to know them. Amalia focused on the inability of the achens from India to relate to their lives and struggles: "Because priests who come from Kerala, they have *no* idea what goes on here. They don't know what college life is like. They don't know what the social life is like here. So how can they relate to us? They know the Bible but you should be able to relate the Bible to what we go through in a normal day's life. To lead us, to say, what you guys did here was wrong, what you guys did here was right." Johnny said passionately, "Pastors should focus more on the youth since they are the future of the church. Currently pastors are very oriented toward adults. Look, they attend the area prayer meetings, and the women's meetings, but not the youth cottage meetings. Shouldn't it be the other way around, I am asking." Several members of the second generation similarly mentioned that they would like the pastors to be more youth-focused in their sermons.

They were also critical of the short terms of the pastors, as they felt their stay was too short to accomplish anything. Reeba had attended a Calvary chapel while she was in college and emphasized the importance of having a long-term relationship with a pastor and having sermons that had a practical application to her life:

> I think the biggest thing at Calvary chapel for the five years I was there, it was one consistent pastor. It was *so* wonderful. So you build your relationship with him, you know his learning style. . . . And the second part is that all the messages we ever heard at Calvary chapel had to do with our own lives. So every day we walked in there with a conviction that something's got to change in our lives to make it more like Christ. You've got to change. Whereas in [her Mar Thoma church], the messages were more like God is good. I wasn't as clear about how it applies to my life.

Johnny made a similar point, telling me, "In fact, Rick Warren in his book says, you want to kill a church, just make your pastor stay in the church for a short term. Three years, four years, what vision can you plan? . . . He comes straight from India. It takes one year to know about everything, to learn about the youth. . . . By the time he is ready [to talk with us] he is packed up and gone."

Many young people felt that important larger issues in their world were absent from the achens' teaching. Mary felt that the church did not put enough emphasis on evangelism. "How many of us are told to go to our workplaces and told to share? How comfortable can we be about inviting people to come to our church? We are not encouraged to do this. And this is part of the great commission; this is what we are called to do." Others complained about the church's not addressing or taking a clear stand on contemporary issues like evolution, infant baptism, abortion, homosexuality, and dating before marriage. For instance, Tom said:

I think the Mar Thoma church currently doesn't have a strong stance on a lot of like key issues. For example, like where does evolution fit in with everything? Where does creationism come in? Like, you know, do we really believe that? Do we just believe in Intelligent Design? Why do we have child baptism? It's just like a lot of whys. Why do we chant the service? Why do we have a liturgy? . . . [We want] more doctrine, more theology, more focusing on like what are *the* issues.

Not only were they critical of what the achens did not say, but several youth were also very critical about the theological messages in the sermons and about what they claimed to be heresies preached in the church. Alex, who still continued in the church because he felt a loyalty to the church of his parents, admitted, "Um, the teaching here is not good. I don't think I've heard a single sermon from our current Reverend that has had any impact on me whatsoever. Jesus Christ should be preached *every* Sunday in our church, and he's not." Preeti was in her early thirties with three young children and attended a nondenominational church which she said she loved. She said she had left the Mar Thoma church because "the gospel of Jesus Christ was not being preached from the pulpit." She continued,

I have even witnessed heresies, completely opposite of what the church was founded on. Even from some priests. Mar Thomites should believe that Jesus Christ is the son of god, the only way to heaven, to the Father, to be forgiven of sin, to be breathed life. . . . There was a priest who believed something fundamentally different, that there are many ways to heaven. That Jesus Christ is *one* way, not *the* way, *the* truth and *the* life.

Second-Generation Perspectives on an Ethnic Church
An Ethnic Church Is Not Christian

In January 2015, an Internet article titled "The Indian Church Must Die," written by a second-generation man of Malayali background, went viral. After a long introduction, the article declares, "This is a piece about culture and why it has no place in the mechanisms of Christianity. . . . You're either 100% for the pursuance of every lost soul, or you're not. If there's

even a 0.01% misapplication of culture thrown in there, you're not 100%
for the pursuance of every lost soul. Culture has no place in the mechanisms of Christianity" (Samuel 2015). This emphasis on a "culture-free"
Christianity is one that I heard many times among second-generation
Mar Thoma Americans. Often, this was expressed in the form of an
insistence on the importance of a "multiethnic" church.

In striking contrast to East Asian American Christians, who are reported as articulating a strong sense of racial marginality (Alumkal 2003;
Min 2010, 152; Yep et al. 1998), as discussed, most Mar Thoma youth
referred to their racial status only indirectly. Although they showed an
awareness of being racially different or "brown," only a small minority
(six) of the second- generation interviewees referred to incidents of racism, most often as something they had to deal with while growing up or
as isolated encounters with a few prejudiced people. Again, unlike East
Asian American interviewees who spoke about feeling marginalized in
the larger evangelical churches (Alumkal 2003; Min 2010; Jeung 2005;
Yep et al. 1998), Mar Thoma youth who attended large nondenominational churches indicated that they were happy and well integrated.
Youth in the Mar Thoma church with friends who had left for evangelical churches described them as active members in leadership positions.
Rather than underscoring or even articulating their ethnic or racial difference from the wider society, throughout the interviews American-
born Mar Thomites implicitly or explicitly contrasted their "American"
identity and their comfort with individuals from a variety of racial and
ethnic groups with their parents' insularity. After rereading the interview transcripts carefully, I came to realize that this was not merely to
show that they were open-minded and "American," unlike their parents.
More important, it was to make clear that they understood pluralism to
be a crucial indicator of a "true" Christian (again, in contrast to their
parents). This can be seen by the importance they placed on having an
"open" church.

Viju, who was in a nondenominational church, emphasized the value
of worshiping with people of other cultures. When asked why that was
important, he replied:

> The main reason is, I mean heaven's gonna be multicultural. And so you
> know, one of the things that we always say about our church is, we want

people to get a foretaste of what heaven's gonna be like and heaven's not gonna be like you're worshiping with people that look just like you, but people from all different backgrounds. Like it says in the Bible, tribes, tongues, you know, of all nations.

Satish, a young man in his twenties who attended the Mar Thoma and a nondenominational church, was looking into seminary schools, since he was interested in going into full-time ministry and becoming a pastor. He said that in the long run he wanted to be at a church based "just strictly on faith" because he felt that the "political aspect" in the Mar Thoma church was a barrier to spiritual growth. Like Viju, Satish emphasized that heaven is going to be multicultural and that his generation recognizes the importance of having a "mixed" church comprising people from a variety of backgrounds, and not just Malayalis. He continued:

I feel like within the [Mar Thoma] church everyone here thinks that it's just gonna be Mallu [Malayali] people in heaven one day, and that's the end! [Laughs] But I can't blame them, 'cause they all did come from a different country . . . they were just taught that . . . it's hard. But like for the next coming generation, we know a lot more, so we can actually think and step out of the box.

His explanation makes it clear that the American-born Mar Thoma youth do not see a mixed church as a compromise that they have to accept because they do not have the numbers to form second-generation ethnic churches. Rather, he and Viju see multiracial churches as a theological mandate rooted in the Bible. This is in contrast with second-generation East Asian Americans who, while emphasizing that the church should abandon ethnic languages and practices and should be open to all, still preferred to maintain a largely ethnic membership. Interestingly, Rebecca Kim (2011) recently indicated that second-generation Korean Americans use the same Revelations verse (7:9) referred to by Viju (about people from "every nation, tribe, people, and tongue" worshiping together in heaven) to argue that if the Bible indicated that ethnic divisions are going to continue until the end of time, ethnic churches were justified!

We can see here that multiculturalism, as interpreted by both Viju and Satish, meant that churches should not be ethnic, but instead should be multiracial. However, a multiracial church would necessarily mean that many of the Mar Thoma traditions that are accessible only to the initiated would have to be abandoned. This multicultural perspective appears to be relatively recent. I did not hear this particular theological justification used by the earlier group of second-generation interviewees, although they had also emphasized the importance of having an "open," nonethnic church. This may be traced to the recent turn toward multiracialism within large evangelical churches, and might indicate that the youth were picking up these discourses from such churches (Emerson 2009).

The interviews with Viju and Satish, from two different Mar Thoma churches (Viju in the Midwest and Satish on the East Coast), were both conducted in 2008–2009. Several other young Mar Thomites who were interviewed after 2007 similarly stressed the importance of having multicultural churches, since "heaven is going to be multicultural." This theme has continued to be important even in 2015. Very recently, some second-generation Indian Americans (both Malayali and non-Malayali) who are linked to American evangelical organizations have sensed "a unique opportunity for Indian Americans to get into the world of gospel-centered, multi-ethnic, church planting"[3] and have started churches in several metropolitan areas of the United States with the goal of reaching coethnics and others. They argue that multiethnic churches are important since this is a mandate "found in the gospel."[4] According to author Sam George, in 2015 there were fifty such second generation-led fellowships or churches in the United States (George 2015).

Many of those who remained in the church also criticized its closed, ethnic nature. For instance, Jacob declared, "I believe in opening our doors to everyone. The Mar Thoma faith doesn't. It is very closed-door oriented. To me, that's not being Christian-like." Jacob was referring to the discomfort of the immigrant generation with members of the local community entering the Mar Thoma church. These and other statements from the second generation indicated that they viewed ethnicity not just as a spiritual distraction but also considered ethnic churches like the Mar Thoma to be anti-Christian for not being open to other ethnic and racial groups.

Valuing the Social Benefits of the Church

Despite their criticisms of how the "ethnic" features of the Mar Thoma church hindered their spiritual growth, most second-generation Mar Thoma Americans, even those who had subsequently left for other churches, talked about how much they had enjoyed being part of the congregation when they were young, for social reasons. Since their parents often forbade them from going over to the houses of their schoolmates, church was their one place of freedom where they could spend time with their friends. The church community had been like their extended family. Reeba remembered it this way: "You got yelled at by your parents, you got yelled at by your friend's parents, so it was very, very community oriented. And I loved it. I absolutely loved it!" Youth who were going to a local college, and consequently continued to attend the Mar Thoma church, often spoke enthusiastically about the nurturing youth group. Comparing her life in the United States with that of her parents in India, nineteen-year-old Rekha said, "We have a different life and different trials here so we have more questions than our parents." But she had found answers to her questions in the Mar Thoma youth group. She concluded, "If not for youth, I wouldn't want to go to church. They are my second family."

Several of the older second-generation members also spoke about how they appreciated the way church members rallied around in times of need. Like Gracy Mathai, who was supported by her church community when her mother died, Shelby, who was in his thirties (and only attended the Mar Thoma church occasionally), recalled how the church community had helped him and his mother when his father passed away: "I like that when there is a tragedy or something like that, the Mar Thoma church is very good about coming together. They will call the person, everybody will go there and meet for dinner and they will have a prayer session there and this and that. That is very, very comforting."

The community orientation and familial nature of the church were the primary factors motivating some second-generation members to continue to attend the services (sometimes in addition to a nondenominational church), to return to serve the youth, or to want to raise their children in the church. Alex said that he had stayed despite the fact that most of his cohort had left for other churches, because his father had

taught him that "your church is your family" and that it was his responsibility to mentor the "younger guys" in church. Similarly, Ravi declared:
"I've gone to a Bible study called BSF, Bible Study Fellowship. And that's
basically where I became a Christian. So I became a Christian outside
of this church. But I still, um, attend here. Because of the fellowship
and the family ties and because I wanna be there for these kids in this
church." Suja, a young married woman with an infant, talked about how
getting married had changed her outlook regarding which church to
attend: "I mean, it's interesting, because, before getting married, I went
to a hundred million different interdenominational churches. But then
after getting married and thinking more like where I would want my
family to grow up, now I'm more leaning towards like an Indian Mar
Thoma church." She went on to say that this change in her outlook was
not just due to family reasons, but also because she and her husband felt
that they had the ability to help the youth in the church.

> We talk about how like . . . there are a lot of young people in our churches
> now, who are just, you know, leaning away from it . . . and we feel like—I
> mean, at least I feel like . . . those are the people that we can reach out
> to best, because we've been through that experience. So I think we have
> something to . . . something unique to offer to a Mar Thoma church
> that . . . is different than what we could offer to, like, a totally interde-
> nominational, intercultural church.

There were also some young men and women who said that they
stayed in the Mar Thoma church to please their parents or to keep in
touch with their friends. Joshua said that he had thought of switching
churches after marriage, but "I don't think I seriously considered it only
because I didn't want to disappoint my parents." And Sally, who attended
a nondenominational church and only came to the Mar Thoma church
once a month with her husband, said that the reason she continued to
attend the Mar Thoma church was to keep in touch with Indian culture,
the Malayalam language, and their friends. She added, "But spiritually,
as far as for growth spiritually, we want to go to the church that we are
going to now." Similarly, Raju, who now attended a nondenominational
church on most Sundays with his wife, described his time in the Mar
Thoma church as "a social fellowship and we had lots of fun network-

ing and partying in the church set-up. But we had very little spiritual growth." Both Sally's and Raju's comments point to a tension that many American-born Mar Thoma youth who have absorbed the individualistic paradigm of evangelicalism feel between their social and cultural needs on the one hand and their spiritual needs on the other. Those that remained in the Mar Thoma church appreciated the ethnic community and social support the church provided, but felt that the Mar Thoma church and service did not provide an optimal environment for spiritual development.

Valuing Ethnicity but in Secular Spheres

This tension was particularly acute because second-generation Mar Thomites valued their Kerala heritage. Most married other Syrian Christians and, like their parents, practically all their close friends were from one of the Syrian Christian denominations. After telling me that her Christian identity was more important than her Indian identity, Sally went on to explain what she appreciated about Indian culture: "Respect for elders, the family emphasis. I enjoy going back to India. The food, the people, and all that. The values, I guess. I think the culture is a lot different from the American culture and when I go back to India I just feel right at home." She added:

> I would want my kids to still hold onto the Indian [values], know that they are Indian, know about where they come from and would like them to keep in close touch with the Indian culture. For instance marriages, we place such a high value on being married and staying married and we have certain times when we get married and a lot of different things that are not the same in the American culture.

Unlike their parents, however, American-born Mar Thomites felt that their spiritual objectives would be weakened if they mixed their religion with secular goals such as learning the language and maintaining ethnic ties. In Johnny's words, "I am all for Malayalam. Learn five languages, I don't really care. But church is not the place to learn language. Teach them at home. But that is not happening." Miriam, who had mixed feelings about the Mar Thoma church and was staying in it because it was her husband's wish, expressed her discomfort with intertwining ethnicity and religion, clearly saying:

> Don't get me wrong. I *love* my culture. I think I am more Indian than most of my friends. . . . But I don't believe that culture and Christianity have to go hand in hand. I think I can teach them [her daughters] the traditions of India and our ancestors without compromising their faith. And sometimes I feel that by going to the Mar Thoma church that's really what I am doing.

In Miriam's understanding of the relationship between culture and Christianity, the concept of a "de-ethnicized" religion was clear: she argued that maintaining Mar Thoma traditions would compromise the Christian faith of her daughters. Similarly Sally, who had waxed eloquent about her appreciation for Indian culture, was adamant that when she did have children, she would send them to the Sunday school at the nondenominational church that she currently attended.

> I wouldn't send them to a Mar Thoma church . . . because above the culture and the identity and all that, we have an identity in Christ and spiritual growth needs to be there. And I think that this [nondenominational] church would provide it. I would still do things with the Indian people. I have cousins. We do a lot of things, but you need to be grounded in the word of God and I think the Mar Thoma church doesn't provide it.

In other words, the second generation who left the Mar Thoma church tried to resolve the tension between their appreciation for their ethnic heritage and their opposition to ethnic churches by arguing that they did not need to go to church to be around coethnics. For instance, as mentioned, Anu, who attended a nondenominational church, had been derisive about some of her friends who continued to go to the Mar Thoma church so their children would have a Malayali community. Responding to a question about whether she thought she might return to the Mar Thoma church once she had children, she said:

> I know I'll always have a Malayali community. . . . But I don't—like my kids won't grow up in the Mar Thoma church . . . or an Indian church

per se. They'll grow up, surrounded by . . . [children of Malayali friends]. None of us go to church on Sundays together . . . most of us. But we all see each other like in social settings, and hanging out, dinners and birthday parties and what not. So, they'll always have other [Malayali] kids around.

Again, Tony, a young man in his early thirties, told me that he had dropped out of the Mar Thoma church because of its "hypocrisy" and had attended a Calvary church for a period. At the time I interviewed him, he described himself as "basically unchurched." However, most of his close friends were Syrian Christian, and he said that he still kept in touch with them by attending secular events. He too did not see the need to attend the Mar Thoma church to keep up with his social community.

Intergenerational Tensions within the Church

Since the first and second generations had such a different understanding of the meaning of being Christian, the two groups were often at odds, both in the church and at home, on the subject of religion. The second generation youth were contemptuous of the "automatic Christianity" model of the older generation. Several of them talked about the fact that the older generation did not really know the word of God well or how to apply the Bible to their lives. For instance, when Johnny, the Sunday school principal and one of the oldest of the second-generation members in the Bethelville church, preached one Sunday, he named three young men as the only committed Christians in church, angering several of the older members.

As in the case of the confrontation with which I began this chapter, the older generation were deeply offended when the youth stated or implied that they, the elders, were not true Christians because they did not have a "born again" experience and did not personally evangelize. Williams (1996, 58) points out that Syrian Christians have traditionally avoided active evangelism, "which may have contributed to their peaceful relations with their Hindu neighbors" and was probably also important for their survival as a minority group in Kerala. The importance of tolerance and of getting along with non-Christians seemed to be a philosophy that even the Metropolitan upheld, since he wrote in one of his pastoral letters from Kerala (which was read aloud in church), that

"Mar Thoma Christians have to realize that we live among those with different faiths and we have to live in harmony with them." Thus, while the second generation was right in saying that their parents' religion was basically about following traditions and rituals, they did not understand or appreciate the context within which these traditions were formed. Dr. Peters, one of the founding members of the Bethelville church, summed up the perspective of many of the older generation when he said, "We are a traditional church. We are not like the Pentecostals who go after people. We believe that it is the obligation of those who are Christians [by birth] to go to their church and become part of the church. And though we may not personally evangelize to non-Christians, our church supports the activities of missionaries who do."

When talking to me, many members of the older generation spoke passionately about the hardships that they had experienced (and continued to experience) due to the process of immigration and relocation. In most cases, they justified these hardships by saying that it had been for the sake of the children (although it was not always clear that this was the original motivation for the migration). Thus, they found it particularly upsetting when the youth in the church were trying to take away the one place where they could re-create home and be validated, and when their children were rejecting all their cherished traditions and becoming strangers to them. The youth, on the other hand, felt that their parents were placing an undue burden on them. As one young man put it, "We didn't ask them to come here. But now that they are here, they can't expect us to act like we are still living in India in the 1960s."

The tensions between the two sides often came to a head over the issue of marriage; this was particularly true in the 1990s, when the community was small and interracial marriages were more common. Many of the youth that I talked to felt that there was a contradiction in their parents' emphasis on the importance of being Christian and of having "Christian values," and their insisting that they should only marry a Malayali Christian. Some parents whose children had married non–Indian American Christians told me that this was the trump card that their children had used in their attempt to persuade them to agree to the marriage. One said, "My daughter asked me, 'Isn't it hypocritical to say that we are Christians and that being Christian is important and then saying that only an Indian Christian is worthy of being married. Aren't we all equal in the sight of God?'" She and her husband had subsequently agreed to the marriage and had come to like their son-in-law, so Tessy Cherian laughed as she narrated this incident to me. Other mothers were not yet persuaded. When I paid a visit to the home of the Chacko family, the topic of marriage came up for discussion. Philip, the twenty-two-year-old son and one of the youth leaders in the church, told me that the most important consideration for him would be that his wife be Christian. "The rest is not so important." But his mother interrupted from the other side of the room to say, "I am very strict about this. I tell them, I love them and will love them until I die but that they must marry a Christian from India." She paused and then added, "a Malayali."

CrossWay, the Second-Generation Mar Thoma American Congregation

The formation of CrossWay, the second-generation Mar Thoma American congregation in Dallas, was an important event in the history of the Mar Thoma church in the United States as it represented an attempt by a second-generation group to stay within the Mar Thoma church as a separate and independent congregation. Their website[5] describes their vision for the church: "Under the framework of the faith and practices of the Mar Thoma Church, CrossWay strives to bring glory to God through Gospel-centered worship, teaching, discipleship, fellowship, and missions. We believe conducting service can be done through a responsive and interactive format that brings out worship in our hearts." Despite coming under the Mar Thoma denomination, we can still see the "open church" emphasis at CrossWay since their vision statement indicates that they welcomed "ALL people, regardless of age, race, culture, background, or stage of life to join us as we live life the way of the Cross."

I was able to talk briefly to one of the leaders of the church, whom I will call Reji Easaw, in early 2016. Reji told me that he had made it clear to the CrossWay leadership team that he personally "could not be part of this movement" to form a separate congregation unless the intent of the group was to remain under the Mar Thoma church. He gave me two reasons for this. First and most important was because the fundamentals of the Mar Thoma church were sound since it followed a Reformed doctrine, which was "very biblical." At the same time, the leadership team believed that the Reformation was not just a one-time event and that the church should adapt to the needs of the believers. Now that the Mar Thoma community was decades into the migration from India to America, they felt that it was important for the Mar Thoma church to change so it could be relevant to believers in the United States. Specifically, they thought that the church needed to modify some of its cultural traditions. Reji explained, "When you try to bring in cultural traditions along with biblical traditions and try to mix them, sometimes you have to pick one or the other. I think over the journey of faith, we have sometimes picked the cultural traditions over the biblical traditions. So we have deviated a little from the perspective of what Christ called us to do."

Second, they wanted to preserve the sense of community that they had been raised in, and which they enjoyed. Reji thought that second-generation Mar Thomites would not be able to obtain this community in a megachurch. The CrossWay leadership team was not interested in forming a separate church since Dallas had "churches in every corner" and there was no need for another church. Consequently, what they decided to do was to "take ownership of the Mar Thoma church" by modifying the worship and messages to be "relevant" to the American-born generation and by institutionalizing local mission activities.

When I spoke with Reji in early 2016, he told me that the CrossWay congregation comprised of 37 families. Most were second-generation Mar Thoma Americans, but it also included a sprinkling of people of other backgrounds, including two or three white Americans. They used English as the primary medium of communication and the language in which they worshiped. Although they had an immigrant Mar Thoma achen who conducted the Mar Thoma liturgy in English every Sunday, the message was usually given by lay leaders. The messages were longer than the traditional messages in the Mar Thoma church, around 30–45 minutes instead of the traditional length of 15–20 minutes. The congregation also sang contemporary praise and worship songs instead of traditional hymns. The leadership team held regular Bible studies for men and another for women, which met at least once a month. Reji indicated that another important "cultural change" they had instituted in the church was that the leaders did not try to portray themselves as believers who had "the perfect life, the perfect family, the perfect environment."

On the contrary, they were willing to be open about the problems they faced and allow God to work through their "brokenness." This meant that people could share "their burdens" and openly pray for situations without being afraid of being judged, and could try to deal with situations before things escalated to an "extreme level of crisis."

Some of the lay leaders had been theologically trained in local evangelical seminaries (the two Reji mentioned were the Dallas Theological Seminary, and Christ for the Nations). When I asked if the theological training he and others had received in the local seminaries was compatible with the theology of the Mar Thoma church, Reji responded that he did not really see a "huge difference." He said that he and the others in the leadership team believed in "the core doctrine of the church" and did not deviate from it since they believed it was biblical. Their theological training was intended to "equip [them] to be able to lead the flock." They did not preach about water baptism, or adult baptism, or anything that was "new age or more culturally connected." Reji also emphasized that their goal was to work with other Mar Thoma churches, and that it was not to "create an exodus from those churches to our church." Throughout our conversation, he repeatedly mentioned how appreciative the leadership team of CrossWay was of the support and leadership of bishop Mar Theodosius who had guided them every step of the way through their "long journey."

Conclusion

It is clear that the American-born generation had internalized the individualistic perspective of contemporary spiritualism and evangelicalism, and consequently viewed the social, cultural, and historical practices of the Mar Thoma church as a distraction from its spiritual mission. In embracing an evangelical orientation, American-born Mar Thoma youth separated their faith and their sociocultural identity. As a result, although most valued their heritage and eventually married other Syrian Christians, preserving the history and traditions of the Mar Thoma church was not a priority.

The expectations of the second generation clashed with Mar Thoma traditions and practices that emphasized communitarian liturgical worship over the sermon; the integration of the social and cultural community with the faith community; and the historical and apostolic grounding of the church, as opposed to its doctrinal position on contemporary social issues. Due to this clash of religious perspectives, most of the American-born generation questioned the religious credentials of the immigrant generation and the achens.

At the same time, they appreciated the friends and community that the church provided, and thus were caught between what they considered to be their spiritual needs and their social needs. I identified four different strategies that such individuals adopted. There was an older group that had left the church in the 1990s (some became unchurched, while others attended evangelical churches); they had few connections with the Mar Thoma community other than their immediate family, and only maintained their ethnic identity in the home (I was not able to speak to anyone in this group). There were also individuals in their late twenties and early thirties like Anu, Preeti, Viju, and Manju, who had left the Mar Thoma church but still maintained close relationships with people of their age in the church. A third group in this age category, like Reeba, Alex, Ravi, Suja, and Jacob, remained in the church but, as we have seen, were critical of many of its central ethnic practices. Some of these individuals tried to transform it, failing which they attempted to create subgroups or organizations like the "young couples group" where they could connect with like-minded second-generation members. A fourth group, like Satish and Chris, comprised a younger demographic, those in their early to late twenties who were unmarried and were either studying or working. These individuals attended both the Mar Thoma church and an evangelical church every week, probably because their lack of family obligations gave them the time to do so.

We have seen that second-generation Mar Thomites grew up in and benefited from the nurturing community provided by the ethnic church. The individuals with whom I spoke who had left the church either did not have children or had children who were very young. Despite their confidence that they would be able to immerse their children in the Syrian Christian community through secular events, it remains to be seen whether they will be able to provide a supportive ethnic community for their children with this type of intermittent contact. The one person in this group, Preeti, who had a child who was a little older (five years of age), voiced this concern in her interview, and had sent her son to the

Mar Thoma Vacation Bible School that past summer as a way to help him get "culturally connected and community connected."

The CrossWay church leadership was clearly cognizant of the importance of community and as indicated above, this was an important reason that they wanted to continue in the Mar Thoma church rather than joining or forming a different church. At the same time, they also emphasized that their church was welcoming of all people. By using English as a language of worship, they wanted to make sure that the church and its activities were open to all believers in the area who wanted to join. In our conversation, Reji indicated that this openness meant that other ethnic groups could join the church, which might even lead to changes in the language of worship in the future. Like other second-generation Mar Thoma Americans, we have seen that the CrossWay leadership emphasized the importance of separating cultural and biblical traditions. They too believed that by being gospel-centered, they could sidestep both cultural and theological differences. Unlike many other second-generation Mar Thomites, however, the members of CrossWay apparently did not object to having a liturgical service, since they saw that the liturgy was based on the Bible. Because the leadership of the church remained in the hands of the worship team and the message was given by lay leaders, the Mar Thoma achen in the CrossWay church primarily became a liturgical and ritual specialist, not the leader of the congregation, a big change from the traditional pattern. In this way, CrossWay was an attempt to integrate the biblical underpinning and community-centered nature of the Mar Thoma church with strong lay leadership, contemporary worship, and messages that were relevant to their lives.

What explains why second-generation Mar Thoma Americans tended to downplay incidents of racism and prejudice and emphasize the importance of multiracial churches in contrast to East Asian American Christians? Perhaps the difference in the racial outlook of Indian American Christians and East Asian Americans arises because second-generation Americans belonging to smaller Christian groups develop more diverse social networks and a different scaffolding for their identity due to their inability to self-segregate into ethnic organizations, churches, or subcommunities within larger congregations. This in turn may make them more comfortable in white or multiracial religious communities. For instance, Mar Thoma America youth who attended evangelical campus groups or churches often mentioned being the only Indian Americans in that setting, yet reported having a network of people within these organizations who would "check in" with them periodically and also pray with them and for them, to keep them "on track." Consequently, it is likely that the worldviews of these individuals were shaped more by white or interracial evangelical groups and organizations that deemphasized racial identity than by their coethnic peer group. This might explain their lack of a racial or ethnic discourse and their stress on the importance of multiracial churches as a manifestation of their Christian and American identities, in contrast to larger groups like Korean and Chinese Americans. At the same time, we see that in the case of CrossWay, currently the only second-generation Mar Thoma congregation, the emphasis on an open church was more theoretical, since most members were Mar Thomite, making it similar to second-generation Korean American churches.

The particular situation of each Mar Thoma parish was somewhat different depending on the composition of the congregation and the nature of the area, so the long-term outcome may also vary. Regardless, the Mar Thoma North American diocese is likely to be substantially transformed through the influence of its evangelically influenced American-born members. If the CrossWay model spreads, it could also bring about a fundamental change in the meaning of a Mar Thoma identity, the practices of the Mar Thoma church, and the role of the achen in the church. Since the denomination is centralized, a change within the American parishes will probably change some of the traditional doctrines and practices of the Mar Thoma church as a whole. This is particularly likely given that American evangelical churches now have branches in India and English-dominant Mar Thoma youth there are attracted to evangelical parishes in Indian cities that have links to American nondenominational churches. Consequently, the conflict between the two paradigms of religion is also taking place within Mar Thoma parishes in India.

4

Class, Culture, and the Performance of Gendered Christianity

In addition to intergenerational rifts, there are also other cleavages and tensions within many Mar Thoma congregations. We have seen that the female-led migration of a significant proportion of the immigrant families resulted in both the downward mobility of many of their husbands and the spouses playing nontraditional gender roles at home, with changes in the division of housework and child care. The church became an even more important space for men in such families to recover their wounded masculinity (see also George 2005, 125) and gendered divisions were very visible in the Mar Thoma church at the time of my research. The economic success of nurses' families also created tensions with the "high status" professional families in the church. Class and status fissures were not so readily apparent, but became evident after I had spent some time in the Mar Thoma church. Each of these axes of difference manifested themselves within congregational spheres through ideas and performances of normative gender, which consequently varied by immigrant and second-generational status as well as class and religious orientation.

Following Candace West and Don Zimmerman's argument that the household division of labor constitutes "the material embodiment of wifely and husbandly roles, and derivatively, of womanly and manly conduct" (1987, 144), there is now a large body of literature discussing the way the relative economic contribution of husbands and wives to their households can shape how they "do gender." The home is only one arena where spouses "do gender," however. "Wifely and husbandly roles" and "womanly and manly conduct" are also performed in front of the social community. In fact, the home may be considered to be a "back stage" arena, and gender displays in a socially significant "front stage" setting might be different from those at home. In addition, the isolation of gender from other important social attributes is problematic. People do not just "do gender." The performance of gender is always shaped by and inflected through other social attributes such as class, culture, and religious identity (West and Fenstermaker 1995).

By focusing on three groups within the Mar Thoma congregations—immigrant nurses and their husbands; professionally educated immigrant men and their wives who are often professionally educated as well; and well-employed second-generation women and men influenced by American evangelicalism—we can explore how each group tried to perform normative Christian identities in very different ways. The first group emphasized female submission and male dominance in church; the second felt that women should be active participants and leaders along with men; and the third group argued that although men should "head" the church, women have important roles to play in "serving" the church. I demonstrate that it is the social class position of the three categories of women and men, their understanding of Christianity, and their desire to distinguish themselves from each other that results in the embrace of different strategies of public self-presentation.

Doing Gender, Class, and Culture in Mar Thoma American Parishes

Traditionally, men sat to the right of the altar and women sat to the left. While men wore Western pants and shirts, immigrant women and many second-generation women almost always wore Indian clothes to church (sarees consisting of six yards of fabric draped around the body with short fitted blouses, or the Punjabi suit: a long top with baggy or fitted pants with a long scarf), For special occasions, men wore Western suits, but women of both the first and second generations brought out their expensive, gold-embroidered Indian clothes and matching jewelry sets: the church was one of the few venues where they could display these outfits and have them appreciated and admired. Only men were allowed to serve as priests, deacons, and acolytes at the altar (the official church position was that this was for cultural and not theological reasons). All lay leaders and most of the executive committee members were male. With the coming of age of the second generation, there were more female office bearers, particularly in the youth (i.e., second generation) organizations. However, a quick Internet search in 2014 indicated that most executive committee members in U.S. Mar Thoma parishes were still men.

Within Mar Thoma congregations (as in most other Syrian Christian congregations), men were viewed as the head of the household and they spoke on behalf of their families. It was mostly immigrant men who spoke during the general body meetings. In the Bethelville parish, for instance, I noted that the men of the households were the ones thanked for the dishes prepared by their wives, and who stood up to receive the congregation's commendation for the food! Anita, a twenty-eight-year-old second-generation member told me that until a few years earlier (when women had finally protested), the men would decide whether or not there would be food for an event, and they would pick the menu, often selecting dishes that were hard to make. Even though women were important or primary earners at home, the men would rise to declare economic pledges on behalf of the family for the special fund raising activities of the church. Some of the immigrant couples I spoke to indicated that the Bethelville parish was actually considered to be "more progressive" in terms of gender than many other Mar Thoma churches around the country. For instance, the Mathais told me that when the thirumeni came to visit their parish, he "congratulated us on the fact that every year we have some women members on the executive committee. Many churches don't have that."

An important space for women within the Mar Thoma church was in the Sevika Sangham, the women's organization. During my research I could see that women within this organization were generally very active. They held monthly Bible study meetings in the houses of different members, organized an annual U.S. conference, and raised funds to support poorer women in Kerala. However, since the meetings were generally in Malayalam, in practice only immigrant women who were fluent in spoken and written Malayalam attended. This meant that there was no women's organization for the second generation and for younger immigrants from India who were raised outside Kerala and did not read and write Malayalam. As an alternative, some of these individuals had taken the initiative to form Young Couples groups for Bible study, discussion, and fellowship.

When I attended the annual Sevika Sangham national conference in 2007, I was struck by the intense religiosity of many of the women and the fact that they seemed to find the conference spiritually and personally invigorating.[1] As far as I could tell, all the registered attendees at the conference were immigrants (around ten teenage girls from two nearby churches came to the conference hotel to attend the only session catering specifically to the second generation). Most were between forty to sixty-five years of age, though some women were probably in their thirties. Some of the older women had been attending for around ten years or more and I noticed how much they enjoyed being able to catch up with friends and relatives from other parishes around the country. Many of the conversations that I overhead were of a religious nature, with frequent references to God and His will.

Toward the end of the conference, a speaker initiated a general body discussion about whether the Sevika Sangham should continue the practice of holding an annual U.S. conference. When they began in 1999, women had few opportunities to meet and really needed a forum to talk about their difficulties and burdens. But now there were so many Mar Thoma conferences (e.g., the regional and annual family conferences) that this need was less acute. So, she asked, "Should we still do this every year—spend 6–700 dollars and leave our husband and children, to attend?" The question elicited strong responses from the audience, with many women getting up to argue forcefully in favor of continuing to hold the annual event (to date, the annual conferences continue to take place). One woman said that she had been coming every year because the conference provided an important opportunity for socialization and fellowship, and to pray for their families. Another person talked about how women had to deal with so much—depression, problems with children, and that some had even contemplated suicide. The conference was one place where they could come to find comfort and the support to lighten their burdens.

Immigrant Nurses and Their Husbands

Immigrant nurses participated enthusiastically in the Sevika Sangham. They also cooked for church events and helped with the cleaning after such events. They generally deferred to the achen and defended the gender norms of the church. For instance, most supported the gender-segregated seating. Welcoming me to a meeting during the annual church retreat where the rules were much more lax, Anna Daniel nevertheless directed me to the women's section, telling me, "We believe in gents sitting on one side and ladies sitting on the other." The women I talked to also indicated that male leadership in the church was the "traditional" pattern and what they were used to. As an example, Sunita Abraham told me candidly, "I prefer that men do these kinds of things. That is the way we were brought up and I feel that is better." Immigrant nurses also felt that their husbands represented them adequately, so they did not need to speak out at church meetings. Explaining this to me, Tessy Cherian, a middle-aged nurse, said, "Women are equal of course, but still we feel we have to be a little submissive." But she went on to add that sometimes she would say or start to say something in church and her husband would nudge her and ask her to be quiet, which seemed to indicate that often men were the ones who enforced the norms. The women also made clear that they were not interested in leadership positions. They told me that even when women were nominated for a position on the executive committee, they would often turn it down for fear that it would interfere with their family obligations.

Immigrant nurses also repeatedly mentioned to me that women in the Mar Thoma church had a "much better status" than women in the Orthodox church (the largest Syrian Christian denomination). This is something I also heard said by Mar Thomites in Kerala. Since Mar Thoma members generally had close friends in other Syrian Christian churches and the Mar Thoma church had broken off from the Orthodox church, it is not surprising that the Orthodox group became the reference point for Mar Thoma members in a variety of spheres, particularly for those who were closely tied to Kerala. As mentioned, immigrant nurses also talked about how they followed strict parenting rules at home with the goal of bringing up their children in the authentic Indian culture.

I occasionally perceived, through their facial gestures, that the nurses (who generally sat together), seemed to be critical of immigrant women who took on leadership positions in church. This was corroborated by many of the women in the professional group, who were eager to have more female leadership in the church. Several of them talked about how the nurse group would gang up together against their efforts. As Dr. Lizy Itty, a doctor with a successful practice, commented, "It is the women who pull me down the most." Jessy Jacob, who worked in a biochemical lab, talked about how the nurse group was envious even of another immigrant nurse who had volunteered to take on the secretary position in the executive committee when no one else (male or female) seemed to be interested. "We ourselves don't try to help other women. There is jealousy."

The husbands of immigrant nurses also challenged women who were in leadership positions or who were outspoken. This did not come up in my interviews with the men, but I heard about several such incidents in my conversations with the educated professional women (both first and second generation) in Bethelville, where I conducted the longer period of my ethnographic research. Dr. Itty told me that while she was speaking in her official capacity as secretary, she would be heckled by some of the men who would ask, "Isn't there a man to do this?" or who would bring up St. Paul's injunction (1 Corinthians 14:34) that women should not speak in church. She also said that some of the men would leave out the "Dr." in her name. This upset her because she knew that they would never do this to a man. A second-generation woman, Amalia, talked about a time when she was on a committee as a youth representative and a man had started shouting at her. She told me that she had declined a subsequent position because of that experience.

> One of the reasons that I didn't want to be secretary was because I didn't want to be up there and get yelled at. I am in the committee meeting and one person is yelling at me and I said I won't have you yell at me. It wasn't anything personal. It was about how they wanted the money spent. But they can't talk *to* you—they disagree by talking *at* you and yelling at you, or talking loud, and there's no point in that.

The husbands of nurses also challenged the status norms of the church by criticizing the committee members of the church and the "high status" or professionally educated men. I had seen a group of men sitting at the back during the General Body meetings who would raise several objections to the proceedings, and had also heard complaints from the professional immigrant group about the disruptive "nurse-husbands who make a lot of noise in church" and the emotional General Body meetings. Apparently in the early days, there were even occasions when participants would pick up chairs during these altercations, threatening to throw them at their opponents.

A nurse, Thankamma Iype, whose husband was one of those who would sit at the back during meetings, explained the status divisions in church and the animosity it created. She described the church as being split into the "high" and the "low," based primarily on education, and said that she and her husband were part of the "low" group. According to her, the "high" group generally sat in front of the church and was closely involved in church administration. There was tension in church between the two groups, and she said that her husband would get involved in these disputes. She herself kept out of this kind of church "politics" by not going to church on days when there were General Body meetings, as she did not see the point in it. In my subsequent interview research I also heard a great deal about this division in a variety of churches around the country from members of the congregation and from Mar Thoma achens. This division, which stems from the Kerala context, is also described by Sheba George (2005) who studied an Orthodox Syrian Christian American congregation.

Thankamma Iype told me that one thing she appreciated about American culture was that there were no such distinctions between "high" and "low" status people. Although Mrs. Iype described the status divisions in the church to me in a matter-of-fact manner, other families who were classified as "low status" were challenging this division and trying to redefine traditional Malayali conceptions of status. An important reason was that in the United States many nurse families were able to become as affluent as those in the professional group. Although the financial situation of the husbands was not particularly strong, because nurses were able to earn a good income (particularly in the 1970s and 1980s) by working at night and doing double shifts, the families were able to do well financially and consequently wanted to be treated with the same respect as those in the professional group. The Mathais told me that one of the reasons the current pastor of their church was unpopular among many in the congregation was because he did not treat everyone equally but made distinctions between people on the basis of their occupation. "For instance," Mr. Mathai said, "I don't have a doctorate, but that does not mean that he should treat me differently from someone who has a doctorate." Mrs. Mathai (who was a nurse) went on to say, "In

India doctors have a high status. But here we are *all* equal." An achen I met in India who had been posted in a U.S. parish corroborated that an important factor shaping the dynamics within the Mar Thoma American church community was the emphasis on the equality of professions and the "dignity of labor," because in the United States "the cook will not let himself be demeaned by the dentist."

The general opinion of the well-educated Mar Thoma American immigrants and the second generation was that the obstreperous behavior of some of the men in church was due to their Malayali "culture" and Kerala upbringing, their lack of education, the fact that they did not work in jobs where decisions were the outcome of discussion and disagreements were expressed in a civil fashion, and because they felt "a lack of control at home" since their wives were the breadwinners. Sarah, a second-generation woman, expressed it this way:

> I think it goes back to our culture. In Mallu [slang for Malayali] culture men have a lot to say, are given a lot of authority, and what they say goes. Men are really arrogant and women have grown up with this. Less-educated men also fight in church when they feel a lack of control in their personal lives here.

Amalia, the young woman who had been "yelled at" during a committee meeting, explained such behavior on the part of men as follows:

> A lot of times, I don't think the men know how to express it and, I hate to say it but a lot of times especially in India where we came from, when we discuss things, it wasn't like sitting and talking rationally. It was always yelling when they express their views and I feel like it is all learned behavior from where they are from.

Both Sarah and Amalia, and most of the second-generation Mar Thoma Americans who continued to attend the Mar Thoma church, were children of nurse families, so they were careful not to distinguish the behavior of men who were the husbands of nurses from the other immigrant men in the congregation. Rather, they attributed the strident and rude male immigrant behavior to their lack of education and their Kerala upbringing.

The well-educated immigrants and second-generation Mar Thomites also repeatedly explained the submissive behavior of the nurses in church as being due to "culture," because in traditional Kerala society "women weren't given a voice." Anita, who was born in the United States, told me, "For a long time, the reason all the office bearers were men was because they thought it was a man's role. The women were intimidated or they just felt that's how it happened. But there's been like five to six years where women have started participating." She added a little later in the conversation,

> It is also a personality thing. There are only a few women who are dominant. I don't mean dominant in a negative sense, but who can speak up and so forth. Because they were either educated here, or they lived here for a long time, or they worked in the kind of environment where they hold lead roles, where they would have to, in order to be successful, be able to converse, and take charge. So therefore when they come here [to church], they felt at ease.

Anita made an insightful distinction between nurses who had administrative experience, such as Mrs. George, the person who had volunteered to be secretary, and those who did not, to make the larger point that women who were used to having authority at work were more comfortable taking on leadership positions in church.

George (2005), who studied an Orthodox Syrian Christian immigrant community in the United States with a class and social composition similar to that of the Mar Thoma church, argues that the church becomes the sphere where both Indian immigrant nurses and their husbands compensate for their nontraditional economic positions and division of labor at home. This dynamic may account for the strong defense mounted by immigrant nurses and their husbands of the gender norms of the Mar Thoma church and of male leadership. However, both nurses and their husbands contested the status norms of the church by challenging women who were outspoken or who were in leadership positions, and by criticizing the behavior of the committee members and other professionally educated men. The well-educated professionals in the congregation for their part criticized the "traditional" gender attitudes and conduct of the women, as well as the "disruptive" actions of the men, attributing both behaviors to the groups' upbringing in Kerala, lack of higher education, and lack of authority at work. Male outbursts in church were additionally blamed on their presumed emasculation at home as they were secondary income earners.

Immigrant Professionals

George (2005) discusses the role of class in giving rise to tensions between families in the immigrant church that she studied. However, she does not provide, except in passing (2005, 13, 144, 151), an analysis of how these class differences affected the performance of gender within church spaces. Similarly, Ebaugh and Chafetz (1999, 607) mention that well-educated, employed women in the congregations they studied were beginning to "question cultural and religious restrictions" on their participation in the religious institutions, on their comportment and clothing, as also their roles at home, and that this was viewed by many as a threat to the traditional familial and religious culture of the groups. Below, we see how class and status differences between nurse families and immigrant professionals shaped ideas and practices of gender within immigrant community spaces.

There was a significant proportion of professionals in a few parishes around the country (I had interview data from several first- and second-generation Mar Thomites from one such parish), but it was clear from discussions with Mar Thoma Americans in different parts of the country that this situation was unusual. In most U.S. Mar Thoma parishes, professionals comprised a small minority in the congregation. Both men and women in this professional group emphasized that they had grown up, or had studied in, cosmopolitan cities outside Kerala or in the United States, and told me how those experiences had shaped their worldview and outlook. Jessy Jacob, for example, was talking to me about divisions among the women in her congregation.

> If you notice, most of the women—I am not trying to put anyone down okay, their basic background, the way they were brought up in India— that has a big role in it. Like Martha, she was brought up in Bombay [Mumbai]. And you can see it when you talk to her. Or if you talk to Geetha. We were all brought up in schools outside Kerala. That has some-

thing to do with it. If you went to a typical Kerala school or lived in Kerala until you came here—that can make a difference.

Similarly, Babu Samuel, who had obtained two higher education degrees from the United States, pointed out that there was a big difference between people like him who had come to the United States to study and those with little education, who came straight from Kerala to work. Anand Mathew, another man who had done his MBA in the United States, made clear that these differences also shaped interaction patterns within the church, telling me, "College-educated people generally have a different worldview from those with a school education and like to interact mainly with other college-educated people." The well-educated group often expressed their vexation at the fact that the church was dominated by people who were not highly educated and who had been brought up in Kerala.

One of the ways in which men and women in this group articulated the difference in outlook made by their education was by describing themselves as "liberal" or "open." Several of the women mentioned that even their parents had been "broad-minded" and "liberal." I have indicated that they were likely to have a different and more permissive child-rearing philosophy from that of nurses. This group was also more likely to have spoken to their children in English while they were growing up, "because we wanted [them] to know English very well, and have no accent at all." This orientation was strongly criticized by nurses but also by the more recent IT workers from Kerala. One middle-aged professional, who had grown up in the Middle East, described the newer immigrants from Kerala as "die-hard Mar Thomites" and wryly referred to their tendency to "look down on us as people who have forgotten our roots, forgot to teach the language, culture, and values to our children."

Both men and women in the professional group spoke about how their open-minded outlook and their comfort with American culture meant that they were able to mediate or help with intergenerational conflicts in the church and to work with the second generation who could not communicate with their parents because of the latter's lack of education and traditional Kerala outlook. The men worked as informal counselors, organizing meetings and events for teenagers and young adults, while the women got involved in the Sunday school as teachers of the younger children. Many of the men also talked about how they were called on repeatedly to get involved in church committees because of their ability, honed through their professional work experiences, to handle conflict through discussion and to run meetings. The men also tended to be quite critical about various aspects of the church—for instance, its hierarchy and the unresponsiveness of the church to U.S. conditions. However, I noticed that many of them would also let me know that they had a close relationship with one or more of the Mar Thoma bishops, which is generally taken as a sign of high status within the Mar Thoma church.

By and large the women in this group tended to describe the church as very "male-dominated" because it insisted on following the traditional pattern in Kerala, and indicated that they were frustrated at the lack of opportunities for women in the church. For instance, Molly Ninan told me that her sister and daughter had left the church because they did not like the fact that women had no role in the church. She continued, "I am not a feminist, but still some of the practices of the church, like achens who stand up and speak without even looking at women, bother me." Jessy Jacob, who was from another Mar Thoma parish, similarly talked about how her daughter had left the church for similar reasons.

> My daughter and some of the other girls were all asking achen why women were not allowed to do more. My daughter went to a Catholic school until the seventh grade. There the women were allowed to go into the pulpit and my aunt's daughter is a minister in [a mainline American church]. So my daughter always thought, if they can do it there, why can't we? Achen said, "Well, that's the way the Mar Thoma church is and until things change, this is the way it will be."

I met Shanti Zachariah and her husband together at a café in the downtown area of a city in the Northeast that I was visiting. They were in their forties and had been in the Mar Thoma church for over ten years but had subsequently joined a liberal American denomination. Mrs. Zachariah described how she felt she "did not fit in" as a woman in the church because she was working on a Ph.D. in the sciences (which was very unusual for a woman in the church), and had come from a very liberal church in India and had even considered going into ministry. In the Mar Thoma church, on the other hand, she could not participate meaningfully as the church had no real options for women. Since both she and her husband were active in the church as youth mentors, they had continued in the church despite her increasing unhappiness, until it got to the point when she felt "assaulted psychologically" and could not take it anymore. They had then switched to their current American church and described themselves as being very happy in it.

Some of the women were also frustrated that only men were generally allowed to preach in most Mar Thoma parishes. Gracy Mathai of the Bethelville parish, who had spent several years in another Mar Thoma parish, one of the few that had a lot of professionals in the congregation and where women were allowed to give sermons, told me that she had preached there once. "But here, the idea is that only a male can speak." Dr. Lizy Itty, who was also from Bethelville, complained about how women were not given any opportunities in the church. She said that although several guest speakers came to give sermons, they had never been allowed to invite a woman to preach. The only time women preach is one Sunday a year, for Sevika Sangham day, when usually the achen's wife speaks.

Some women in this group were able to get into church committees and take some leadership positions, but they wanted to see more equality for women in church. However, their activism was criticized by some of the more recent immigrants who had attended American evangelical churches in metropolitan India. Nirmala Lukose said disapprovingly, "In the Mar Thoma church some women [she clarified later that it was more of the 'old timers'] feel that they need to be very vocal, they believe in women's liberation. It might be because of the influence of American culture. But they don't know that the real churchgoing American women feel differently—that there is a role for women and a role for men." She felt that women were equal to men, but at the same time she thought they should follow St. Paul and that women should not get involved in arguments in church or in confrontations with the achen.

In short, the well-educated professional immigrants distinguished themselves from "nurse" families by emphasizing their upbringing and education outside Kerala, their cosmopolitanism, and their liberal outlook regarding gender, child rearing, and intergenerational relationships. The women chafed at the lack of opportunities in church and wanted more equality for women, though more recent immigrants, influenced by evangelical Christianity, might be more conservative with respect to the role of women in church. Many of the well-educated women were teachers in the Sunday school, and some were also able to obtain positions on church committees.

The Adult Second Generation

While transnational norms of gender and class may complicate the lives and behavior of immigrants in community spheres (George 2005; A. Kim 1996; Purkayastha 2012; Suh 2004), this does not necessarily mean that gender relations among immigrants will be more traditional than among their children. In fact, in their studies of Korean and Chinese American religious communities, both Alumkal (1999) and Yang (2004) argue that the second generation who had imbibed American evangelical ideas were more conservative than immigrants when it came to the role of women in the church and in the home. Yang (2004) also indicates that the younger generation used biblical references to undercut the authority of the older generation. We see somewhat similar dynamics in the Mar Thoma church with the second generation criticizing the older generation for religious ideas and practices that were not biblical. In some respects, they were also more conservative than the immigrant professional group.

I have mentioned that the second generation that remained in the Mar Thoma church as adults were mostly the children of nurse families, both because such families comprised the largest section of the immigrant population in the church and because the children of the immigrant professionals tended to leave to attend nonethnic American churches. The second generation group in the Mar Thoma church comprised well-educated professionals influenced by American evangelical ideology. In general, both men and women supported gender roles in church that they believed were based on the Bible. They felt that they had a "higher understanding" about Christianity than the immigrant generation because of their exposure to evangelical organizations, their education in American schools and colleges, and their biblical knowledge. For instance, Alex George, a twenty-nine-year-old man, referred to a highly educated immigrant woman in his parish who had come up in front of the church to make a short presentation.

> Like the aunty that led up there . . . I would prefer her to cover her head [a traditional practice for women in the Mar Thoma church] but she didn't. And she never does. And she's one of those people that like you know, I am a woman hear me roar. . . . There's a lot of the feminist movement where you know, for a woman to submit to her husband [is something negative]. . . . For me, the thing is, I want to teach them why God instituted . . . you know why Paul taught about covering your heads. You know, what it means spiritually, and things like that, but a lot of women just don't know what it means and they think, oh you're trying to put me secondary, so I'm not gonna do it.

Although Alex criticized the older woman for not covering her head and for being a feminist, he had no problem with her taking a leadership role in the church. Generally, the American generation supported women being involved in the church in the Sunday school, leading intercessory prayers, giving sermons, and being on committees. Miriam, a second-generation woman, mentioned that she generally liked to challenge some of the gender norms of the immigrant generation by sitting on the men's side during General Body meetings.

> Somebody asked me, why do you always sit on the guys' side? I'm like oh well, the guys' side is where there's power. (Laugh) And that's the truth! You know, women don't really talk, they don't, you know, really voice their concerns, and everything is mellow. So nobody really pays attention to what goes on in there.

Like several other second-generation women, Miriam said that she made it a point to try to speak up during General Body meetings and she felt that it was easier to do this from the men's side of the room. For the most part, second-generation men and women tended to subscribe to what Anita had said above, that the church was open to participation by women, and that the primary reason for Kerala-raised women not to get more involved in the church had to do with their culture rather than the structure of the church. This was, in fact, very like the official position of the Mar Thoma church as a whole. The Mar Thoma leadership maintains that women are not permitted to take leadership positions or be ordained in the church due to cultural, not theological, reasons (the church is in full communion with some churches which have female pastors), and that the majority of both male and female Mar Thoma members would be opposed to having a woman pastor. They indicate that when a majority of the church's representative assembly (which includes representatives from each parish) supports female ordination, the leadership would make it possible. For the present, the situation is summed up by Simon, a young man in his mid-twenties, talking about the older generation:

> SIMON: I would just say from a cultural aspect, it's the men who do and the women that follow. Um, there are you know, exceptions to the rule, but I mean the majority of women, they just, they don't wanna lead.
> *And do you think that is different for the women who grew up here?*
> SIMON: Oh yeah. Oh yeah. Yeah. Wait till you talk to Reeba. Yeah. Yeah.

In contrast to the well-educated immigrant women who felt that the church was very male- dominated, only three of the twenty-five second-generation women interviewed for this project felt that women were treated as "second-class citizens." Several of the women expressed their exasperation with the culture of the women, men, and achens of the immigrant generation, however, arguing that it created barriers to the involvement of younger American-born women in the church. Gigy, who was going through a divorce, spoke bitterly about how the church members had pushed her out of her Sunday school teaching position but had supported her husband's continued involvement in the church. But she said that the thirumeni had been supportive of her and that she was planning to fight to get her Sunday school position back. And Reeba, who had been the secretary of the Sunday school, said that she finally resigned as "there was a lot of drama and a lot of politics about it because our church doesn't like it when our generation steps up." Consequently she felt that her age and being American-born were the real barriers to involvement in the church, not gender.

Suja, like other American-born members, complained that "some of the ideas of the older generation are based on the culture, like you know our Malayali, Indian culture. Not necessarily based on what they think is biblical, which can be frustrating for the next generation." Referring to a praise and worship service that the second generation in their parish had organized before the main service on the days when the main worship was in Malayalam, she explained,

> For example, today I was talking to one of the leaders of the Divine Service and about my possibly doing some speaking for the service. . . . And they said, "Oh, we're so excited about that. But we'd have to see if it's okay for a girl to . . . to do the speaking." You know? And like we'd have to make sure that Achen was cool with that and . . . the rest of the church was okay with that.

Suja went on to say that as a rule, women were only allowed to be "adjunct" speakers for the youth worship service and could not be part of the regular group of people who gave sermons (since that would need official approval). This example shows how the second generation had to get the approval of the achen and the immigrant congregation even for a service that they were organizing themselves.

Although most members of the younger generation were open to women taking a much more active role in the congregation when compared to the immigrant nurse group, with few exceptions they did not support women approaching the altar. This in turn meant that they did not think that Mar Thoma women could be deacons or pastors. While some said that this restriction was due to cultural reasons because the congregation was not used to female priests, a significant number indicated that there was a "biblical" basis for the prohibition against women entering the sanctuary, though most could not articulate what it was. For instance, Satish declared, "There is a biblical reason [laughing] but I can't . . . There is a verse, I can't pinpoint exactly, but there is." Alex similarly said, "There is a line, *literally*, in the sanctuary, that women can't cross . . . it is not allowed," but could not explain the reason.

Two young women and one man provided biblical arguments to explain why women could not enter the sanctuary but gave three different reasons for the prohibition. Rekha, a senior in college, said that the prohibition came from an Old Testament verse (she thought it was from Deuteronomy) that said that women were considered to be "unholy or unclean" while they were menstruating. However, she acknowledged that "there are pastors who are women in the American churches," and although she was not sure she would want to be a pastor in the Mar Thoma church, she said wistfully, "I think it'd be really cool to be a deacon and you know, wave the incense [censer]." To a question about whether the rules about women's menstrual uncleanliness applied in present-day America, she replied that this had been brought up in a discussion in the women's group in church.

> Somebody did say that women aren't supposed to talk in the church, and some aunty was like "You know the Bible is outdated," and another aunty was like "How can you say that?" So, um, I mean, there have been disputes about that. . . . And I—I don't think that the Bible can be . . . outdated. It's the word of God. If it's outdated, is God *wrong*? No, He can't be wrong. He is all-knowing.

This conversation with Rekha shows that the position of women in the church had been discussed a great deal and that it had led to disputes between the liberal and the conservative groups.

Ruby provided a different biblical basis for women not being able to be priests. When asked whether women could be priests in the Mar Thoma church, she replied, "That would never happen. And I'm okay with that. Because of its biblical origin. In the Bible it says Aaron and the sons of Levi, *sons* not daughters, will be the priests in the temples. That's why I am okay with women not being priests." Titus provided yet another biblical justification for why women in the Mar Thoma church did not enter the sanctuary:

> TITUS: In the church women do not go past the curtain, ever. That is
> a place where only men can be and the reason I believe is because
> it says in the Bible a man represents Christ and a woman repre-

sents humans. . . . So in that view, women are a little lower. But in all the other areas women have the same thing, in the GB [General Body], and in other areas. There are certain positions [forbidden to women]—obviously the deacon, and a woman cannot be an achen. They can go and give a message if they want to, or read a lesson. They can sing in the choir, be involved in the youth group, in any commit-tee, in that sense they are all equal.

Is there a reason that men symbolize Christ?

TITUS: It is said in the scripture. The only explanation I have is that when Christ came into this world he did not come as a woman, he came as a man. The first person to be on this earth according to Christianity was Adam. . . .

And then if you look at it from the perspective of the first sin that was caused in the world [it was] by Eve listening to Satan and obeying Satan and she tempted Adam. In that sense, sin came to the world because of her.

Do you think that translates into women . . .

TITUS: Today? It's tough. It even says in the Bible, women are not sup-posed to speak in a place of worship. Paul says it specifically. Women are supposed to keep quiet. When it comes to decision making, men are supposed to be the only one. I think for women today it is very . . . it is a hard message. But for the girls and women in our church when it comes to service time I think they realize their position, the guys realize their position. . . . That is not a topic that is brought up to our own bishop—never. [This was actually not the case—I heard it brought up at a Family Conference I attended and some others I interviewed told me that it was a topic that was regularly brought up.] There isn't that sort of resistance to that . . . to the whole ideology.

Is there a greater responsibility with being a man?

TITUS: When you look at it from a Christian perspective, no. Men and women both have equal duties. When it comes to service, there are certain things a woman can't do, a guy can't do. A lot of girls can sing much better than I can. There are lots of girls who can make decisions better than I can. They just have different talents than I do. Each person is given their own special gifts. And in that perspective, no, everybody is equal.

I present the discussion with Titus at some length since it illustrates the somewhat contradictory position of the second generation that women were "a little lower" than men in some respects, but that they were also "equal" to men from a Christian perspective. The related argument that men and women had different "roles," but that it was also important to recognize and use everyone's gifts and talents in the church, was one that I heard repeated many times in different ways by second-generation women and men. Ruby brought this out in her response to the question, "So what do you think about the roles of women and men . . . in the church?"

> Well, definitely . . . in our community, men have more of the leadership, and, and things like that. When I was younger, that frustrated me . . .'cause I just felt like you know if a man can do it, a woman can do it, you know? Just learning more biblically what God's roles are for a man versus a woman . . . you know . . . and the husband versus the wife . . . that God wants man to be the head [helped me accept these practices]. But that doesn't mean that women couldn't help. Um . . . everybody's given different talents and . . . sometimes it's hard for people to see oh, you know . . . the women should teach Sunday school . . . and help out with . . . you know when there's things to do . . . with you know, food . . . or preparation—those kind of things, you know . . . the women should take care of it and . . . the men will do more of the manly work.

Here, Ruby talked about her initial struggle to understand the reason that men were the leaders in the church. Once she realized it was biblically based, she indicated (indirectly) that she was able to come to terms with it. We see her struggling with reconciling two different points of view, one of "traditional" Malayali custom, the other of the more progressive ethos of the larger society in which the younger church members were living. Ruby continued, pointing to the two "extreme" positions among the immigrant generation in the church:

> Sometimes you know, people take the extreme. Oh, well, women should just be silent and should just be in the background taking care of the kid's needs, you know . . . and the men should be the leaders. And I don't mind that, [men] being leaders, but you know, they should utilize everybody's talents. And sometimes we miss out on that.

And there are other women [who go] even to the [other] extreme—
Well, if a man can do it a woman can do it. And there are some things
God says that men can't do and women can't do. And sometimes we lose
sight of that. So you lose that humbleness that God expects from us, you
know? And, you know, just wanting to be there to serve the church. It's
like when you're serving someone, you're not actually leading. You're
doing what they want you to do.

In this thoughtful and poignant account Ruby pointed to the divisions
between the nurse families who are conservative about gender roles and
the well-educated professional immigrants who advocate for women's
equality in church. She ended with a distinction that I heard a lot of the
second-generation women make between "leading" and "serving" in the
church. In contrast to the immigrant women professionals who were eager
to have leadership roles in the church, women in the second generation
generally used the word "serving" when they talked about their own participation. For instance, Reeba described how she and her husband were
involved with the youth in the church and that it was their "ministry": "I
always felt that I was called to serve. My husband is the same way. It brings
me joy knowing that I am supporting the youth and showing God's love
in this way. It brings me joy knowing that I'm supporting my husband in
his ministry." The conversation then turned to a discussion of the roles of
women in the church. There was a pause and then:

> REEBA: I think women have a strong position in the church. I think
> women are looked upon as—I guess enforcers of the faith. You
> know? Um, a lot of the responsibility of raising children in the faith
> go on the women. Um, so women are looked upon as you know,
> strong, you know role models for—for the growth and development
> or spiritual development of the child. . . . Um, *definitely* they are
> submissive . . . to their husbands. They're supposed to be submis-
> sive to their husbands. Um, they can hold offices in the church, but
> I don't think they can. . . . you know, take on like—I've never seen,
> like women take on like being the vice president of the church or
> something, you know.
> *Do you think that should change? Or do you think that there's a reason for*
> *that?*

REEBA: I think it can change. I mean, I think—I mean it's more recently
that I've seen more women taking on positions in the church. Um, so
I think that it's just a matter of time, that eventually a girl or a woman
will be the vice president. Especially with the newer generation.

Here again we have a discussion of womanly roles in church and at least
a provisional acceptance of wives' submission to their husbands. But
we also see that Reeba, like many others in this generation, still feels
that it is possible for women to hold the highest lay position in the Mar
Thoma church, that of the vice president (the achen is the president).
Perhaps the beginnings of change took place on January 4, 2015, when a
young woman was permitted by diocesan bishop Mar Theodosius to be
a deacon for the Holy Communion service in a parish in Massachusetts,
and to enter the sanctuary. Jesudas Athyal (2015b), who wrote about
this event, indicates that "this was perhaps, the first time that a woman
served as the deacon for the regular Holy Communion service in a parish church . . . as the very entry of women in the sacred space of the high
altar was considered taboo."

I asked Reji of the CrossWay church about the role of women in the
leadership team of the church. He told me that their Sunday school and
Outreach coordinators were women and that women also led some of
the prayer ministries and the intercessory prayer time (they had intercessory prayers during noncommunion Sundays). However, at the time
we spoke, he said that the church did not have theologically trained
women or women who gave the message. But he mentioned that one
woman was studing at Dallas Theological Seminary and that she would
be giving the message at an upcoming Sunday service at CrossWay.
According to Reji, CrossWay was not theologically opposed to having
women leaders as "We are a Mar Thoma church and the church has accepted women coming into leadership. There may not be a woman pastor, but there's leadership positions that they have been given." I asked
whether CrossWay believed that women should not approach the altar
and he replied that such ideas were "more of a cultural thing," and that
this was one of the barriers that the current bishop had broken (likely
referring to the above case in Massachusetts).

Second-generation American Mar Thomites women who identified
as "liberal," seemed to be a very small minority in the church. I gathered

that most ended up being pushed out due to the conservative orientation of the second-generation members who remained in the church.
For instance, Sneha, whom I met by chance when I went to visit her
parents' home, talked about how she had been disturbed by the Mar
Thoma Sunday school (run by the second generation) which focused
on fear of hellfire and sin as the means to make children stay in the
church. She said this was when she dropped out of the church because
she did not want her daughter attending that type of Sunday school. But
she had been "raked over the coals" by her Mar Thoma cohort when
they learned that she had started attending an Episcopal church. "They
were amazed and asked, how can you do that, it [Episcopal Church] is
a church that believes that gays and lesbians are all right. I said I believe
that too, and they pounced on me!"

No one I talked to self-identified as queer, gay, or lesbian, and the topic
of sexuality rarely came up in my conversations with Mar Thomites. The
one exception was during a conversation with a young woman, Rachael,
who identified as a Mar Thomite and said that she had a deep concern
for gender and sexuality issues in the church and hoped that there would
be a change in the Mar Thoma culture around these matters. Rachael
told me that she was slowly trying to "uncover" the Mar Thoma LGBT
community, but this was hard work as there was so much silence and
shame around sexuality within Mar Thoma circles. While some LGBT
individuals had left the church, "not everyone wants to leave their family, their community, and go through social death to be themselves. So a
lot of people will have a death of themselves instead. They will hide who
they are and how they feel."

The only occasion when I heard sexuality openly mentioned was in a
public forum at the August 2015 conference on Indian Christianity, when
a member of the audience asked the thirumeni of the North American
and Europe diocese whether the church was having discussions regarding how to deal with the legalization of same-sex marriage in the United
States. The thirumeni affirmed that these discussions were taking place,
but did not reveal the position of the church on gay sexuality. However,
people outside the church (either Mar Thomites who had left the church
or Syrian Christians of a CSI background) indicated that there was a lot
of "policing" of sexuality by achens, immigrants, and even the second
generation within the Mar Thoma church, leading people who were gay

or supportive of gay issues to leave. For instance, a CSI Malayali achen whom I know told me that an older Mar Thoma woman had asked him to "intervene" to talk to her son who identified as being gay. Clearly this matter was being kept confidential, as she told him that he should not tell anyone else about the matter. The CSI achen talked to the young man and advised him to attend a more open church. He then tried to explain the situation to the mother, who had apparently hoped that the achen might be able to persuade her son that he was not gay.

In this section we have seen that the evangelically oriented adult second generation tended to be more progressive than immigrant nurses and their husbands regarding the involvement of women in the church, as they supported women taking up any position except for deacon and priest. At the same time, they were critical of the "feminism" of the well-educated immigrant women and did not support their goal of a gender-equal church. They believed that their perspective was biblically grounded, unlike that of the older generation, which they criticized as being an outcome of secular influences such as Kerala culture or the feminist movement. Even when second-generation women did take on leadership roles, they usually described what they were doing as "serving" the church, thereby making a distinction between "leading," which was a manly role, and "serving," which women could undertake since they were doing what the church community wanted them to do. Sexuality seemed to be a charged issue in the church with most people taking conservative positions, but it was also an issue that was rarely discussed.

Conclusion

We see here that gender is a key factor shaping the central dynamics not just within Mar Thoma homes but also within Mar Thoma American parishes. The literature on how men and women "do gender" has focused largely on the household, where the practical necessities of juggling child care, household chores, and paid work may trump gender ideology. But gendered behavior might be different in community spaces, and men and women are more likely to perform normative gender roles in arenas like the church. The broader literature on gender in religious institutions makes the case that although such institutions often reinforce patriarchy, women have also been able to use religious spaces to build social support networks and to "argue for equality" (Ebaugh and Chafetz 1999, 586). I give a more nuanced account above, showing that gender norms vary depending on educational and class background, work experiences, ethnic culture, and religious orientation.

In the case of nurses and their husbands, women might have been trying to compensate for their higher economic contribution to the household by being submissive in church, allowing their husbands to take a dominant role. However, another reason for their lack of interest in church positions might also be that they came from Kerala cultural backgrounds where they were used to women remaining in the background in church, showing how transnational norms influence the gender ideologies of immigrants. It could also be that they were too busy with their work schedules and housework to take on additional responsibilities at church. The reverse of all this was likely to have been in play for well-educated immigrant women, accounting for their different ways of doing gender. The educational and professional background of individuals and their experience with authority in the workplace were further reasons why well-educated women and men of both generations were more likely to take on church positions.

We also see the significance of understanding the performative aspect of gender within community spaces. In Mar Thoma congregations, the notion of being a "good Christian" was defined by norms regarding how women and men should behave in church. While the literature on immigrant congregations tends to discuss them as though they are homogeneous spaces, I have shown that they can be differentiated by class and generation and also how social class and culture influenced gendered performances, leading to disagreements about the role of women in church organizations and committees. In this context, it is also important to distinguish how spouses relate to each other in community spheres as opposed to how they perform gender, class, and culture more generally. Despite the differences in the ideology and performance of gender of the three groups in the church, I noticed that their spousal interactions tended to be fairly similar across the board, with women being careful not to appear to be dominating their husbands (see George 2005, 150). This is also shown through Reeba's quote about women being submissive to their husbands but still being able to take positions in church. Finally, this study demonstrates yet another way in which evangelical Christianity has impacted the Mar Thoma church. Whereas other research has focused on either progressive or conservative changes as a consequence of migration and generational transition, we see that the internalization of evangelical Christian ideas had complicated consequences for gender and sexuality, which cannot be reduced to a one-dimensional movement.

5

Religion, Social Incorporation, and Civic Engagement among Generations

Unlike Hindu, Muslim, and Sikh Indian American groups that became politically active in the United States around homeland issues and developed umbrella organizations to unify and mobilize, Indian American Christians seemed to actually become depoliticized as a consequence of immigration. Even though Indian American Christians are substantially overrepresented in the United States and many were in the early wave of post-1965 immigrants, it was only in late 2000 that a national organization, FIACONA (Federation of Indian American Christians of North America), was formed to represent all Indian American Christians. This was thirty years after Indian American Hindus, sixteen years after Indian American Sikhs, and eleven years after Indian American Muslims had formed similar organizations. Since the largest group of Indian American Christians is from Kerala, many leaders of FIACONA were Kerala Christians. Some of the founders of the organization were of Mar Thoma background, including from the Bethelville church. However, there seemed little interest in the organization within the Bethelville church or the wider Mar Thoma American community.[1]

The precipitating cause for the formation of FIACONA was the rise in violence against Christian churches in India after the Hindu nationalist party, the BJP (Bharatiya Janata Party), came to power in 1998. Kerala is a state that seethes with political activity, with a highly educated and mobilized electorate, alternately sending to power either the Communist Party of India-led Left Democratic Front (LDF) or the Indian National Congress-led United Democratic Front (UDF). Christians and the Church are important players in state politics, on the side of the Congress Party. As mentioned, I had originally undertaken this study as part of a larger project on Indian American political mobilization around issues in the Indian subcontinent. Consequently, I wondered why Mar Thoma American congregations tended to be apathetic about the defeat of the Congress by the BJP in India and the attacks against Christians, and why they did not support their fellow Mar Thomites who were organizing locally and nationally around these issues. This was the puzzle that first led me to begin my research in the Bethelville congregation.

I learned over time that the factors that account for this disinterest were to be found both in the nature of Mar Thoma church politics and in the cleavages between immigrants and the second generation. From around 2007, a burgeoning literature emerged on immigrant religion and civic activism, arguing that participation in religious institutions facilitates the civic engagement and incorporation of contemporary immigrants. In the case of the Mar Thomites, however, I discovered that the different Christian traditions embraced by the first and second generations—Eastern Reformed and American evangelical—not only led the two generations to develop opposing ideas about the relationship between their ethnic and religious identities and the meaning of these identities; they also shaped how the immigrant and American-born Mar Thomites defined their communities, drew boundaries between themselves and others, and delineated their social obligations to their respective communities. This chapter shows how both church politics and negotiations and disagreements between the generations shaped the civic engagement of the multigenerational Mar Thoma Christian congregations. The second generation developed ideas of American identity and Christian obligation in interaction with and often in opposition to those of their parents' generation, with the result that contradictory forces affected the civic engagement of these multigenerational congregations.

Transnationalism, Identity, and Political Activism

Many Mar Thoma immigrants who are involved with the church are also passionately interested in church politics. The intensity of interest and involvement of first-generation Mar Thoma members is heightened in the United States due to immigrant nostalgia and because the church becomes the primary social arena for immigrants. We saw that there were frequent altercations between the immigrant professionals and the nurse families. Connections with bishops and other highly placed church officials in the Mar Thoma hierarchy in Kerala became important resources in these status struggles.

Although many immigrant Mar Thoma members are actively involved in intra- or interdenominational Kerala Christian politics, unlike the case of other Indian minority groups in India this is not a politics that generally translates into any larger national political narrative. Since Syrian Christians in Kerala are a well-integrated and prosperous minority with a very distinct sense of their identity and of their high caste status, they usually do not identify with lower-caste Christian converts in other parts of India (the majority of Indian Christians), who have been the primary targets of violence. This seems to be why there was very little awareness about FIACONA or support for its activities among the wider Mar Thoma American public.

Second-generation Mar Thoma Americans for their part were turned off by what they perceived to be the pettiness and emotionality of denominational and church politics, and this was a factor in the decision by many of them to leave the church. Because their parents formed close friendships with Kerala Christians from a variety of denominational backgrounds, second-generation Mar Thomites developed an understanding of what a Kerala Christian identity meant. But because Indian Christians are a minority in the United States, the second generation was unlikely to encounter Indian Christian Americans from other Indian states besides Kerala, and so they did not develop a larger Indian Christian identity. Although both they and their parents often referred to themselves as Indians, in practice "Indian" meant "Kerala Christian." Perhaps this was the reason that second-generation Mar Thoma Christians did not show any particular interest in Indian history or in contemporary developments in India (quite unlike the second-generation Hindu Indian Americans whom I was also interviewing at the time). Two conversations that I had during a period when attacks against Christians in India were in the news sum up the perspective of many of the Mar Thoma youth.

During my conversation with Sam in 1999, he said that he considered India his "homeland" but that he was not in touch with Indian news and had not heard that the BJP party had taken control of the Indian government in 1998. He told me that he would be "concerned" if India became a Hindu state but he added that he did not see himself mobilizing or leading a movement around that issue. When I asked him whether, if he knew that there was a group of people who were mobilizing, he would support them, he said he would. But he added, "I don't think I would do anything out of my way, to be honest. I don't think I would go to rallies and things like that. I am not counting out that I would, but it would be one of those things that fits into my schedule and that type of thing." Sam's lukewarm response was typical of the attitudes I encountered among second-generation Mar Thomites.

On another occasion, also in 1999, I had an interesting conversation with Mr. Chacko and his son Philip when I visited their home. Mr. Chacko was unusual among Mar Thomites in that he thought that it was very important for Indian Christians in the United States to speak out against attacks against Christians in India (by this time attacks against Christian priests, nuns, and Christian institutions had become widespread). Philip, however, did not seem to feel any such obligation. He elaborated, "I think the church should speak out because it is a human rights issue when Christians are killed for their beliefs. But I would feel the same if it happened in Indonesia or Thailand since I don't know the people in India. It is not like it is happening to my uncle or father or anyone I know personally." Mr. Chacko was upset to hear this and said, "Oh, but *makkale* [child], there is a problem there." He tried to explain that the Indians who were being attacked were "only one step removed" from the relatives Philip knew personally, but Philip would not budge from his position, and again said that he did not feel any special tie to India as such but only to his relatives. His father got emotional at this point, saying, "Son, look at me, I am only a naturalized citizen here. Tomorrow if they tell me to go back, where else can I go to [but India]?" Mr. Chacko was implying that this was why it was important for him to support the cause and for Philip to support it too.

In short, immigrant Mar Thomites maintained their transnational connections and eagerly participated in church politics, but this involvement depoliticized them and made them less interested in engaging with larger Indian (and American) political and social issues. The second generation did not feel any connection with India as a whole but only with their relatives in Kerala, and did not develop larger identities on the basis of their ethnic heritage. Instead, as we will see in the next section, their identities and communities were constructed from scripts provided by the American milieu.

Religion, Immigrant Incorporation, and Civic Engagement

Large, multifaith studies conducted in different metropolitan areas of the United States which focus on how religion shapes the civic incorporation of contemporary immigrants, have shown that participation in worship communities often has a positive impact on immigrants' involvement outside their congregations.[2] This literature focuses on how religious organizations can facilitate the social and civic incorporation of immigrants by providing "bonding" and "bridging" social capital (Putnam 2000), which connects individuals with others in the community and to people in other communities. These studies have found that the level and type of civic engagement of immigrant religious institutions vary depending on whether the theological orientation of the tradition emphasizes social justice, and whether the leadership encourages social activism.[3] These findings are corroborated by research showing that mainline Protestant and Catholic churches of first- and second-generation immigrants were more civically engaged than evangelical churches as they were more concerned with social justice issues than evangelical churches, which were primarily focused on personal salvation and individual transformation.[4] When they did become involved in social justice issues evangelicals, unlike mainline Protestants and Catholics, tended to approach social transformation through what Christian Smith (1998) has described as a "personal influence strategy," which stressed the importance of caring relationships and personal example in bringing about positive changes in the individuals one knew. This in turn, evangelicals believed, would cumulatively result in larger social change.

If civic engagement is taken to mean the involvement of individuals and groups in the larger community of which they are a part, based on a feeling of obligation to "give back" to the community and to improve conditions within it, the effort is inextricably linked with the way individuals and groups perceive their identity and community, and their social responsibilities to this community. Civic engagement of immigrants is also closely related to social incorporation, as it is a manifestation of a sense of belonging, or of wanting to belong, to a community.[5]

As a Reformed church, the Mar Thoma denomination emphasizes that "Christian commitment" includes working for social and economic justice, and lay members are encouraged to seek vocations that will allow them to serve the community. They are also strongly urged to contribute financially to the denomination's many social service projects in India. Currently, the denomination's website indicates that it owns forty-seven social welfare institutions, fourteen homes for the destitute, and nine hospitals, in addition to fourteen colleges and four industrial training centers.[6] Under the influence of the British Anglican missionaries, we have seen that the Mar Thoma church developed an evangelical mandate and started outreach among lower-caste Hindus through church-sponsored evangelists as part of its Christian and social justice mission. The church has played an active role in humanitarian projects both in Kerala and in other parts of India. It has several "mission fields" in Kerala and in some other Indian states to reach out to underprivileged, lower-caste communities, who continue to face many disadvantages in India. The goal is to bring about socioeconomic community development in addition to spiritual growth. The work of reaching out to lower-caste communities, however, is carried out by specially trained evangelists funded by the church, and lay members are generally not closely involved except through their financial contributions. Converts in these outlying communities fall under the aegis of the Mar Thoma church, but since these communities are often in locations far away from the founding Mar Thoma church, they are formed into separate parishes and continue to worship in their own native languages with a translated Mar Thoma liturgy. Consequently, despite the British Protestant–inspired outreach and evangelical mandate of the denomination, mainstream Mar Thoma parishes in India largely maintain their ascribed upper-caste ethos.

Mar Thoma Identity and Social Obligation: The Immigrant Generation

The immigrant generation's Mar Thoma Christian identity defined their community and also their social responsibilities to this community.

While immigrants often spoke about their faith to friends and relatives, they did not believe in personal evangelism to strangers—they felt that it was a difficult and delicate task, best left to specialists. Only among Pentecostals and Jehovah's Witnesses (both viewed negatively since they were not episcopal and consequently were not viewed as legitimate), they believed, did lay members go after outsiders, trying to get them to "convert." Consequently, Mar Thomites did not evangelize and certainly would not want to do this in the United States. But several immigrants told me that they believed that an important part of being Christian was the call to perform service to the community, and indicated that they had chosen their professions—whether as a doctor, nurse, social service worker, or missionary—partly for this reason.

In my interviews, the immigrant generation generally self-identified as Indians or, more commonly, as "Malayalis living in America." I have heard even highly educated immigrants describe the second generation as "Kerala youth living in the U.S.," indicating that that they did not recognize that their children were Americans (of Kerala ancestry), rather than "Kerala youth." Although they lived and worked in the United States, they felt that as Mar Thoma Christians their primary responsibility was to "give back" to the poor and needy in Kerala and in other parts of India who were much less fortunate than the poor in this country. Mar Thoma achens and even some bishops strongly reinforced this argument. As I have heard many times in their sermons and speeches in U.S. parishes, Mar Thoma achens and bishops emphasized the importance of giving to the Indian missions of the church. Many of these missions and projects had been initiated because of the remittances from Mar Thoma members outside India and the church was dependent on their support to continue these projects. Some new projects had been introduced by the *Valiya* (senior) Metropolitan, Philipose Mar Chrysostom, a much loved and respected figure, currently in his nineties, and the immigrant generation felt an obligation to respond to his call for donations. Every year, Mar Thoma Americans sent money to support several Mar Thoma-run social service projects in many parts of India. The members of U.S. parishes constituted only a small proportion of the denomination as a whole, yet a substantial amount of the money for the denomination's charitable projects was generated by this group (Lincoln 2008).

Evangelicalism and Social Obligation: Second-Generation Mar Thomites

Although a few studies suggest that generational activism patterns among Christians shift from conservative to liberal between the first and second generations,[7] most U.S. studies of religion and civic involvement of immigrant congregations do not focus on variations in patterns across generations or on the civic involvement of the second generation. Elaine Ecklund's (2006) and Sharon Kim's (2010) research on second-generation East Asian American evangelical churches are the exception. Both maintain that second-generation Korean American congregations engage in outreach activities partly to distinguish themselves from the first-generation congregations, which were focused on serving the needs of the Korean immigrant community. Both indicate that the congregations that they studied stressed the importance of serving the needy in their local communities and that evangelism was the primary goal. This outreach involved conducting religious services and providing social and economic help to individuals living in poorer areas of the city, rather than bringing these individuals into the church. Sharon Kim (2010, 132) explicitly argues that this outreach was intended to emphasize that second-generation Korean Americans saw themselves as "full members of American society . . . that despite their involvement with ethnic institutions, they truly are 'American' and they do care about the welfare of America." However, neither Ecklund nor Kim develops this generational contrast further, since they focus on second-generation congregations. This Mar Thoma case study demonstrates how attending immigrant-dominated churches impacts the ideas and practices of civic engagement of second-generation American Christians. Specifically it details the ways in which the outlook and traditions of the first generation become the foil for the second generation to define their identity as Christians and as Americans and shape their corresponding outreach activities.

As we will see, in discussions about their obligations as Christians, second-generation Mar Thomites demonstrated most of the social characteristics of American evangelicals described by Christian Smith (1998): a sense of value distinctiveness based on their personal relationship with Jesus and adherence to "Christian morals," an emphasis on the responsibility to evangelize, use of a "personal influence strategy" to effect social change, and the drawing of strong boundaries with nonevangelical Christians (in this case, immigrant Mar Thomites). They supported a "seeker-church" model where informal, antiliturgical worship is a form of outreach that targets religious seekers. They viewed such outreach as a central function of worship and believed that enabling other racial and ethnic groups to participate in worship services was a crucial mission of the church. Sharing the individualistic focus of nondenominational American evangelicalism (see Smith 1998), most second-generation Mar Thoma Americans have not viewed religion as a platform for broader civic engagement. However, they interpret the evangelical mandate of showing the love of Jesus and bringing others to him as a personal obligation. Since Christianity is the dominant religion in the United States, their outreach is not directed toward members of non-Christian religions, as in the case of Mar Thoma evangelism in India. Instead, they target "unchurched" youth and young adults, both in the church and outside, through their Christian witness and personal morality.

The Immigrant-Dominated Church and Its Impact on Local Engagement

Few Mar Thoma parishes seemed to encourage the second generation to participate in church committees, except as the mandatory "youth" representative. This was the case in the first parish and to some extent in the second parish where I conducted participant observation. Discussions with achens and the youth at the national conferences I attended indicated that this situation was common around the country. The issue was explicitly addressed by the bishop of the North America and Europe diocese at the annual Family Conference in 2008. Speaking to the immigrant group, he said, "Why don't you entrust more responsibility on the second generation instead of holding onto committee positions? They will do a better job than you." Only one of the six parishes that I studied, "Hope Mar Thoma church," had lay leaders from the second generation in important "trustee" positions, and this was the only parish where a large number of the older second-generation members remained in the church. It was also the only parish among the six studied that was civically engaged with the local community.

Second-generation Mar Thomites in the other parishes provided several reasons for their exclusion from church committees. First, committees tended to be filled with recently retired members who needed something to occupy their time, as well as seniors and underemployed men intent on maintaining their positions of control in the church. Another problem was that the older generation continued to view the American-born generation as "youth" members even though many of the latter were about the same age as the newer immigrants, who were often welcomed into committee positions. The fear of change seemed to be an important motivation for excluding the second generation. According to Becky, "Our church doesn't like it when our generation steps up. And they don't like it when you are vocal. They don't like it when you understand how the political system works and how to work it. They just expect things will always go the way it has always gone. They don't want anyone who will like ruffle the waves or whatever."

Even when a second-generation member did take on a committee position through the urging of a section of the church, there were others in the church ready to criticize them. I heard of several cases, both of women and men, who had stepped down from their positions because of criticism from the older generation or because they felt that they were wasting their time. Vivek, a second-generation man in his mid-thirties, talked about the experience of his friend.

> Our vice president was like this guy that was in his thirties, and grew up here. And, during committee meetings, he was never taken seriously. . . . Because everybody else is like you know seventy years, and they've been in a Mar Thoma church for like fifty years of their lives, and they do things like, you know this way. And if you come around and say no, we should try doing it this way, it's not gonna fly.

According to Vivek, the dropout rates of the youth from the church were high "because the second generation doesn't have much of a say in church. So people leave to find a place to serve." The exodus of the second generation meant that the church remained immigrant-oriented.

But the problems were not only generational. Varkey, a second-generation man from another parish, explained the role of the achens, whose orientation remained India-based. "A lot of the way things run, the achens that are brought here, you know, whatever programs are happening are kind of still done within their leadership and their plan and their vision . . . which really works well for them, but doesn't necessarily work well for the next generation." As another young man, Thomas, argued, "I feel like the Mar Thoma church runs out of India to the point that all the ideas are focused there and the needs of the local community or even the members are not being met." Miriam, a member of yet another Mar Thoma church, echoed the same sentiment, "Everything is related to India. And this is such a problem for those who grow up here because India is foreign." The Indian focus was reinforced by the three-year terms of the achens (the bishop of the diocese has a longer term, usually around eight years), which led to a lack of American-based leadership. Peter told me, "You know the one—the *big* problem I have with our current achen is that all he cares about is raising money to send back to India. . . . You know . . . like *every* Sunday, it's the same thing . . . we need money . . . You should give money. You've been given this. Give money. You know?" Bijoy, a member of yet another church, said that too much of the Mar Thoma funds were going to India "but when we want to do some local community outreach the achens say, 'No, this is an Indian church.'"

While most of the achens had this orientation, this was not the case with all of them. Beena, a member of the same church as Bijoy, mentioned an achen they had some years ago who had explicitly asked them to be involved with the local community. "He said, you have been here twenty-plus years and what have you done for the community? And we had an open-air concert for people in the neighborhood. We started doing car washes, but then it died because he left. We saw him in India and he had heard that there is no youth group and things are going downhill." Beena's account illustrates how dependent the churches are on the orientation of the particular achen from India who is in charge for the three-year period.

The U.S. context and the influence of evangelical Christianity led the youth to adopt very different ideas of identity from those of their parents. We have seen that in contrast to their parents the second generation identified as American and were comfortable with people from a variety of racial and ethnic backgrounds. Their American evangelical identity also shaped the second generation's ideas about their community and their social responsibilities to it. Unlike their parents, they felt strongly that their social obligation, as individuals who grew up in the United States, was primarily to friends, coworkers, and members of the local community, rather than to people in Kerala.

As part of the Mexico mission, initiated in 2002, the church adopted the communities living in two small islands off the east coast of Mexico, close to Brownsville, Texas, with 90 families and 150 children. Diocesan parishes raised money and members built ninety-two houses for the families, but the islands were submerged in the 2005 hurricane and all the houses were destroyed. The parishes raised money again (the youth raised $46,500 and another member contributed $19,500) and the diocese bought new land for houses as well as a mission center and dorms for children on the mainland. Individual parishes were asked to sponsor the cost of building new houses and sent teams to build them. Ninety new houses were built by parish teams. The church plans to maintain a long-term involvement with this community, and has also been working to address their health, economic, vocational, and educational needs (*Mar Thoma Messenger* 2008; Varghese 2008).

The Mar Thoma church currently has Native American mission projects in Alabama, Oklahoma, and Louisiana. Mission work here involves organizing a Vacation Bible School for the children, some programs for the youth and young adults, and organizing visits by Native Americans to their nearest Mar Thoma parishes. These missions were structured much like the ones in India and focused on the community development of rural, socioeconomically disadvantaged groups at some distance from Mar Thoma churches. Teams from throughout the United States took turns visiting these communities, mostly over the summer. Each team only spent about four days at the mission.

Although the members of the second generation were happy about the Mexico and Native American projects of the Mar Thoma church, for the most part (with the exception of members of Hope church) social service ideas did not come up spontaneously when the second generation was asked about what obligations to the wider community they had as Christians. This is true even though they grew up in and in most cases still attended the Mar Thoma church which, as Peter mentions above, constantly emphasizes the importance of "giving back" to the less fortunate in society (in Kerala). The question about community obligation generated quite a wide range of responses, elaborated below, but few dealt directly with volunteering or social service. As in the discussion about identity, the second generation constantly contrasted their views regarding Christian obligation with those of their parents.

Christianity as a Personal Relationship and Not a "Works-Based" Faith

When asked whether they felt they had social obligations as Christians, several second-generation Mar Thomites mentioned that, unlike their parents, they understood that Christianity is not about what you are supposed to *do* but about a personal relationship with Christ. Many of the youth explicitly contrasted their understanding of Christianity, which some claimed was "more biblical" or "on a higher level," with that of their parents' "works-based" faith.

Susan explained:

> I think I am on the same level as them [her parents] culturally, but about faith, I have learnt more especially through our Bible study class and I am . . . a little above my parents. I know that it is not just about work or deeds but it is more about having faith. . . . Like, my Pappa would say, "It says in the Bible that whatever good deeds you do, it will be passed onto the children. Whatever bad deeds you do, that curse will be passed to the children." He goes toward the Old Testament-side teachings about how to lead a family.

Susan attributed her father's emphasis on good deeds to an "Old Testament" perspective on Christianity that clearly contrasted with her "higher-level" New Testament perspective. Elsie made a similar comparison between herself and her father, though without explicit criticism, saying, "Daddy showed it [his faith] in his works . . . that he did for the church, in his compassion for other people, in how he helped other people in church and [outside]. Wherever. I believe he practiced it in his works." James similarly said, "My mom has a strong faith and commitment. She does a lot of things for the church. And she actually went with me on a missions trip to Mexico. She retired this last week, and one of her goals is to go and do a missions trip to India and serve the poor people there." However, he went on to say later that for his parents the emphasis was on God while for him it was on Jesus Christ.

Although they did not focus on their parents, both Titus and James contrasted the message that they received from the older generation and from many achens in the Mar Thoma church with the "true" message. According to Titus, "The whole message is based on you and what you have to do to attain salvation, and what you have to do to be a good Christian. But the important thing is to realize that Christ has already done the work, all you have to do is to believe in that." James said that the large evangelical church that he now attended taught that "Christianity is not a religion, but it's a relationship. And so, focusing on that relationship is probably the most important thing. It's not about the things that we're supposed to do." When I asked him what he thought people were "supposed to do" in the Mar Thoma church, he said, "You know, I think, you know honoring your parents, being good people, doing well in your school or your work, you know giving back to the poor. . . . Just being well-rounded people, you know, obeying what God has told you to do, those kind of things." In the evangelical church, he said, "I think the main emphasis is developing that relationship with God . . . and then through that these other things of serving the church, serving the community, loving people that don't know God . . . come out of that."

James seemed to be saying that the Mar Thoma church had it backward in its emphasis on all "the things that we're supposed to do" (including giving back to the poor) as Christians, instead of focusing on teaching that being a Christian meant developing a personal relationship with Christ.

An "Open" Diverse Church Instead of a "Closed" Ethnic Church

Unlike the immigrant generation, who did not personally evangelize to people outside the Syrian Christian community and who considered the Mar Thoma church to be an ethnoreligious worship community, the second generation interpreted their primary Christian responsibility as "spreading the Word," "bringing others to Christ," "witnessing for the Lord," or being a "disciple of Christ." Following the "seeker-church" model, they believed that such Christian outreach should be the main goal of worship services. They felt that the church should be a faith community, not a social group.

Anisha, for example, argued that the youth in her church felt that it was important for the Mar Thoma congregation not to be "so closed-in." She continued, "And I think that is going to entail [crossing] a language barrier. Definitely we're going to have to get services that are in English if we're going to reach out to the community at large. So changing the language and then there's a lot that's going to go into opening the minds of the older generations as well." Having the worship service in English every week would thus serve the dual purpose of making the church accessible to members of the wider American community and breaking down a major barrier to having an "open" church—the mind-set of the immigrant generation.

Although having an open church might not look like civic engagement, the Mar Thoma youth felt that inviting members of the local community into the church was an important way to make a difference in the community within which the church was located. Once they got to personally know some of their neighbors by welcoming them into the church, they could learn their needs (both spiritual and nonspiritual) and try to address them. This approach resonates with the "personal influence strategy" of bringing about social change through personal relationships that Smith (1998) describes.

Personal Outreach to the Local Community, Instead of "Checkbook" Outreach to India

Related to the "open church" idea, some second-generation Mar Thomites, particularly those attending urban churches, mentioned that local outreach was part of their Christian obligation, usually as a means to evangelism. For instance, in response to the question about what kind of obligations to others Christians have, Beena said, "We are called to be servants. So youth have helped in clothing drives, soup kitchens, mentoring programs. We have also done nursing home visits." She added, "Our first mission is to spread the Word. But we can reach out to others through . . . using our medical skills." A few youth groups around the country had taken the initiative to visit local soup kitchens and nursing homes and to organize periodic clothing drives; a large Mar Thoma church in Dallas had such activities (Brettell and Reed-Danahay 2012, 104), and this church was discussed within Mar Thoma youth circles as an exception. Such practices seemed to be nonexistent or sporadic at best in most of the parishes that I studied, and in 2009 did not seem to be institutionalized in any of the six parishes except in Hope Mar Thoma church. Some second-generation leaders around the country expressed an interest in local outreach, usually in the context of discussing what changes the youth wanted to see in the Mar Thoma church, but admitted that few churches had regular outreach programs. However, recently youth in more Mar Thoma parishes seemed to be participating in local mission activities, with the support of the current diocesan bishop.

A few youth besides those in the Hope Mar Thoma church mentioned participating in community service when asked about their obligations to others, but they had a somewhat unusual definition. When asked about his obligation to others, for example, Satish said, "I would say like community type of service. And I like to just go out . . . have a Bible study with certain people, or just share my testimony which I have, in different churches." Asked specifically if he had done some community service, he said, "Yeah . . . I actually worked with uh, this ministry . . . they work with abortion clinics . . . they pretty much tell the kids who are pregnant not to go through abortion . . . so I have done little community service like that . . . try to reach out to our community over here." In short, for Satish community service meant participating in Bible study and picketing abortion clinics. He also mentioned going to help out in the local area by offering to help clean backyards, paint, and bring in groceries as a means to build relationships, but apparently this had only happened once. But what is particularly notable is Satish's definition of "our" community as the local American community outside the Mar Thoma church.

A Religious Obligation to Maintain Personal Morality

When pressed about what further obligations toward others, beyond sharing the gospel, were involved in being a Christian, many second-generation Mar Thoma Americans talked about an obligation to model the example of Christ in their lives. Sometimes they brought this up in the context of what they described as the "hypocrisy" of many of the immigrant members of the Mar Thoma church, individuals who "did things outside the church that were shocking" but still maintained leadership positions in the church, or those who regularly picked fights with others during the congregation's General Body meetings. In this case, Mar Thoma youth brought up the importance for Christians to model Christ to make the point that these churchgoing immigrant members were not "real Christians." Other individuals brought up modeling Christ to contrast themselves with their classmates or coworkers who were "not religious."

Whether the contrast was with the immigrant generation or with secular peers outside the church, however, what is important to note is that with the exception of members of Hope church (discussed further below), the second generation interpreted trying to "behave like Christ" to mean demonstrating personal morality by not swearing, drinking, smoking, or having premarital sex, rather than working for social justice, as Mar Thoma bishops understand Christlike behavior. For instance, in Matthew's words, "Showing God's love is important. I think it was Saint Francis who said, preach the gospel and if necessary use words. So actions, just show it from your actions." What actions? I asked. "No drink, no premarital relationships, don't curse." Similarly, Shirley responded that being Christian did affect how she related to other people and then referred to her personal values:

> Like my values in life are different I'd say from an everyday human being. Um . . . especially in terms of dating, like . . . I won't have sex before marriage and like, being sexually permissive or promiscuous, like, I won't do any of that. There are these certain boundaries, I would say, I set myself for as opposed to like non-Christians. Like, I want to save myself for my husband and like . . . stuff like that, I feel like I'm different in that sense, yeah.

Asked if she felt that being Christian affected how she related to her community, Shirley said, "Yeah, like I don't swear, I don't curse, like stuff like that. I feel like you should conduct yourself in a more . . . I don't know, morally defined way."

Although many second-generation American Mar Thomites brought up the issue of personal morality to distinguish themselves from some members of the immigrant generation as well as their coworkers and classmates, a few also talked about how they used religion to reach out to others. For instance, Jacob, a member of Hope church, said that he was viewed as being "religious" by others in his workplace and mentioned that he had had an opportunity that very day to emphasize Christian values. He explained that his coworker was in a relationship but had talked about finding herself attracted to someone else. "So I said if you are unhappy in a relationship, you should let the person know you are not happy and then move on. For you to go behind his back and do it is not Christian-like." Similarly, Reuben, also a member of Hope church, said that he tried to "role model after Christ" and was able to reach out to others in his workplace where he was part of a Christian fellowship. He said that coworkers who were not religious were interested in finding out "what's different about you. So people would approach me at work" and he made it a point of being available to them.

Hope Mar Thoma Church: The Importance of Second-Generation Leadership

As mentioned, Hope Mar Thoma church was the only one of the six that I studied that had initiated a regular local outreach program. They hosted an annual Labor Day barbeque to have "fellowship with people from the community for a couple of hours," with several youth volunteers available for "anyone who comes and wants to talk, or be prayed for," a Christian band, and a short message. The Sunday school children gave out school supplies at the event. The youth also gave out turkeys to homeless shelters and food pantries in the neighborhood over Thanksgiving. Hope church was also the only one among the six that had actively tried to "open up" to include other racial and ethnic groups. We have heard Jacob (who was from the Hope Mar Thoma church) earlier discussing the importance of an "open" church because he felt that a "closed-door oriented" church was not Christian. When asked what he meant by "opening our doors," he explained, "If we are in a city, it should be open to anyone and everyone who wants to come and worship the Lord in the city. . . . You shouldn't go up to them and say, 'Can I help you?' They know it is a church. They see it from outside. They come in for a reason. No one needs to go there and ask you, can I help you with anything." Jacob made it clear that in his view, the Mar Thoma church had an obligation to welcome everyone into the church. The interview continued with a discussion of the reasons that the older generation might turn away visitors. When it was suggested that they might simply not be used to non-Malayalis coming to the church, Jacob thought it was more than that: "Well you've lived in this country for thirty-some odd years. You've got to be used to other cultures, other types of people. I think it is mostly because they just don't want different ideas coming into the church. Maybe they don't want their kids getting involved with different types of people." But although this might explain part of the uneasiness of the older generation when non-Indian visitors entered the church, Jacob did not recognize that the primary reason was that the Mar Thoma church model is based on an understanding of worship as oriented toward those within the religious tradition—the liturgy and rituals are not easily accessible to outsiders—unlike the seeker-sensitive services of evangelical churches.

When their initial outreach efforts toward the adults did not succeed, the second generation turned their attention to opening their Sunday school to the children in the community. This did not work very well either, because, as Sheila explained:

> When kids come in they are *really*, really poor. Most of them are from broken homes or drug abuse homes. But when they come to our church, they see everybody so well dressed; they see a huge difference between the community kids and our kids. When we go to church, I make my kids dress up really well. . . . That's how we were brought up. You give your best to the Lord. . . . And the community kids see all that and after a while they don't want to come anymore.

Sheila concluded by saying that they were working on dealing with this problem.

The four second-generation members from Hope church who were interviewed for this project, all in their thirties and married, made it clear that these outreach projects were organized by the second generation, "all kids who grew up here." Like most of the other Mar Thoma American youth, each of the four had been influenced by evangelical Christianity. Sheila (who was quoted earlier saying that her Christian identity was foremost, before her Mar Thoma identity) and Reuben mentioned growing as a Christian during their college years when they were exposed to campus Christian fellowships and groups; Alice and Jacob had attended evangelical churches after marriage. However, unlike most of the other Mar Thoma youth, each emphasized the importance of reaching out to the community as part of their Christian obligation. Jacob said this was important "to make sure your love for Jesus shines on others." Likewise, Reuben tied local outreach "to make sure that kids have education or those that need shelter or food . . . the church can be there to help them" to modeling Christ, stating, "Christ liked to reach out to people in need, to people around." Alice praised the "mission-orientation" of the Mar Thoma church but emphasized that their generation wanted to help the local community instead of sending money to India, and Sheila similarly said, "We've been trying to hammer this . . . we've been trying for so many years to get our church involved in the community. Finally it took youth members to just get them involved."

Each also indicated that this local involvement was possible because their church, unlike most Mar Thoma churches, had, in Reuben's words, been "open to letting the second generation take leadership positions and helping and nurturing them to take ownership of the church." This in turn had led to a large proportion of the youth staying in church and had even brought back some of the older second-generation members who had left years earlier, which probably resulted in enough of a critical mass in church to organize community outreach projects. While praising their church for permitting the second generation to be incorporated in important leadership positions, Jacob, Sheila, Reuben, and Alice also made it clear that achieving second-generation leadership had not been easy as there had been resistance from some sections: "There are still a lot of people who don't want the changes in church. It's a battle that we fight every day." However, many members of the immigrant generation had been encouraging; the two immigrant church members I interviewed were supportive.

That their local outreach was a consequence of the way the second generation defined their identity and community as opposed to the first generation was made amply clear by Sheila and Alice, who were primarily responsible for the outreach projects. For instance, Sheila indicated that local outreach was important to the second generation in the church, "because we are growing up in this world. We are going through the same things that they are going through. We are more into their culture. This is our culture." Her friend Alice echoed the same theme while also poignantly referring to the racialization she experienced while growing up:

> The difference is that I grew up here. No matter how hard it was to assimilate into American society. I could watch as many cartoons as I want to learn English perfectly but when someone looks at me they are not going to say that I am an American. Unless I start speaking. . . . But I feel like I am an American. And I feel like my problems are not just about what happens in my little community. It is what is going around in my city, what's going around in my state.

Both Sheila and Alice contrasted their orientation to that of their parents. In Alice's words:

> My parents only wanted to deal with the Christian, Indian, Malayali community . . . [whereas] I think my generation wants to deal with *the* community. Not just the Christian community but the whole entire community. Our church is in an urban, low-income area. The thing that we are more looking toward is bringing the church together so they can do something for the people who live around us. And then make an impact on our little section of the globe. . . . We are more about bursting the bubble and moving forward.
>
>   Whereas our parents . . . they wanted to make little duplicate communities. Take a portion of Kerala and bring it to America, live in this little bubble, have their kids speak Malayalam, only eat Indian food. . . . And then just bring them all back to India so when they go back, they still look like Indian girls, they still look like Indian boys, they still eat Indian food, they still speak Malayalam. [So that] there's no way you could tell the difference. . . . And whatever extra we had, the money would go back to India.

Alice contrasted the immigrant generation's idea of community with that of the second generation, and she also contrasted the difference between the older generation's outreach via charitable donations with the second generation's personal outreach. Sheila similarly contrasted the first generation's "checkbook" civic involvement with the orientation of the American-born generation:

> You write a check for whatever the amount is and you send it to different places in India. As long as we don't have to do the work, as long as you don't have to get your hands dirty. Write a check, large amounts, no problem. And as long as it is going overseas to our country, to India or Kerala, it is not a problem. But nobody cared about our community, our surroundings right outside our doorstep.

The Hope church case seems to indicate the importance of second-generation leadership in initiating and sustaining local outreach in Mar Thoma parishes. As discussed, youth from around the country talked about their frustration at being excluded from church leadership and some also emphasized the importance of developing local outreach projects. What is remarkable about Hope church is that all four second-generation members who were interviewed articulated a strong commitment to helping the local community as part of their Christian responsibility, in contrast to most other Mar Thoma American youth. It may be that the incorporation of the second generation in leadership positions gave the youth of Hope a sense of "ownership" of the church that allowed them to weld together the Mar Thoma church's emphasis on social justice with their "personal influence" evangelical outlook. It is also interesting that Hope church members were involved in reaching out, as Christians, to their coworkers. Perhaps their experience with local outreach empowered them to be active in other arenas as well.

The second-generation Mar Thoma CrossWay church also stressed that being involved in local missions was one of their "cultural" differences from the traditional Mar Thoma American parishes. Reji, the leader from CrossWay whom I spoke to, told me that the Mar Thoma church had global missions (referring specifically to the Mexico and Native American missions), and that some of their church members participated in the Native American mission on a regular basis. However, CrossWay emphasized the importance of "serving the needs of people around us" which they did through one activity a month. Taking responsibility as Christians to minister to the local community, Reji told me, was a "core value" of their church.

Conclusion

We have seen that Mar Thoma immigrants took an "ethnic" church model for granted since religious and even denominational affiliation is traditionally determined by birth in India. As individuals from modest backgrounds who had been able to "make good" in the United States, many felt a strong sense of obligation to contribute to the poor in India. They had a strong commitment to the Mar Thoma church and the Metropolitan, were proud of its projects, and knew that the denomination depended on their contributions to support them. Contributions to Mar Thoma projects in Kerala also earned them status, since their friends and relatives in the area often heard about their donations. This was why they felt that supporting Mar Thoma projects in India ought to be the priority of the Mar Thoma church and its members.

At the same time, many immigrants were happy about the church developing the Mexican and Native American mission projects. They wanted their children to stay in the church and they could see that going on mission trips was common practice among Christian youth in the United States. It is expensive and difficult to send young people to the Mar Thoma Indian mission fields (although more youth have started going to these recently), so having mission projects closer to home was the ideal solution. Again, these projects were like the traditional Mar Thoma projects—at a distance from the Mar Thoma churches, which meant that they did not affect the homogeneity of the church or its practices. Most immigrants did not object to their children getting involved in local projects; it was just that the first-generation church leaders did not know how to go about getting these up and running. Consequently, second-generation leadership is very important for local outreach. And support from the church trustees is central in order to get the church to move some of its resources to local outreach. Often even worthy projects get blocked because of the internal politics and factionalism among the church trustees.

Second-generation Mar Thoma Americans consistently drew on evangelical ideas to contrast their perspective on the meaning of Christian identity and obligation with that of their parents. Most of the second-generation members felt that Christianity was primarily about a relationship between themselves and Jesus, and that faith or belief was more important than good works. Many explicitly contrasted this "higher-level" understanding of Christianity with their parents' and the Mar Thoma church's stress on social service. Their emphasis on their religious identity as distinct from, and more important than, their ethnic identity also led them to contrast their interest in forming open faith communities with their parents' ethnic religious community. Although Alice and Jacob were very critical of their parents' resistance to opening up their church and phrased their critiques rather strongly, they were right that many immigrants want to preserve and reproduce their cultural traditions and do not want their children to become "too Americanized." They also wanted their children to marry other Malayali Christians. Consequently, it was important for them to preserve the church as an ethnic space where they could transmit their culture, language, and religious traditions to their children. For all these reasons, immigrants resisted opening up their church to outsiders.

The immigrant generation delegated the task of evangelizing others to church-sponsored evangelists, but the second generation felt that their Christian obligation was to spread the Word and to maintain personal morality. Despite repeated probing, only a few individuals, with the exception of those in Hope church, mentioned outreach to the underprivileged, generally tied to evangelism, as a Christian responsibility. Their identity as Americans and their view that the church should be open to religious seekers and that church members should be directly involved in social and spiritual outreach rather than just through financial contributions meant that they were interested in getting involved in the neighborhood rather than sending money to missions in India.

Like the second-generation Korean Americans in Sharon Kim's (2010) study, second-generation Mar Thoma Americans distinguished themselves from their parents by emphasizing their concern for people in the wider society. But the big difference between the East Asian case and that of the Mar Thoma is that only Hope Mar Thoma church, among the six that I studied, had an active outreach program led by the second generation. This appeared to be because Hope was the one church where the second generation was incorporated into church leadership and had input into church activities. CrossWay Mar Thoma church also emphasized the importance of local outreach because the church was led by the second generation. Mar Thoma youth in immigrant-dominated churches probably adopted an individualistic evangelical identity, focusing on personal morality, as they did not have leadership opportunities within the church nor the ability to develop local outreach projects. The diocesan bishops have recognized the needs of the youth (their longer U.S. terms and their travel to parishes around the country provide them with a better understanding of the American context than the achens) and have been working to ameliorate this problem. The previous bishop initiated Mexican and Native American projects, and the current bishop, who started his term in 2009, helped second-generation youth establish local projects. Consequently the civic activism profile of Mar Thoma churches is beginning to change.

We can see from this discussion that the civic engagement of immigrant religious groups is shaped by ideas about identity and community, as well as by the immigrants' relationship to political issues in the homeland. In addition, generational differences within congregations between immigrants and their American-born children influence patterns of activism. This issue has so far been overlooked, as most of the literature on religion and civic activism has focused on either the first or the second generation. The few studies that did examine immigrant generational activism patterns indicated a shift from conservative to liberal. In the Mar Thoma church, however, the older generation embraced a liberal version of Christianity with a social gospel emphasis, while the second generation had internalized a more conservative evangelical Christianity focused on individual transformation. Many congregational studies also seem to assume that ethnic churches are homogeneous and that members have a common understanding about their theological tradition and social activism. This study shows that this may not be true, and why it is important to understand how negotiations between generations shape, for example, outreach activities.

In the Mar Thoma case, the immigrant-controlled nature of the denomination has resulted in a substantial part of its resources being directed toward projects in India. Despite the fact that the second generation had very different ideas about outreach, they were not able to implement these ideas because they were in churches dominated by the first generation. Thus the type of civic engagement of a congregation depends not only on its ideology, or even whether the leadership encourages social activism. Civic engagement is also shaped by the ability of different groups within the congregation to implement their ideas about social activism.

We also see that religion can be a powerful means of promoting social incorporation and of demonstrating belonging in the wider society. Although many second-generation Mar Thomites may not have been civically engaged, they did use religion as a means to connect with other Americans through their personal morality, Christian outreach, and participation in large evangelical congregations. Consequently, it is important to examine the different ways that religious involvement, particularly in the dominant tradition, can act as a "bridge to inclusion" into the wider society (Foner and Alba 2008). Despite growing up and, for most, continuing to worship in a liberal church tradition with a strong social justice orientation, the second generation still internalized American evangelical ideas to such an extent that their responses were indistinguishable from those who grew up in evangelical churches (as described by Smith 1998). Ironically, the second generation's lack of civic engagement was a consequence of their assimilation into the framework of individualistic piety of some of the influential versions of evangelicalism. What is particularly surprising is that these ideas led them to feel such a strong sense of identity with other American Christians that race and ethnic differences did not pose barriers, unlike for their parents. In fact, the sharp religious boundaries they drew were with immigrant members of their own church. It appears that the experiences and understandings of race and ethnicity among new immigrant groups are more complex and fluid than many scholars of contemporary immigration have recognized.

6

International Migration and Its Impact on the Mar Thoma Denomination

In *The Next Christendom*, Philip Jenkins (2002, 2) makes the case that the "center of gravity" and the religious dynamism of global Christianity have swung to the South. Expanding on this perspective, Robert Wuthnow and Stephen Offut (2008) argue that an important factor in the rise of the new religious dynamism is the role that international migrants play through their networks and remittances, and by forging connections between churches in the North and South. The profound social, economic, and political transformations in sending countries as a consequence of migration is documented in studies of international migration and transnationalism (Kurien 2002; Vertovec 2004). Few studies, however, have examined the ways in which religious communities and institutions in sending countries are impacted by the international migration of their members.[1]

The emigration of Mar Thomites has had major repercussions on the Mar Thoma denomination and on Mar Thoma communities in Kerala. This is despite the fact that only 133 out of 1,206 of its parishes are outside India, 86 in North America and Europe, 27 in Malaysia, Singapore, Australia, and New Zealand, and 19 in the Middle East (the majority or 741 of the Mar Thoma denomination's parishes remain in Kerala; the denomination has another 332 parishes in other parts of India).[2] These repercussions became clear to me during my fieldwork in three areas of central Travancore, Kerala, in 2006. Subsequently, I continued to examine this issue through discussions with Mar Thomites during later visits to India, through conversations with Mar Thomites in the United States, and through online research.

In 2006, most of the houses I visited in Kerala consisted of middle-aged or older occupants whose children were in the United States. Every single Mar Thoma achen I talked to in Kerala and in Bangalore had either been posted in the United States for a term or had spent time in the United States visiting relatives (this is despite the fact that I did not intentionally select achens based on their U.S. experience; my goal was only to speak to achens who were based in India). I attended a Mar Thoma church service in a small village in central Travancore, with around a hundred adults in the congregation, more women than men. As per the custom, the presiding achen called congregants who were celebrating their birthdays and their wedding anniversaries that week to the altar rail. When it came time for the wedding anniversary blessing, I saw several young women go up to the altar rail by themselves. I realized that the presence of these young married women in church without their spouses was a consequence of emigration from the region: their spouses were either temporary migrants in the Middle East, or American im-migrants who had started the long sponsorship process for their wives to join them.

There are two sets of theories that can help us understand changes in religious institutions as a consequence of large-scale migration. Theories dealing with the impact of transnationalism on sending communities focus on the ways in which financial and social remittances of migrants have been responsible for the introduction of new religious practices back home (Ebaugh and Chafetz 2002; Levitt 2001). However, most of the changes in religious practices in the Mar Thoma church have taken place outside the home base. More generally, the transnational perspec-tive does not consider the role of church leaders in instituting or resist-ing particular changes. Consequently, it cannot explain why leaders of religious institutions in home countries are not responsive to some con-cerns of migrants and why they sometimes bring about changes that are not demanded by their members.

Theories of religious organizations, on the other hand, use organi-zational frameworks to explain how leaders of religious institutions re-spond to opportunities or constraints in the environment (DiMaggio 1998; Stark and Finke 2000). However, they largely focus on national contexts and also ignore changes such as those caused by large-scale migration, as they do not view lay-driven changes to be significant. Ac-cording to the religious economies perspective elaborated by Rodney Stark and Roger Finke (2000), competition posed by new religious sup-pliers encourages religious dynamism by forcing religious leaders to work harder to attract and maintain members.[3] Religious institutions that do not do this eventually start to decline, often as they become more institutionalized. In such cases, the financial and social rewards of professional clergy increase and their religious motives decline, diminishing their ability to inspire their congregations.[4] In addition, the theological training of ordained clergy can hinder their connection with the laity, since their intellectual messages may not resonate as well as the emotional messages of lay preachers. Then fresh religious suppliers arise and newer clergy and church members who desire a more intense spiritual experience leave established churches for vibrant religious groups, or "sects," seeking religious rewards.[5]

Assessing the causes of decline in religious institutions differently, scholars in the neo-institutionalism paradigm recognize that leaders are constrained by the structures and conventions of institutions and are often more interested in stability and legitimacy than in efficiency and growth. Consequently, neo-institutional theorists believe that institutions do not respond to changes quickly but instead change "glacially" (DiMaggio and Powell 1991, 10), often in unanticipated ways. In examining the impact of the Mar Thoma migration on the home church, it is useful to draw on theories of migrant transnationalism and on theories of change in religious organizations, but I will also point to some of the limitations of these theories.

International Migration and Its Impact on the Mar Thoma Denomination

We have seen that the length and formality of the liturgy and the holding of Malayalam services became issues for American-born Mar Thomites in the United States. But through my discussions, both in India and in the United States, with Mar Thomites who had grown up in metropolitan Indian cities, I learned that these were issues that had come up much earlier in Mar Thoma parishes in cities like Mumbai, Delhi, Chennai, and Bangalore. Mar Thomites raised outside Kerala were less likely to be fluent in Malayalam. There were also many churches in these cities with shorter, more informal English services that were attractive to Mar Thoma youth. In response, the Mar Thoma church had started offering weekly English services in metropolitan parishes. In 2006, I met a Mar Thoma achen in India who had been posted in Mumbai in the early

1990s. He told me that Mar Thoma parishes in that city had been offering an English service every Sunday (in addition to a Malayalam service) "for decades." The youth had also been allowed to have their own praise and worship service once a month and to draw up their own order of service. An immigrant in his fifties whom I met in the United States had grown up in Mumbai and corroborated that his parish had taken many measures to make the youth feel involved in the church. He indicated that unlike in parishes in the United States, in Mumbai the congregation had no problem accepting youngsters in positions of power. The parishes in Mumbai were not unusual. Parishes in Chennai and Bangalore had also made similar changes to accommodate and incorporate the English-dominant generation. Why, I wondered, had Mar Thoma parishes in metropolitan India been able to incorporate changes to accommodate youth brought up outside Kerala much earlier and with less controversy than Mar Thoma parishes in the United States? I came to realize that this was not because of the policy of the church leadership, but instead had to do with the desires of the lay members.

Although the Mar Thoma church did try to bring about modifications to deal with the needs of its foreign-born members, it was constrained by its need to be responsive to the demands of its primary constituency in the diaspora: the Malayalam-speaking migrants who were its most loyal members and its financial base. Since migration is ongoing, the first generation continues to comprise the dominant group in the parishes in the Middle East and West. The control this group had over the Mar Thoma leadership became clear to me at the annual U.S. Family Conference that I attended in 2008. In his address, the bishop of the North American and Europe diocese said that he felt that the churches in the diocese should increase the number of English services to three times a month (from the current two). But he mentioned that if he tried to implement this, there would be *behalam*, an uproar, in the parishes (i.e., among the immigrant generation). He continued, stating that he had advised the American-born youth that they should attend the General Body meetings and express their opinions, as the church would only be able to change with their active participation, when they "own the [Mar Thoma] church." But, he said, the problem is that the second generation "still thinks of it as their parents' church." In other words, the difference between the practices of the Mar Thoma church in metropolitan India and the United States seemed to arise because the immigrant generation tended to guard their traditional practices more fiercely than their coethnics in India. This is not surprising. A variety of studies indicate that as a reaction to the alienation experienced through relocating to a new and very different culture, immigrants tend to romanticize their earlier lives in their home countries and to cling to tradition, particularly in the religious sphere (Hirschman 2004, 1211; Smith 1978, 1174–1175; Williams 1988, 11).

As we have seen, the Mar Thoma church has made modifications to deal with the establishment of new parishes and dioceses around the world, and it has brought about specific changes in the North American context to address the needs of its American-born members. All these changes have had some impact on the denomination as a whole. But my fieldwork in Kerala illuminates that international migration had brought about fundamental changes in the home communities and in the functioning of the denomination for two other reasons. First, migrant members made significant financial contributions to the church, which led to adjustments in the orientation and functioning of the denomination and its clergy. Second, the large-scale emigration had indirect effects. International networks and the affluence of the population, along with a rise in social problems caused by migration and consumerism, have led to the rise of evangelical and charismatic transdenominational churches in Kerala that challenge the traditional episcopal foundation, hierarchical organization, and Eastern worship rituals of churches like the Mar Thoma. The Mar Thoma leadership was trying to bring about changes to address these developments, but they were constrained by the tradition, structure, and the mission of the churches.

New Financial Resources and the Impact on the Church

While the global spread of the church resulted in many dilemmas and problems for the Mar Thoma church, it also provided an unexpected financial windfall, as most of the revenue of the church came from the diaspora, particularly from North America (Lincoln 2008). Achens who obtained overseas assignments benefited the most from this development. Although their salaries abroad were modest in terms of the local currency, it was a substantial amount in Indian rupees. Furthermore, most of their expenses (housing, utilities, phone, transportation, and health insurance) were met by the church. The achen's wife (who was not allowed to pursue employment abroad due to visa restrictions and church policy) obtained a small monthly stipend, and achens were given a generous "purse" of at least four months' salary at the end of their term. In addition, they received lavish tips from the members of the congregation for the house visits and services that they provided to individual families. As a result, most achens were able to save enough from one assignment abroad to buy a nice house and a car on their return to Kerala, and sometimes even to fund their children's higher education. Thus, overseas assignments were highly coveted, prompting the Mar Thoma leadership to shorten rotation terms (both internal and external) from five, to four, and finally to the current three years, to make sure that more achens were able to obtain foreign postings.

While the rapid growth and enrichment of the Mar Thoma church materially benefited achens, older members of the Mar Thoma church in Kerala and in the United States felt that it negatively affected their orientation and motivation. These Mar Thomites recalled an earlier period when achens had been highly educated (at a time when educational levels were generally low) and had chosen to forgo lucrative and secure government positions to live a life of poverty out of a commitment to what they believed in. Over and over, interviewees commented on how the priesthood had been transformed from a "calling" or "vocation" to becoming a commercialized "profession." Consequently, Mar Thomites believed that many present-day achens were less committed than achens in the past, and that they went into the priesthood not because of a desire to serve God, but for money and status.

Many Mar Thomites in Kerala said that achens in the contemporary period received a good dowry when they got married (one man mentioned that the "going rate for achens these days" was ten lakhs or one million rupees, enough at the time to build a house in rural Kerala), in contrast to an earlier period when parents were reluctant to marry their daughters to achens due to the financial hardships that the wife of an achen would have to endure. People now recognized that being a Mar Thoma achen was a well-paid, secure position and that an achen's wife would be given preference for a position in one of the Mar Thoma-run educational or social welfare institutions. An older Mar Thomite in

Kerala, Thomas Idiculla, who was on the Mar Thoma selection committee for the Bachelor of Theology (locally called BT) course in the seminary, told me an anecdote to illustrate this change. An achen he knew had contacted him to ask for his support to get his son into the BT program. When Mr. Idiculla asked the achen why he was going to the extent of canvassing selection committee members for a BT course, the achen had replied:

> This is one profession where you get a job immediately. You don't even have to lose one day after getting your BT. Very few professions are like this. Also, if he [the son] marries a woman who has or will get a B.Ed., she is guaranteed a post in one of the many Mar Thoma schools [this selection is decided by the bishop]. He will also get a good dowry and job security.

Mr. Idiculla concluded that people had now become very cynical about Mar Thoma achens. Since I had noticed that the church services I attended had been full, I asked why people would go to church in such large numbers if they did not respect the achens. Mr. Idiculla replied, "People come to church because their minds are full of problems and they want to place them [the problems] before God, not before the achen." He meant that spiritual reasons and not the qualities of the achens were responsible for people's church attendance.

Even as foreign postings proved to be a boon for achens, the Mar Thoma church as a whole benefited from the remittances that flowed in from its overseas members. These remittances allowed the denomination to substantially expand the number of institutions it owned and the projects it funded. Special monthly offertory collections were taken in Mar Thoma parishes around the world to support the denomination's various projects. Overseas members also provided generous donations to their home churches for renovation activities. Given that Mar Thomites received public acknowledgment for their donations, this was one way to obtain status and prestige within their home communities.

Ninan Chandy, one of the middle-aged Mar Thomites I interviewed in Kerala, mentioned another reason for the large contributions:

> People have money now and they pour out a lot in support of the church and various charitable causes as a way to be absolved of their sins. For

example, there is a large orphanage nearby. It costs 5,000 rupees to sponsor a lunch there but it is always booked way in advance. People fall over
each other to sponsor such events, but not because they have any special
feeling for orphans!

Mr. Chandy meant that people made substantial donations to charitable
causes not because of their interest in charity per se, but rather in the
hope that God would overlook their shortcomings and ensure their continued success. With the large amounts of money flowing into parish
projects, Mr. Chandy talked about how achens tended to start on some
kind of construction (such as renovating the church or building a parsonage) when they received a posting. Like Mr. Idiculla, Mr. Chandy
said that people had become cynical about achens and believed that they
used building projects as an excuse to say they were too busy to go on
house visits, or to try to siphon off some of the money (Mar Thoma
parishioners abroad often sent money in the achen's name and they did
not always ask for receipts).

Mar Thomites had also introduced several new ceremonies in Kerala at which they gave donations to the church. According to Mrs. Lilly
George, an elderly parishioner, "Now there is a ceremony at the start of
the school year when children go up in front and get blessed and parents give covers [envelopes] with money." Similarly, events like baptisms,
confirmations, birthdays, and the launching of new businesses were os-
tentatiously celebrated with the involvement of several achens and possibly even a bishop. All this meant that achens and bishops traveled a
great deal as part of their priestly duties.

Congregants complained that achens hardly got to know the members of the parish during their three-year terms due to their increased
travel and administrative responsibilities. A middle-aged woman in Kerala gave me two personal examples. She said that a family member had
been sick and she had called and asked the achen to pray for her. He did
that, but she said that he did not "even bother to come and visit." When
her mother died, she informed the achen, and he said that he would "try
and come" for the funeral (he did not). She said that she had not made
an issue of it but had been upset. Mar Thoma bishops were even busier,
and Mar Thomites in Kerala said that it was hard for lay people to meet
them as they were always rushing around from one appointment to an-

other. In the past, when the bishop would come for a function in a locality, he would interact with all the members of the parish, trying to get to know them personally. But now, when bishops attended a function, they would leave even before the function had finished so they could attend another one. Consequently, Mar Thomites felt that the clergy had lost the "personal touch" that the denomination had been famous for earlier.

To summarize, international migration brought significant new financial resources to achens and the denomination as a whole. Overseas assignments resulted in substantial financial rewards for Mar Thoma achens; international remittances and the enrichment of Mar Thomites in Kerala also led to a tremendous growth in the number of projects run by the church and an increase in the scale of the life-cycle celebrations performed or presided over by Mar Thoma clergy. These changes negatively impacted the relationship of Mar Thoma achens and bishops with their membership in Kerala.

All these developments can be viewed as an outcome of the economic and social changes of Mar Thoma members due to their international migration and are understandable through the lens of transnational theories. Theories of religious change shed further light on these developments.

International Migration, Mar Thoma Leadership, and Theories of Religious Change

The religious economies theory argues that as churches become institutionalized, the financial rewards can start to become a more important motive for religious leaders than religious rewards, and their ability to inspire their members diminishes. This seems to be taking place in the Mar Thoma church due to the economic benefits flowing in because of international migration and the large number of projects it has instituted with the remittances of migrant members.

Neo-institutional theory argues, on the other hand, that leaders are constrained in many ways and are often more interested in maintaining the stability and legitimacy of their institutions than in growing them (DiMaggio and Powell 1991). An important constraint on the Mar Thoma church was the structure of the central decision-making bodies of the church, the Mandalam and its Sabha Council or executive committee, which comprised all the Mar Thoma bishops as well as elected members. The Mandalam is very large, consisting of over 1,400 members, and meets once a year for a three-day period. One prominent Mar Thomite, Dr. Samuel Paul, wrote an article (in English), published in the church's Indian magazine in 2004, in which he suggested making changes to the Mandalam meetings. In the article, Dr. Paul critiqued the "unwieldy" size of the Mandalam and the fact that most of the three days was spent on the "ritual" of presenting annual reports from the multitude of organizations run by the church and on discussing local issues and operational matters. The article concluded, "The end result of an overcrowded agenda is that the time available to discuss serious church-wide policy issues gets squeezed" (Paul 2004, 15). Several other Mar Thomites who had attended the meetings as Mandalam members also told me that the bishops "dominated" the sessions and that there was little opportunity for lay members to talk. Moreover, the Sabha Council that implements and oversees Mar Thoma policies is composed of members who are largely from central Travancore, as the Council meets regularly. In our conversation, Dr. Paul pointed out that this was an additional "constraint" on the operation of the Mar Thoma church, as these members could not relate to the issues faced by parishes outside Kerala (currently 465), which meant that many of the concerns of such parishes were not addressed. Consequently, even though the Mar Thoma is a global church, he said, "it still functions as though it is a central Travancore church" and is reluctant to change. This is in line with the neo-institutional theory of religious change.

The background of the achens and the mission of the church were additional barriers to change within the Mar Thoma community. The Mar Thoma leadership had not publicly commented on the perceived commercialization of its clergy, but individual Mar Thoma leaders that I spoke to argued that since the clergy had families to support (only bishops are celibate in the Mar Thoma church), they needed to keep up with the changing economic environment. They said that it was unreasonable for members to expect achens to live in poverty when everyone else was living in luxury: earlier achens had lived very modestly, but so had most of the others around them. Again, some clergy were children of Persian Gulf or other international migrants who had grown up in comfort in Kerala. (If both parents were working in the Middle East, the children were often sent to live with relatives and attend schools in Kerala. This was particularly true in the 1970s and 1980s when there were no good English-medium schools in many places in the Middle East.) Although such individuals had not turned to priesthood for economic reasons, they took a middle-class life for granted.

In a discussion on the culture of the achens, part of wide-ranging conversations with two Mar Thoma scholars which were compiled into a book (Athyal and Thatamanil 2002), the Metropolitan of the church, Philipose Mar Chrysostom, however, seemed to agree with some of the complaints by Mar Thoma members (both in the diaspora and in Kerala) about the achens' lack of attention to the needs of the congregation and their authoritarian style of functioning. The Metropolitan admitted that the church needed to review its pastoral ministry and make it a central concern, as "meeting people, entering into their needs is not a priority today" for achens (2002, 67). Instead, "an Achen's capability is assessed by how many church buildings and parish halls he has built. If there are no churches to be built, old ones are pulled down to build bigger ones! That is considered as the main ministry of an Achen. This is true about the bishop too. . . . [A]ll of us have become victims of this building culture" (131–132). To a question about obstacles to change in local congregations, the Metropolitan replied:

> The basic problem is that our Achens are not ready for any changes in the traditional patterns of liturgy and worship. . . . The fact is that many of our present Achens are trying to build up the traditional images of leadership; that is, the image of the patriarch who demands unquestioning obedience from his children. . . . Times have however changed; the people have now come of age. They have questions and they are not prepared to give anyone unquestioning loyalty. (131)

In other words, although the Metropolitan showed that he recognized the need for change, he made it clear that neither he nor the Mar Thoma bishops had much control over the achens or even the culture of the church. Since Mar Thoma achens have to be fluent in Malayalam, most have grown up in Kerala. Consequently, they may not have had much exposure to other types of environment. This is yet another limitation on the ability of the Mar Thoma leadership to bring about change. In this respect it appears that the religious economies theory of Stark and Finke (2000) overstates the extent to which religious leaders have the ability to make changes. The neo-institutional perspective seems to be more on target in recognizing the constraints on leaders, including the fact that they may be more interested in meeting the mission or goals of their organization than in efficiency and growth. However, the religious economies theory is helpful in understanding the impact of the financial resources on the Mar Thoma church. As Stark and Finke (2000) argue, the bureaucratization of the church's administration and the professionalization of the clergy brought about due to increased affluence had changed the culture of the church. The clergy and bishops became more like secular administrators, which diminished their personal connection with members and their religious influence over them. Consequently, people in Kerala were becoming increasingly disillusioned with established churches like the Mar Thoma and were turning to new religious options.

The Rise of New Generation Churches in Kerala

A series of developments linked to international migration and financial prosperity transformed the social environment in Kerala and also created new problems and anxieties. The separation of family members due to international migration led to tensions within migrant households, while the competitive consumerism and material expectations unleashed by a remittance economy increased the strain on middle- and lower-class households of both nonmigrants and migrants. Among both migrants and nonmigrants it was common for both spouses to work outside the home, which resulted in changed gender and parent-child dynamics. Perhaps not coincidentally, rates of alcoholism (Biswas 2010; Harikrishnan 2011), suicide (Kerala State Mental Health Authority 2010; Sauvaget et al. 2009), and divorce (Scaria 2010; Shanavas 2012) in Kerala were among the highest in the country in the recent period. Lay Mar Thomites and achens recounted these developments to me and, like Mr. Iype and Mr. Chandy previously quoted, opined that these problems were responsible for a rise in religious fervor.

While the services of the traditional denominations continued to be well attended, foreign networks, together with the recent restrictions on foreign evangelists brought about by various Indian states trying to limit proselytization (Fernandes 2011), the enrichment of the population, and the increase in religiosity led to the rise of new evangelical and charismatic trans-denominational churches in Kerala that challenged the functioning of established episcopal Christian denominations like the Mar Thoma. These transdenominational churches were locally called "new generation" churches. Some were independent, while others were affiliated with international evangelical or Pentecostal churches. Many were led by individuals who were not ordained or even trained in theology. Most targeted a Malayalam-speaking audience, but some focused on a younger, primarily English-speaking group who had studied in the elite English-medium schools and colleges that had become the rage in Kerala after the large-scale migration was institutionalized.

The rise of charismatic, evangelical, or Pentecostal churches is a global phenomenon (e.g., Miller and Yamamori 2007, Miller et al. 2013) and can be seen all over India. Several Indian newspapers and magazines have recently reported on the growth of independent churches in Kerala (Bhattacharyya 2008; Lakshman 2010) and around the country (Rahman 2011). In the central Travancore Christian belt, new generation churches were attracting non-Christians but were also drawing away adherents from traditional churches (Bhattacharyya 2008; Lakshman 2010; Rahman 2011). Although there are a large number and variety of new generation churches in Kerala, some of the first were initiated by return migrants. Many of the new churches in Kerala and around the country are also believed to be thriving due to the contributions coming in from evangelicals in the West, particularly the United States (Bhattacharyya 2008; Rahman 2011). Consequently, international migrants and foreign connections have played an important role in initiating and sustaining these churches (Wuthnow and Offut 2008).

One of the earliest of the new generation churches in Kerala is the Sharon Fellowship Church (SFC) founded in Tiruvalla in the early 1950s by a Syrian Christian man, P. J. Thomas, who had completed a master's degree in comparative religion at Wheaton College, Illinois. While working in Illinois he felt a calling to return to Kerala and serve the Lord. After establishing the Sharon church, P. J. Thomas also started a Sharon Bible College in Tiruvalla. The SFC now has several affiliated churches in other parts of Kerala and in several U.S. states.[6]

The largest and most noteworthy new generation church in Kerala established by an international migrant is the Believers Church, also headquartered in Tiruvalla and formed under the auspices of the Gospel for Asia. It was founded by a Syrian Christian man, K. P. Yohannan, who went to Texas for theological studies in 1974, founded Gospel for Asia (GFA) there in 1979, and then returned to Kerala to focus on mission work in India. Gospel for Asia currently has 67 Bible colleges in South Asia to teach and train "national missionaries" to proselytize co-nationals without the cultural barriers and state restrictions faced by foreign missionaries.[7] The Believers Church received large foreign contributions, Rs.10.44 billion over a period of fifteen years, which it used to buy 2,880 acres of land in Kerala. Since land is scarce and expensive in the state and land holdings are limited by strict laws, this purchase was reported to be under investigation by the state government in 2008 (Bhattacharyya 2008).

Parra ("Rock") was another new generation church in the Tiruvalla area founded by the son of Middle Eastern migrants, who, according to locals, was wealthy enough to be able to devote himself to starting a church without having to give up a comfortable life. Parra targeted English-speaking youth who had studied in English-medium schools and colleges in Kerala or who had grown up abroad (usually in the Middle East or Africa).

Doulos Theological College, established in 1996 in Alwaye, Kerala, was also founded by return migrants: a husband-wife team who had studied at Fuller Theological Seminary, California, and felt called to plant churches in India.[8] Another well-known church in Kerala, Heavenly Feast in Kottayam (where 15,000 people worship together on Sundays), was not founded by a migrant but still had international connections. The founder indicates that he was inspired to form the church by the visit to Kerala in 1998 of Rev. Reinhard Bonnke, a German Christian evangelist with an international following.[9] This church received large foreign donations and was also being investigated by the Kerala government for possible misuse of these funds (Bhattacharyya 2008).

Although there were differences between the new generation churches, they were all characterized by "spirit filled" worship, with clapping, dancing, ecstatic singing, and sometimes faith healing, in stark contrast to the solemn liturgical services of the episcopal churches. Many subscribed to a "prosperity theology" that was attractive to the upwardly mobile and those aspiring to upward mobility. Most important, they provided the kind of "personal service" for members that the more established churches with their bureaucratic structures were no longer able to provide, reaching out to the poor, those who were sick, and the psychologically needy.[10]

Mar Thoma members in Kerala brought up several factors to explain why the new generation churches posed a challenge to churches like theirs. One evening, I talked with four middle-aged Mar Thomites (two men and two women) who had attended some services and revival meetings of these other churches. They indicated that a powerful draw was the faith-healing claims of individual preachers, and they told me of some of the faith healing they had heard about, seen, and experienced personally. But even in cases where there was no faith healing, they mentioned that the homilies of the preachers had been far more powerful than those of the Mar Thoma achens. Mrs. Abraham extolled the preaching at an all-night meeting that she had attended the previous week. "My, what a message that was! It was forceful and moving! I took notes and then came home and read through the notes" (but she could not give me any specifics, despite my probing). Apparently, the preacher had focused on the same verses that the local Mar Thoma achen had used for his sermon a few days later that past Sunday, a sermon that had been rather tepid, from what I gathered. The group also told me that people found the singing and dancing in the churches to be therapeutic. As Mrs. Varghese put it, "Now people have money, but don't have peace of mind so these churches provide the intense spiritual experience that they crave."

Another theme that came up in every discussion about the new churches was how leaders and members of these churches would come and spend a long time praying for those who were sick, had an addiction, or were in psychological distress. In the words of Mr. Easaw, another middle-aged Mar Thomite, "They come regularly, and in large groups to provide support. So this is attractive to those who have problems. In the Mar Thoma church, the achen and some others will visit once, but that is about it. But the new churches have people to do this outreach work full time." Over and over, the individuals I talked to mentioned that people in Kerala had a large number of problems (financial or health issues, but most often family tensions) and did not have "peace of mind." The search for mental peace led them to turn to the new spiritual providers.

The churches in Kerala oriented toward the English-dominant speakers (mostly young adults) were similar to evangelical churches in the United States. Like the older Mar Thomites, the younger, English-speaking group mentioned that they had a lot of problems (such as "boyfriend-girlfriend issues") but no one to talk to, as they could not bring these questions up in the Mar Thoma church or with parents. But in the evangelical churches they could talk to any of the leaders, who would provide guidance and counsel. These churches also had wider discussions of issues that were important to youth.

As I noted earlier, the Mar Thoma church had instituted English services in metropolitan India and had given the youth the autonomy to develop their own praise and worship services once a month. However, evangelical churches were still drawing English-dominant Mar Thoma members away from Mar Thoma churches in these areas. Churches that seemed to particularly draw younger Mar Thomites away in these cities in the 1990s and 2000s included the Vineyard Church in Chennai (with links to the American Vineyard churches), the All People's Church in Bangalore, one of the "new generation" churches, led by a pastor who had relocated to India from the United States in 2000, Methodist churches, and also Pentecostal churches. The attraction seemed to be the informality of the worship, the rousing singing with the use of drums and guitars, and the longer, practically oriented sermons that the youth found more relevant to their lives.

In 2006, I spoke with several English-dominant younger members of the Mar Thoma church in Bangalore. It was clear that they had imbibed many evangelical ideas. Elsa, a young woman in her late twenties, complained, "If you are born again, you are so excited but the rigid Mar Thoma service dampens your excitement. You don't hear the passion and zeal in church." Aji, her husband, criticized the length of the liturgy, "The liturgy is long but only 10 minutes are given to the speaker. In other churches the structure is not so formal. There is a shorter liturgy and the speaker is given a longer time. This is the meat of the service, so you at least feel that you are getting something." Yet, Elsa and Aji still remained in the Mar Thoma church despite feeling that they were not getting enough "spiritual food" from the church. Aji explained, making a very interesting distinction between his relationship with God and the importance of corporate worship, something I did not hear from second-generation Mar Thoma Americans. According to him, "Spiritual food depends on the relationship between me and God. So I depend on God for food. I rely on the church for fellowship and corporate worship. For fellowship and spiritual support, you really need a group you can grow with." In this quote, Aji emphasized the importance of fellowship and corporate worship as important components of the church, while he viewed spiritual food as deriving from a more individual relationship with God. He seemed to have a different understanding of the role of the church than second-generation Mar Thoma Americans. His wife, Elsa, similarly stressed that the fellowship developed through a strong Youth League could keep young people in the church despite the formality of the service, saying, "If you have a strong Youth League, then you don't mind staying [in the Mar Thoma church].

At a subsequent discussion with four youngsters in their late teens and early twenties belonging to the Youth League of a Mar Thoma church in Bangalore, Rajeev, a youth leader, told me that several of the youth who were older than them had left the Mar Thoma church for the All People's Church. In order to find out why the older youth preferred the All People's Church, some of them attended a few services at that church. Rajeev described his experience at that service: "I could feel the presence of God. Everyone was singing from their hearts and I could close my eyes and forget everyone around me. I felt a little self-conscious at first, but I quickly realized that everyone else was raising their hands and completely absorbed in worship. After the service I felt satisfied, and cleansed. The worries of the week just seemed to have rolled away." Rajeev said that when he came back to the Mar Thoma services, he felt that there was something lacking and he talked to his father about it. His father encouraged him to talk to the achen. It was through Rajeev's initiative that the achen had reinstituted the monthly youth-led praise and worship services that had been abandoned due to the leadership vacuum caused by the "committed Christians" in the older cohort leaving for the All People's Church. Rajeev concluded that he was now happy in the Mar Thoma church as he was able to have the same worship experience during the monthly youth-led praise and worship service that he had had at the All People's Church.

Another interesting difference between the Bangalore-born youth and the American-born youngsters was that the Bangalore group was not against liturgical services per se. They just wanted a shorter liturgy.

In fact, a majority of them told me that they thought the Malayalam service was "more beautiful," that they could "feel the spirit more," and that it came "closer to worshiping God" even though they could not understand the meaning. The four youngsters speculated that this difference could be related in part to the fact that there were more people in church for the Malayalam service, which meant that the singing was louder and more enthusiastic.

While several Mar Thoma members attended the services and meetings of the new generation churches, only a small proportion of Mar Thomites in Kerala and even in the metropolitan areas officially "left" the Mar Thoma church. They still wanted to have baptisms, marriages, and funerals conducted by an ordained priest (as mentioned, Syrian Christians in episcopal denominations place a lot of importance on the ordination ceremony, as they believe that the ritual of the laying on of hands transmits an unbroken line of apostolic succession), and to be buried in a Mar Thoma cemetery (the new churches did not have cemeteries of their own). Given the difficulty of obtaining local jobs, positions in Mar Thoma institutions were greatly valued and individuals needed recommendation letters from achens indicating that they were active in the church to get these jobs. For all these reasons, many people who were drawn to the new generation churches still maintained a formal relationship with the Mar Thoma church and continued to attend services at least occasionally and to make some financial contributions.

Although achens and bishops privately acknowledged that new generation churches were drawing away some of their members, the Mar Thoma church had not officially addressed the issue at the time of my fieldwork. However, I know that individual achens tried to provide information to Mar Thomites to counter the claims of these churches. For instance, I attended a service in Bangalore where the achen focused on explaining the Mar Thoma churches' rationale for infant baptism during the sermon (most of the new generation churches practiced a "believers'" adult baptism). Several of the youth members also acknowledged the efforts of the Mar Thoma achens to retain the youth. Elsa remarked during our conversation, "The more they [Mar Thoma achens] see you moving to other churches, the more they try to make sure that you come back." Mar Thoma achens also emphasized the importance of clergy training and ordination and pointed out that new generation churches

did not have a constitution, financial or accounting structures, or democratic oversight by members, in contrast to the Mar Thoma church.

New Generation Churches, Mar Thoma Leadership, and Theories of Religious Change

Two propositions of the religious economies model can be examined
in the context of the rise of the new generation churches in Kerala.
First is the question of how and why such churches developed in such
large numbers. Proponents of the religious economies paradigm take
the stability of people's religious needs for granted and argue that the
increase or decrease in the supply of religious providers is a result of
opportunities and constraints created by state regulation policies. In
the Kerala case, we see that large-scale migration had brought about
major shifts in the circumstances of religious consumers, increasing the
demand for religious and therapeutic goods and their financial ability
to support such efforts. Consequently, the rise of the new generation
churches was at least partly due to these demand-led changes. However,
state regulation policies that increased restrictions on foreign evangelists
and transnational resources that helped to subsidize the start-up costs of
new religious institutions were also important in stimulating the supply
of a large number of domestic religious entrepreneurs (Rahman 2011).

The second issue concerns the relationship between long-
institutionalized churches and newly established religious groups or
sects. The religious economies theory helps us understand why individuals might turn to new religious organizations in search of greater religious
rewards and why the messages of lay preachers may be more inspiring
to ordinary members that those of professional ecclesiastics. However,
we also see that although many members of established denominations
were attracted by the new generation churches and attended their events
and services, only a small proportion of members of churches like the
Mar Thoma actually "left" the Mar Thoma church for the new generation
churches. They wanted the respectability and legitimacy that the mainstream church provided when they needed to mark life-cycle events and
its resources when it came to jobs. This is the advantage that established
churches have over "sects," an advantage that has not been adequately
recognized by the religious economies paradigm.

Theories of transnationalism emphasize the changes that immigrants were able to bring about in the home church, but in the Mar Thoma case most changes had taken place in churches outside Kerala. Why was the Mar Thoma church willing to make some changes to respond to the demands of overseas members and those in metropolitan cities, but not to the needs of its local membership? The transnational cultural differences preventing the Mar Thoma church from being responsive to the needs of its foreign-born generations were not a barrier at the local level. Neither was the opposition of the older generation an issue, since the new generation churches were attracting a wide age-range from the middle-aged to the youth. Both the religious economies theory and neo-institutionalism argue that long-established institutions are relatively resistant to change. However, the influence of the global charismatic movement has led many Protestant, Catholic, and Orthodox churches worldwide to incorporate charismatic elements into their services (Miller 2013). Why then has the Mar Thoma church been so resistant to doing so?

Certainly, since Mar Thoma services in Kerala are well attended and the church is financially strong, there is probably no compelling need for the leadership to bring about change. However, there are additional reasons for the church's unwillingness to make modifications in response to the rise of new generation churches. For one thing, the Mar Thoma church, like other episcopal churches in Kerala, still largely operates on a (castelike) "monopoly" model (Stark and Finke 2000, 201), where individuals remain in the church that they are born and baptized into as infants and switch denominations only as a result of marriage (with women adopting their husband's denomination). This model is reinforced by the fact that few of their Kerala members actually "leave" the church. Consequently, while new generation churches might be genuine competitors for Mar Thoma members, most Mar Thoma leaders preferred to view the turn to the new churches as a temporary fad that people were passing through before returning to the Mar Thoma church.[11] This is particularly the case because the Mar Thoma church (and other Syrian Christian churches in Kerala) deem Pentecostals to be "upstarts" (since they do not have the long history of the Syrian Christian church), lacking in theological legitimacy because their clergy are often not theologically trained or ordained. As the line between Pentecostals and new generation churches is slippery (see Miller and Yamamori 2007), this perspective is extended to the latter as well (Rahman 2011).

Finally, the Mar Thoma church is constrained by its tradition and mission. Due to the theological liberalism of the Mar Thoma leadership, they do not endorse the religious exclusivism of the new generation churches and even of many Mar Thoma achens who have been influenced by the contemporary evangelical turn in Indian Christianity. Yet it is hard for them to supplant some of these ideas. In a long discussion with me (in English) on June 14, 2006, Metropolitan Chrysostom, in his characteristically gentle way, articulated some of the disagreements he had with Mar Thoma clergy.

> God is the God of the universe. Not of Christians. To say that Jesus is God of the Christians is the worst heresy ever produced. But mostly we say it. God is the God of Christians. This is misunderstanding and heresy. . . . M. M. Thomas [a famous lay theologian of the Mar Thoma church] used to say: "Building a Christian religious world is only the center, not boundary. God has redeemed all people. Christians are people who have understood and acknowledged this redemption in Christ." So there is no Christian apart from the non-Christian except in heaven. Until the second coming of Christ, there will be some people who don't belong to the Christian fold. But they are still people of God.

He continued, talking about how Mar Thoma achens often responded with perplexity when he articulated these views.

> I get heaps of questions when I say these things and I have found it difficult to answer them. Because I can only discuss the matter . . . . There are some people who say there is salvation only in Jesus Christ. And I believe them. And I ask them, is there any reality outside Jesus Christ? Can you say that this man was not created by Christ? Then you are saying there is a God other than Christ, isn't it? And then they say—Thirumeni, you are twisting the logic and you are pulling us into a knot so that we cannot untie it so easily!

Due to its nearly two thousand-year history as well as its Orthodox liturgical traditions and worship theology, it is also difficult for the church to include significant charismatic elements into the service: the church cannot change to such an extent that it loses its fundamental identity. Metropolitan Chrysostom also made this clear in his discussion with me. He said:

> The church is very slow in changing. It has to be. . . . Church is the institution where people are defined . . . [so it cannot] keep on changing like people change their fashions. The stability of the church is necessary. . . . The world changes very fast. As Alice in Wonderland said, you have to run very fast to stay where you are. That is true. But we cannot change like that . . . it would be dangerous . . . the church becomes very unstable. Therefore church changes will be very slow and should be very slow, I would say. But unless it changes, the church ceases to be the church.

I asked him how the church would then decide when to change. Is there a critical mass that is needed? He replied, "Two things. First you wait on the Lord and you listen to God." The second criterion, he went on to say, was that the church needed to be "future" or "telos" oriented and should only change to reach a definite future goal, not to keep up with the competition or with every worldly circumstance.

In short, the Mar Thoma church leadership had many constraints on their ability to bring about modifications to the church. They also seemed to be more resistant to change in their central Travancore home base because the leadership continued to operate with traditional paradigms regarding the nature of the church's identity, its membership, and that of its competitor churches, unwilling to recognize the new developments that were affecting Christians in Kerala. The leadership seemed to be more open to acknowledging that the church had to make modifications (however limited) in dioceses formed in cultural contexts outside Kerala.

Culture, Mar Thoma Leadership, and the Participation of Women in the Church

At the same time, the Mar Thoma leadership has been able to bring about some major revisions to church rules that have impacted Mar Thoma parishes around the world. I have mentioned the reduction in the terms of its achens from five to three years to give more of them the opportunity for a foreign assignment. Here I discuss another change, the mandatory integration of women into the Mar Thoma Mandalam beginning in the early 2000s.

We have seen that the Mar Thoma church does not permit the ordination of women and that the leadership maintains that this is for cultural and not theological reasons. However, this emphasis on upholding the culture of its Kerala members seems to be at odds with the leadership's position that the Mar Thoma church should not be viewed as an "ethnic" church as it had a commitment to transcending "the barriers of caste, race and language" (Athyal 2015a, 4). Despite articulating that he was against the Mar Thoma remaining an ethnic, Kerala Syrian church (Athyal and Thatamanil 2002, 119; Athyal 2015a, 4), Metropolitan Chrysostom, in my discussion with him, was very candid about how the Syrian Christian culture of central Kerala had shaped the policy regarding women's leadership in the church:

METROPOLITAN CHRYSOSTOM: Legally there is no rule [in the Mar Thoma church] to prohibit the ordination of women. But so far we have not ordained and we will not ordain. Supposing you now apply for ordination. You have all the qualifications [but] we will not select you. . . . The other day some of my priests said, Why don't you allow women to be lay leaders in the church? We don't allow.

Why, you don't think people are ready?

METROPOLITAN CHRYSOSTOM: This is what I am saying. I live in Kerala. You know in the CSI all dioceses have ordained women. The only diocese which has not ordained women is the Central Kerala [diocese]. . . . Why? See, the Central Kerala CSI is very much a Syrian constituency. . . . So it is all culture. Culture is a very strong force. And to leave culture is to some extent to dehumanize. Culture in many cases is dehumanizing. I agree. But you see, when you become decultured, you are becoming alienated from society because culture is an integral part of the society. . . .

And now slowly we are changing. Formerly, we never allowed women to read lessons in the Sunday service. Now in all churches at least one lesson is read by a woman [see below]. And formerly we did not allow women to assist in the Qurbana service. But slowly now in institutions where there are only women . . . we allow [women in the sanctuary].

In the early 2000s the Mar Thoma church passed a rule requiring that at least 20 percent of the seats in the Mandalam should be held by women. It also required that if a parish was allotted two Mandalam memberships (this depended on its size), one had to be a woman. Consequently, more than 20 percent of the Mandalam members were women after the rule was passed, whereas earlier there had been very few women in the Mandalam. This requirement was passed at a time when the Government of India had mandated that 33 percent of the seats on the panchayats (village councils) were to be reserved for women (this amendment was passed in 1993, in 2011 it was increased to 50 percent). The reservation of seats for women in the Mandalam may have been in response to long-simmering discontent on the part of some of the activist Mar Thoma women's groups in Kerala. However, it did not seem to have been the direct result of any mobilization but was, from what I gathered, a top-down initiative to bring the church into compliance with local (and national) rules regarding reservations for women in representative democratic assemblies. Sheba George (2005, 193) indicates that even the much more conservative Orthodox Church was considering making similar changes, "pushed by external forces" such as the Indian Supreme Court and the World Council of Churches. Mar Thoma parishes were also asked to make sure that one of the two Bible lessons for the Sunday service was read by a woman. These rules were applied in Mar Thoma parishes around the world.

By the time of my fieldwork in Kerala, this rule had been in effect for several years. Some of the Mar Thoma women whom I talked to thought this change had come about because women had the "best status" in the Mar Thoma church (compared to the Orthodox churches), something they said the Metropolitan and the bishops emphasized many times. Others thought it was to recognize the important economic contributions of women to the church. For instance, the Sevika Sangham in Kerala seemed to be very active with a range of projects, funded and led largely by women. I brought up the 20 percent rule during my conversation with the four middle-aged Mar Thomites in Kerala. One of the men said it was because women were more docile and did not challenge the achens or bishops (another man had said something similar during an earlier discussion). But Mrs. Abraham, who had a leadership role in the Sevika Sangham, disagreed, saying that while women did not fight and argue (unlike the men), they often stood their ground and refused the demands of achens. She gave a few examples of how they had done this in her parish. The other man in the group, Prakash Koshy, said it may be because Mar Thoma women were "very good at getting things done." The women agreed with this. As an example, Mr. Koshy talked about how it had taken men twenty-five years to get the local YMCA built, but the women were able to get the YWCA built in six months. When I asked how they could do this, the group told me that it was because women were very good at raising funds from their children abroad to support church projects in Kerala. Men on the other hand might ask their children for funds for personal matters, but not for the church.

Conclusion

The effects of migration on the Mar Thoma church have obviously been profound. Some of these effects were due to the leadership's having to accommodate the needs of its international membership, while others were the unintended consequence of the church developing the infrastructure to manage and use the inflow of remittances. Yet others were due to larger transformations caused by migration and rapid social change.

There has been much discussion of the role of global linkages in the rise of charismatic, evangelical churches around the world, as well as the vibrancy of churches in non-Western countries; we see above how these phenomena are related in Kerala, as the theological training and financial resources that many new generation church initiators received in the United States was crucial in enabling them to introduce new types of religious institutions in their home communities.

Based on the Kerala case, it appears that the religious economies model overstates the power of religious leaders and their ability and desire to bring about change. Leaders of churches are limited by the constitution, structure, and traditions of their organizations, but also by their dependence on pastors and lay members. The religious economies model is also based on the assumption that denominational affiliation is a matter of personal choice (Stark and Finke 2000: 114). However, in many parts of the world it is viewed as an ascribed characteristic, determined by one's family of birth. The neo-institutional paradigm recognizes constraints on religious leaders in bringing about change, particularly their interest in legitimacy and stability. These issues are of particular concern to leaders of traditional religious institutions. In the Mar Thoma case, the legitimacy of the church rested on its believed apostolic origins (from Saint Thomas), its episcopalism, the maintenance of its ancient liturgy, and its Orthodox traditions. As the Metropolitan made clear, stability is also important for religious institutions because the church is the anchor for people's identities. At the same time, the neo-institutional paradigm might be placing too much importance on the constraints faced by religious leaders and might be underestimating the agency of leaders. For instance, the reservation mandate for women in the Mandalam was a radical change introduced by the Mar Thoma leadership, which was passed without opposition.

Theories of religious change have emphasized transformations initiated by the leaders of religious institutions, maintaining that the demand for religion stays constant. However, as we have seen, not only have individuals shown a greater need for the church as a consequence of the changes initiated by large-scale migration and rapid social transformation but they also have had new demands for the type of religion and the type of leadership they want. Theories of transnationalism focus on the impact of economic and social remittances on religious institutions and practices in the home communities. The financial remittances sent by migrant Mar Thomites greatly increased the social service projects of the Mar Thoma church and the size of its administrative structure and the social remittances, or the theological resources received by church-planters from overseas, were crucial to kick-starting many new generation churches. However, transnational theories underestimate the agency of religious leaders in the homeland in determining what types of changes they want to make in response to these remittances. Each perspective focuses on an important dimension, but looking at them together allows us to see the interaction between demand-driven and supply-driven factors, the agency of the laity versus that of the leadership in bringing about or resisting change, and the constraints on organizational development.

Conclusion

Transnational Processes, Immigrant Incorporation, and Religious Change

This book has traced the movement of a Kerala Syrian Christian tradition from its formation as a result of encounters with Portuguese Catholics and British evangelicals, to its transformation due to global dispersion and interaction with American evangelicalism in the United States and India. There are a number of larger lessons to be learned from this study.

First, the research has shown that it is crucial to study religion from a global perspective to appreciate the variety of ways that transnational processes affect religious organizations and the lives of members, both in the place of destination and of origin. Within the field of international migration, there has been a vigorous discussion about the role of transnational or "cross-border" connections (Waldinger 2015) in shaping immigrant incorporation. In a recent book on the topic, Roger Waldinger (2015, 15) argues that the discussion so far has been trapped between the views of the "globalists" who emphasize the continuing connections that emigrants maintain with their home societies, and the "methodological nationalists" who focus on how immigrants gradually assimilate into their new societies of settlement. Instead of being trapped in this binary, Waldinger contends that a better approach would be to examine the factors "that promote *and* supplant cross-border involvements" (Waldinger 2015, 55). His book provides a framework for a study of the longitudinal process of change through which emigrants from one country become nationals in another as a result of the "dialectic between immigration and emigration" (Waldinger 2015, 37). This inquiry has presented one attempt at such a longitudinal study by looking at how institutions like the Mar Thoma church with achens from the homeland factor into the process of immigrant settlement and incorporation.

Additionally, this book extends the frame to understand the dialectics and tensions of migration by viewing it also from the perspective of the sending society. When examining the large-scale emigration from the vantage point of central Kerala, we see the role of religion in shaping the outflow of migration but also the big changes that have taken place in religious institutions in Kerala and other parts of India where Mar Thomites live, as a consequence of the out-migration. Financial remittances and the opportunities for foreign postings have brought about fundamental transformations in the Mar Thoma church, including the shortening of the terms of the achens to three years. International migration has also led to the establishment of "new generation" churches in Kerala and in other parts of the country, initiated through connection with the United States and evangelical and charismatic traditions.

Impact of the Kerala Background on the Mar Thoma American Community and Church

This book has shown that the central dynamics of the Mar Thoma American church community were profoundly shaped by its Kerala, Syrian Christian background. The migration of a large proportion of Mar Thomites to the United States, at least until the 1990s, took place through female nurses and their networks. The reason that almost all the nurses from India were Syrian Christians and that Mar Thomites had the highest migration rate of all Kerala groups was because they were able to take advantage of educational and occupational opportunities in missionary educational and medical institutions in Kerala and in other parts of India through their Anglican connections. The Mar Thoma church's links with Anglicans also provided the opportunity to surmount caste pollution and gender taboos that prevented women from other groups from going into the field of nursing. The migration of several Mar Thoma men was also directly facilitated by Mar Thoma networks, as these men had arrived for higher education, including Christian theological education, at Christian universities and colleges affiliated with Bible colleges that the Mar Thoma church was connected with in south India. Others, including Mar Thoma achens, were admitted into American Protestant seminaries because of the ecumenical connections of the Mar Thoma leadership.

We have also seen that the adaptation of Mar Thomites to the United States was enabled by Kerala Christian relatives and friends who often sponsored their immigration, and sometimes housed and fed them for months until the newcomers had the resources to move into their own homes. Ideas of gender and class from India shaped household dynamics among immigrants. Female nurses often became the primary income earners in the United States and many of their husbands were not able to get good jobs, resulting in the reversal of traditional gendered economic roles. While this sometimes caused tensions at home, being part of a Mar Thoma American community where many other couples were in the same situation provided support for such families. The Mar Thoma church also served as a site where couples could compensate for the gender reversal at home by following traditional gender scripts. The anomie of migration and resettlement made many parents even more insistent on upholding "the real Indian culture" while bringing up their children, using child-rearing practices and gendered expectations that had been prevalent when they were growing up in Kerala. More recently, a second-generation achen told me that many Mar Thoma homes had Malayalam television serials (from satellite providers such as Asianet and Surya TV) playing for many hours a day in an attempt to maintain a Malayali atmosphere at home and to ensure their children's fluency in the language. The achen, however, felt that this practice had deleterious consequences for the children's educational progress and English language skills.

Immigrant understandings of Christianity and the role of the church were formed by their upbringing in the Mar Thoma church in India (or other Syrian Christian churches in the case of women who became part of the church upon their marriage). Consequently, they saw their ethnic and religious identities as being interlinked, and in the diaspora the church became their primary social community. Most of the immigrants who had been raised in the Mar Thoma church also had a deep attachment to the Mar Thoma Malayalam liturgy. Over and over I heard from Mar Thomites and Mar Thoma achens that English services tended to have a much lower attendance than the Malayalam services as the immigrant generation was less likely to attend them.

Divisions based on class, education, gender, the region of India from where members had migrated, and connections with the Mar Thoma leadership were imported into the American context, shaping internal schisms within Mar Thoma congregations in the United States and sometimes even the way achens related to different groups. Although the church was primarily supported by nurses and their husbands in the diaspora, this was a segment that was often belittled by other groups in the church, leading to tensions and confrontations in church spaces. We have also seen that the Mar Thoma leadership deferred to the central Kerala culture of the majority of Mar Thoma members, particularly in matters such as women's participation in the church. This in turn meant that norms of the Syrian Christian community in central Kerala were imposed on the Mar Thoma community living in other contexts as well.

The Kerala background of Mar Thoma members also had a fundamental impact on the civic and political engagement patterns of the Mar Thoma American church. Although religious institutions in the United States are often the means through which immigrants become civically and politically involved with their home countries and with the wider U.S. society, the upper-caste Kerala background of the membership and their passion for denominational politics meant that they were less concerned about attacks against lower-caste Christian groups in other parts of the country. They also had a strong commitment to the Mar Thoma church and the Metropolitan, were proud of Mar Thoma projects that they supported in Kerala and in other parts of India, and knew that the denomination was dependent on their contributions ("if not us, then who?") to finance these projects. As individuals from modest backgrounds who had been able to "make good" in the United States, many felt a strong sense of obligation to contribute to the uplift of the poor in India, particularly in Kerala. Consequently, they felt that the priority of the Mar Thoma American church and its members ought to be to support the charities that the Mar Thoma church had already established in India. A further incentive was the fact that contributions to Mar Thoma projects in Kerala earned immigrants status, as friends and relatives back home often heard about their donations. The first North American projects of the Mar Thoma church—the Native American and Mexico mission fields—were structured like the traditional Mar Thoma mission fields in India in lower-caste or Dalit communities at a distance from Mar Thoma parishes, which meant that reaching out to these groups did not affect the homogeneity of the church or its worship and social practices.

It was not just the immigrant generation that was shaped by its Kerala background. The Malayali heritage of their parents, of the Mar Thoma church, and of the Mar Thoma achens impacted the second generation in many ways. Parents' attempts to raise their American children in a "Kerala bubble" was sometimes resented and questioned by children who had to deal with very different expectations between home and school. At the same time, many showed an attachment to their relatives in Kerala. My interviews with the second generation always began with discussions of their family background and the migration history of their parents. In this context, many talked warmly about their extended families in Kerala and said that they enjoyed visiting them. Most of the American-born Mar Thomites manifested a strong ethnic identity and married other Syrian Christians. Kerala remained the fallback option for "pure" spouses for both men and women in the second generation if they were unable to find their ideal partners in the United States. The second generation also went to India for mission trips facilitated by the Mar Thoma church. When I met an immigrant member of the Bethel-ville church many years later at a Mar Thoma Sevika Sangham conference, she told me that her daughter had gone to south India on a mission trip during which she had "some experiences" that made her decide to abandon her plan of going to medical school and instead turn to working for the InterVarsity Christian Fellowship. Second-generation members also sent money back to India. Sheila and Alice from Hope Mar Thoma church said that in addition to their personal involvement in local outreach they also sent money to support Mar Thoma projects in Kerala. However, Alice pointed to a difference between her orientation and that of the women in the immigrant generation. Referring to her mother and her mother's friends in the Sevika Sangham, she said,

> Their whole mission since I have had any awareness of them, you know, has been to give money to India. Always to Kerala girls to teach them nursing, to get them married. I mean, these were the most important things to them. Whereas women like me would never give a woman money to get married. We would give money so she could get educated. I'd rather edu-

cate a woman than give her money to get married. Because that does not empower her. So, I mean that's the ... that's I think the biggest difference.

Despite their attachment to their ethnic identity, the second generation also critiqued the insularity and patriarchy of Kerala culture and had adopted the distinction made by the immigrant generation between the differences in outlook between Syrian Christians raised in Kerala versus those raised in Indian metropolitan cities. Although they were often critical of the liberal orientation of immigrant generation members (particularly women) who had grown up outside Kerala, when it came to individuals of their own age, they felt that they had more in common with the cosmopolitanism of Syrian Christians raised in metropolitan India than with immigrants who were raised in Kerala.

The American-born generation mostly viewed the Mar Thoma church as a warm and nurturing space while they were growing up, where they could be in the company of others of their age who had the same type of background and upbringing. Like the immigrants, they tended to refer to the church community as their extended family. Once they got older, however, many became more critical of the church congregation. For instance, one woman in her late twenties described her parish as a space where the older generation "was mainly interested in maintaining and policing being Indian, being Malayali." Others referred to the gossip and the marriage pressure on young people, particularly women. Many were critical of the fact that the leadership of the church still continued to be retained by the immigrant generation. As we have seen, the American-born youth often tended to find fault with the Kerala-raised achens who were posted in their parishes. However, this was not always the case. They also praised individual achens who had taken the trouble to reach out to their generation. For instance, Sheila and Reuben from Hope Mar Thoma church both talked about how they had been rather shy and "in the background" and said that their involvement in youth leadership came about because an achen had reached out to them and entrusted them with the responsibility of leadership. Sheila described her feelings eloquently:

I don't know, there was something that he just either saw in me, or ... and then I felt this change come on ... I feel the Mar Thoma church gave me my platform to becoming the person that I am. . . . Like that achen, he really gave me my wings. To this day, everything that I do I think I do because of that one, you know that one step-off.

Many second-generation Mar Thoma Americans did not understand or appreciate the Mar Thoma liturgy. However, here too there were differences. In the Cornerstone Mar Thoma parish, a young second-generation man who had taken it upon himself to do some research on the Mar Thoma liturgy held a class for the youth to educate them about it. The two second-generation Mar Thoma members I interviewed from that church who had attended the class spoke about how it had given them a deep appreciation for the liturgy. Alex, one of the two, explained that after going to the class,

> I've learned to appreciate my church a lot more. No disrespect for like other churches, but the structure [of the service] that we have in our church is very, very valuable. . . . And then just, just the environment that we have . . . our service is focused on the message of Christ crucified. And that is something that I've only realized with this class. . . . It's a message that's been in our church since—well since Saint Thomas was here. Since Saint Thomas came to India and, and brought about the church. . . . The liturgy, the service that's being chanted, every single week, I think is very, very, very beautiful, it's, it's amazing. All of it, all of it is Bible based. Everything is scripture. You can find every single sentence there in the Bible. And it's so beautiful.

During my 2015 interview with a second-generation achen, he pointed me to an Internet article that had been making the rounds within the Mar Thoma American community titled "My Apology to the Mar Thoma Church." In the article, the young man, Shawn Varghese, wrote that he had grown up in the Mar Thoma church and had left it out of frustration with its practices, had attended a U.S. seminary, and had then got into leadership positions in a nondenominational church. But he said that after some time, he found himself frustrated with the nondenominational church approach as well, because of "the lack of the grand narrative—the full redemptive/gospel story of our God" in their services. He then moved to an Anglican church, where he came to understand that "liturgy can give the church the meta-narrative that she needs." He ended the article by apologizing to the Mar Thoma Church for not realizing the value of its liturgy. "There is something absolutely beautiful about liturgy when the heart is truly worshipping Jesus and the words are based on God's word" (Varghese 2015).

We have seen that it was not just the Kerala-raised immigrants who upheld the idea that women should not cross into the sanctuary and hold positions as deacons or as pastors in church. Several second-generation Mar Thoma Americans, both men and women, also articulated these beliefs. In many of these cases, it was evident that they had picked up their ideas from the immigrant generation or from achens, for instance about the "line that women could not cross" and about menstrual pollution. In all cases, however, they attempted to provide biblical justifications for the prohibition. Where they heard these biblical justifications, however, was less clear. The more liberal second-generation women were critical of the prohibition on women being in the altar and most left to find other churches where they could have a more meaningful role, which meant that the Mar Thoma church was depriving itself of the contribution of such women to the community.

Amanda Mathew,[1] a second-generation Mar Thomite who self-identified as "liberal" but was still within the Mar Thoma church when I spoke to her (she admitted she was unusual in that respect), had spent an extended period of time in Kerala studying at the Kottayam Seminary. She told me that she had the experience of being "physically and verbally accosted" there in several churches when she tried to take communion with her head uncovered. These experiences made her more understanding of why the Mar Thoma church leadership would fear that the church would "break apart" if they allowed women at the altar. She continued, "For me, I understand if you don't ordain women today. But you need to be explaining to people why it is theologically fine and ethically important for women to be ordained as soon as possible. Start a discussion, even admit that this topic is open to discussion. I think this is the responsibility of people at the top." In other words, her critique was that the Mar Thoma hierarchy was not playing a leadership role in preparing the Mar Thoma membership for change but was instead willing to allow itself to be led by the prejudices of the membership. Amanda argued that some of the other churches had been willing to affirm "the people on the margins," even when this caused the big donors to turn away and the masses to leave, since this was the way Jesus practiced his ministry. But, she concluded, "Our church is not there."

Perhaps the most important way that Kerala culture and ethos has continued to impact the Mar Thoma American community, both immigrants and the second generation, was through the constant supply of Mar Thoma achens and bishops sent by the Mar Thoma synod to the United States. The terms of the achens were shortened from five to three years to give more of them the opportunity to have an overseas assignment. But the shorter term in turn meant that achens did not have the opportunity to adapt to their new society and to understand the differences between the lives and contexts of Mar Thoma members in the United States and in India. Since achens possessed a lot of power and influence, their outlook and perspective had a big impact on Mar Thoma American parishes. In his 2015 discussion of my article on the Mar Thoma church, Jesudas Athyal indicated that the Mar Thoma church had a decentralized structure and that "virtually all decisions pertaining to the Church in the United States are taken by appropriate bodies *within* the country" (Athyal 2015a, 7, emphasis in the original). However, with the exception of the formation of CrossWay church, some local outreach, and the establishment of social service projects in North America among Mexicans and Native Americans, this local autonomy was hard to discern during my fieldwork and my discussions with the membership and the achens. The organizations within each Mar Thoma American church, the structure of the service, what they should do with their weekly collections, and even the structure of lectors reading Bible lessons was laid down by the decision makers in Kerala. At the same time, I have indicated that it is also possible that the adherence of Mar Thoma American parishes to the Kerala model had as much to do with pressure from the immigrant members of the congregation to maintain tradition as it did with the centralized authority structure of the church.

The history of the Kerala Syrian Christian tradition also shaped religious adaptation and incorporation patterns of Indian Christian churches in the United States. Religious groups in the diaspora often practice an "ecumenical strategy," a variety of subgroups coming together under the umbrella of a religious institution, at least in the early period of settlement, due to small numbers and the high expenses involved in renting or building separate institutions for each group (Williams 1992, 239). However, in the Syrian Christian case, the putative founding of the church by Apostle Thomas, the upper-caste status of the Syrian Christian community, the emphasis on the historical episcopate through an unbroken line of legitimate ordination, and the ancient liturgy meant that identity, tradition, and practices were deeply entrenched. Also, the Indian immigrant congregations were formed on linguistic lines based on region of origin in India. For both these reasons, there were few pan-Indian Christian congregations among immigrants, except in areas where Indians were concentrated in the United States, where the services would be held in English (which meant that they only attracted English-dominant Indian immigrants). This pattern of immigrant church formation by Indian Christians contrasts with that by Korean and Chinese American Christians, where a common language and a more recent history of Christianity in the homeland meant that immigrants from a variety of regions of origin and denominations were able to come together to form American congregations (Min 2010; Yang 1999).

The colonial and postcolonial history of schisms and cleavages within the Syrian Christian community was a further factor influencing the religious formations of immigrant Syrian Christians. The long history of Syrian Christianity in Kerala has led to deep denominational divides that are difficult to transcend, even among groups that are "in communion" with each other, as in the case of Mar Thomites and CSI members. For these reasons, the first Mar Thoma-CSI congregation to come together in New York on the instructions of the Mar Thoma leadership, dissolved after only two years due to disputes that resulted in "fist fights" in church (Thomas and Mattackal 2008, 41).

Other aspects of the history of the Mar Thoma denomination have been central in shaping its relationship with nonimmigrant Christian churches in the United States. Since the Mar Thoma denomination is part of the Syrian Christian branch that rebelled and broke away from its Portuguese Roman Catholic yoke, and subsequently also broke away from the Orthodox group to embrace Reformed ideas and practices, Mar Thomites see themselves as a group that is theologically distinct from and opposed to both Roman Catholicism and Eastern Orthodoxy. Consequently, despite the similarities in liturgical worship traditions and social outlook, Mar Thomites, even those fluent in English, would

not consider becoming part of U.S. Roman Catholic or Eastern Orthodox congregations. Because of its Anglican connection and the centrality of its Reformed identity, the Mar Thoma church has a relationship
with several mainline churches (Episcopal, Presbyterian, Methodist) in
the United States and, as we have seen, it encourages its membership to
integrate with such churches, particularly in areas where there is no local
Mar Thoma church. However, there is a disjuncture between the conservative culture of most immigrant members and second-generation
evangelicals, and the liberal orientation of these mainline churches, particularly around issues such as gay rights and gay marriage. As a result,
many Mar Thomites, even if fluent in English, would not feel comfortable in such churches. Due to the episcopal and communitarian history
of the Mar Thoma church, the leadership is opposed to the individualistic evangelical orientation of many contemporary Christian groups in
the United States, but these are precisely the groups to which the second
generation is attracted. All these historical elements of the Mar Thoma
church lead to tensions and barriers to religious integration into mainstream American congregations, even for English-dominant immigrant
members and for the second generation.

Impact of the American Context on the Mar Thoma U.S. Church

Of course, the Mar Thoma church and the Mar Thoma community are
not hermetically sealed Kerala bubbles relocated in the United States,
despite what some of the immigrant members would like to believe. The
American context has a powerful influence on them. This is true even
of the immigrant generation, who in the United States were fighting
back against Kerala conceptions of occupational status by invoking the
concept of the "dignity of labor" and were also challenging some of the
traditional norms around gendered housework.

The second generation, not surprisingly, has been particularly impacted by the American context. Second-generation Mar Thoma
Americans have embraced the "new paradigm" of religion and ethnicity prevalent in the United States in the contemporary period, which
inverts the earlier model of immigrant incorporation. While immigrants to the United States at the turn of the twentieth century were
expected to assimilate to the culture of the host society in the public

realm, they were able to maintain their cultural traditions by establishing their own religious institutions. This was because the understanding
was that religion embodies and maintains the core values of an ethnic
group (Greeley 1972; Herberg 1960; Smith 1978). Large-scale contemporary immigration, however, spurred multiculturalism "from above,"
as states tried to manage racial and ethnic diversity, and multiculturalism "from below," as new modes of communication provided effective
mediums for minorities to advocate for racial, cultural, and religious
rights (Joppke 1996; Vertovec and Wessendorf 2010). The prevalence
of multiculturalism means that immigrants and their children find an
identifiable place in American society by remaining ethnic and group-
identified (Dhingra 2007, 82). Like the denominational structure that
permitted earlier groups of ethnics to be incorporated in American society while maintaining their religious difference, multiculturalism per-
mits contemporary groups to become American by becoming ethnic.
Multiculturalism also legitimates "the expression of and organization
around home country loyalties" (Waldinger 2015, 12), or the continued
maintenance of transnational connections.

While the maintenance of ethnicity has been embraced in secular
spheres, scholars have documented that inherited patterns of belonging and a commitment to institutional religion have eroded among the
native-born post–World War II generation, giving rise to an emphasis
on personal choice and meaning. Individuals are encouraged to actively
choose their religious tradition rather than just accepting inherited
practices, as inherited culture and tradition are seen as a liability in the
spiritual sphere (Heelas 1996; Houtman and Aupers 2007).

Based on his research among a variety of U.S. religious communities
(Protestant, Catholic, Jewish, and neo-pagan), Richard Madsen (2009)
argued that there was a "pervasive, hegemonic understanding" of religion among the communities he studied. According to him, American religious culture was characterized by individualism and voluntary
choice, but was also constrained and shaped by connections with inherited traditions. Specifically, the individuals he studied described feeling
alienated by their parents' religion, which they characterized as being
based on tradition, performed in an "unthinking" or "rote" fashion.
While the interviewees remained within the religions of their families,
in their self-narratives they spoke of "leaving behind the faith of their

parents" (Madsen 2009, 1283) because they sought new, more demanding ways of practicing their religion. While Madsen (2009, 1265) depicts this religious culture as typical of the contemporary "American native-born white middle class," the description he provides of the younger generation breaking away from the religious practices of their parents captures the central dynamic that we see among second-generation immigrants in the United States, and also in Europe.

Beginning around the mid-1990s, scholars researching religion and ethnicity among new ethnic groups in the West began to notice that while most second- and later-generation immigrants stayed within their parents' religions, unlike their parents, many who were religious separated their ethnicity from their religion. These individuals distinguished the "pure" religion they practiced from the "cultural religion" of the immigrant generation and were sloughing off the customs and observances of their parents. Although such individuals did not compose a large proportion of the second generation, scholars noted that they were a significant minority whose ideas and actions were having a profound impact on their communities and on the wider societies in which they were located (Glynn 2002, 969; Kibria 2008, 245; Schmidt 2002). Since then, the tendency of many second-generation immigrants to embrace a "decultured" religion, purified of the cultures of their parents' homeland traditions has been widely discussed in the literature, particularly studies that focused on Muslims in Europe (Mandaville 2007; Roy 2004; Salih 2004). However, this trend has been observed among a variety of religious groups such as Armenians, Muslims, Hindus, second-generation American Christians, and Sikhs in North America as well.[2] Similarly, the emphasis on an individualistic, textually based religion, shorn of most ritual observances is a characteristic of not just Christian groups but also of second-generation members belonging to a variety of religious traditions (Cesari 2004; Kurien 2007; Nayar 2004; Roy 2004). Consequently, it appears that the "remaking" of inherited religion that Madsen (2009) noticed among American white, middle-class youth might be a feature of contemporary Western religious culture more broadly, which in turn has influenced the Western-born second generation from a range of religious backgrounds.

Although members of the second and later generations who turn to culture-free religion believe that they are embracing a "pure" religion free from the cultural baggage of their parents, what is actually taking place is that they are shedding the ethnic languages, theologies, and worship cultures of their parents and assimilating to the dominant form of the religion. In the case of second-generation Americans who are Christians, disentangling religion and ethnicity involves shedding ethnic languages and worship cultures to adopt those of white, upper-middle-class American evangelicals.

The embrace of evangelicalism by the second generation has in turn shaped the central features of the Mar Thoma American parishes. It has created intergenerational tensions within churches as the two generations embrace different models of Christianity, and has led large numbers of the second generation to leave their home church. Many of the criticisms that the American-born generation have leveled against the Mar Thoma church stem from the fact that they have internalized the evangelical paradigm of Christianity and are consequently critical of Eastern Orthodox understandings and practices. The integration of the social and cultural community with the faith community; the liturgical worship that includes ritualized gestures and the idea that communitarian worship is a valued tradition; the concept that worship is an end in itself and that the sermon is less important; and the fact that the church is not defined by its doctrinal position or stand on social issues, all stem from the Eastern, or Syrian Orthodox paradigm of Christianity. Many second-generation individuals like Preeti, who maintain that Mar Thomites should believe that Jesus Christ is *the* way and not just *one* way, may not understand that most Mar Thoma bishops do not support her theological position. Recall that the Metropolitan brought up his discomfort with Christian exclusivism during my discussion with him. He has also made his position clear in more public venues. For instance, in a DVD issued in 2007 on his ninetieth birthday, he said with characteristic humility,

I believe in one and only one God. I do not consider that there is a God for the Hindu, one for the Muslim, and another for the Catholics. It is possible. I am not aware because I am not an authority about the person of God. But it is my understanding that there is only one God and that God is differently understood by different people. (Mar Thoma Syrian Church 2007)

The evangelical influence can also be seen in second-generation Mar Thoma American understandings of appropriate gendered behavior, particularly in religious spaces. Most of the men and women who remained in the church seemed to adhere to some extent to the belief that women should be submissive to men, particularly their husbands. We have seen that this was articulated even by outspoken individuals like Shirley (when she was talking about how she had trouble dating Indian American men because they wanted women to agree with everything they said). However, instead of seeing this norm as being rooted in Malayali tradition, as the immigrants did, the second generation considered it to be a biblical principle and therefore important to uphold. Consequently, they were critical of what they perceived to be the "feminism" of some of the immigrant professionals. At the same time, they challenged the conventional Mar Thoma community understanding that women should take a back seat in church. They upheld the right of women to take some leadership roles, though the women who undertook these positions usually described themselves as "serving" the church community rather than "leading" it.

Evangelical Christianity also led the second generation to espouse a different model of Christian outreach and social obligation from the immigrant generation. They felt that their primary obligation as Christians was to develop a personal relationship with Christ, which in turn would lead to their modeling the example of Christ by maintaining personal morality, and by serving the needy in the community. They contrasted their "higher" understanding of Christianity with that of the immigrant generation, who they described as having a "works-based faith" which emphasized the Christian obligation to help others. Second generation members, on the other hand, emphasized that their personal obligation was to "spread the Word" by evangelizing to others. Consequently they saw outreach as being essential for the Mar Thoma American church. This meant having an open church so they could invite the local community as well as their friends and coworkers to worship with them. They also considered local outreach to be important because they saw themselves as Americans, which meant that their community comprised members of the wider society around them rather than people in Kerala. Consequently they had a very different model of civic engagement than the immigrant generation. While their local outreach strategy likely had a greater personal impact than the "checkbook activism" of the immigrants, it is not clear whether their sporadic outreach activities actually brought about any significant changes in the communities within which they worked. Mar Thoma projects in India, on the other hand, were designed with the goal of bringing about a total transformation of the unprivileged communities that were adopted by the church, by providing socioeconomic, educational, and occupational opportunities, in addition to spiritual support.

While there are variations in how Mar Thoma parishes across the country are affected by the evangelical turn of their youth, the Mar Thoma North American diocese can expect to be substantially transformed by the influence of American evangelism. We have seen that the classes and the organizations oriented toward the second-generation youth draw on resources provided by American evangelical groups. Since the theological outlooks of these organizations are very different from those of the Mar Thoma, they are bound to have deeper consequences for the church. The Mar Thoma church leadership also has to deal with a variety of challenges as it tries to deal with the competing demands of the different constituencies in its American parishes. The immigrants who form its hard-core base are those who are Malayalam-dominant. Consequently, they want to maintain the traditional structure and Malayalam liturgy. However, many second-generation members want a more open, seeker-oriented church with English services in the American evangelical model. At present the church is trying to accommodate both groups by having Malayalam and English services on alternate Sundays and by including more praise and worship sessions for the youth. However, it is not easy to fully meet the needs of either generation within this structure, leading immigrants to complain and many second-generation Mar Thomites to leave the church.

The formation of CrossWay in Dallas by second-generation Mar Thoma Americans is the first organized attempt by a second-generation group to come together on their own for Sunday worship on a regular basis. For three years, the group held contemporary praise and worship services, drawing on the resources of evangelical organizations.[3] They had an immigrant Mar Thoma achen who conducted the liturgy, but in every other respect they were led by lay second-generation leaders who delivered the message, led the worship songs, the Bible studies, and the outreach activities. Reji told me that their current achen was only as-signed to them temporarily, until they became a parish (they had been classified as a "congregation" initially) which they hoped would hap-pen in the next year. I asked him whether CrossWay was trying to get a second-generation achen and he replied that they had requested an achen who could "understand the needs of our congregation" and were also trying to see if there could be some flexibility about the current three-year term. But by emphasizing lay leadership, Reji said that they were trying to make sure that the church did not become too dependent on the achen "and his leadership or lack of leadership." Perhaps develop-ing strong lay leadership is one way that individual parishes could try to ensure that the church meets the needs of its American membership while still receiving Mar Thoma achens sent from India. There is no doubt, however, that if more churches adopt the CrossWay model the administrative structure of the denomination, its control over parishes, and the meaning of a Mar Thoma identity will be completely changed.

While many second-generation Mar Thomites were happy about the development of the CrossWay congregation, Rachel, a "liberal" second-generation woman who remained in the Mar Thoma church, was critical of the evangelical turn of her peers and described the Mar Thoma American church as "schizophrenic" for trying to maintain an "ultra-traditional Indian sort of institution" on the one hand, while also "pandering to millennial evangelicals" (referring to the CrossWay con-gregation) on the other. She thought the church should instead work harder to integrate both groups into one religious community. But as we have seen, this is a difficult task given the very different interests of the two generations. Based on a study of Japanese immigrant institutions, Mullins (1988) argues that ethnic churches that relied on priests from the homeland were likely to lose their membership over time as the second and later generations become more assimilated. Thus, the transnational character of denominations like the Mar Thoma may hasten the demise of the American dioceses in the long term. At the same time, if the Mar Thoma church accommodated so much to the American environment that it abandoned its distinctiveness (currently maintained by its con-nections to Kerala and by its Malayali achens), it could also become ir-relevant and lose its membership. As another second-generation Mar Thoma American pointed out, "If the Mar Thoma church became like any of the other churches, we could just go down the road to the nearest church. There would be no need to drive sixty miles every Sunday." It is clear that the Mar Thoma American church has to perform a delicate balancing act to remain viable in the long term.

The long-term survival of the Mar Thoma church in the United States will also depend on immigration patterns in the future. Some evidence seems to indicate that immigration rates, particularly of Indian Christians, are falling (George 2015). If immigration continues, the Mar Thoma church and similar Indian Christian American churches may continue to be revitalized by the newcomers and might gradually change to accommodate the changes that are taking place in both India and the United States, thus retaining many more of its youth. It has been able to do this in other parts of the world, such as in Malaysia, where the first Mar Thoma church was established in 1936. In 2015, several generations later, the Mar Thoma website indicates that the church still had nineteen parishes in the Malaysian region. The Mar Thoma church is not unique in attempting to maintain an intergenerational congregation. In fact, intergenerational immigrant churches are more common than the generationally segregated Korean American churches (Gornik and George 2015). The Mar Thoma leadership should engage in dialogue with leaders of other intergenerational American churches to learn what practices work best.

While the Mar Thoma leadership has tried to bring about changes in the church to meet the demands of its membership in the United States, right from the inception of its North America and Europe diocese many Mar Thoma leaders have also made it clear that they wanted its members to join and merge with local denominations with which the church was in communion, rather than trying to maintain a separate identity. In Metropolitan Chrysostom's 2001 discussions with Athyal and Thatamanil about the diaspora church, he reiterated that in the interests of its mission of ecumenism, the Mar Thoma Church must be willing to lose itself. Consequently, he maintained that he wanted the "diaspora community to become the local community" (Athyal and Thatamanil 2002, 116–117) and that he would be "very happy to see that there is no Indian church in America. That is what we want. The people should become part of the land" (2002, 125). At the same time, Mar Thoma leaders are not happy when they lose members to nondenominational evangelical churches whose theology and approach they do not endorse. The formation of the CrossWay congregation in Dallas was likely an attempt to prevent this from happening.

There is now a substantial body of literature showing that contemporary second-generation Americans obtain several social, psychological, and economic benefits from participation in ethnic religious institutions. In particular, such participation seems to help them deal with the racialization and identity issues that they have to confront, focus on educational achievement, and avoid assimilating to popular American teenage norms that emphasize social success over academics (Ebaugh and Chafetz 2000; Kurien 1998; Zhou and Bankston 1998). Stark and Finke (2000, 125) argue that the close community ties created by ethnic churches mean that those who leave the church will suffer heavy social and emotional costs. Second-generation Mar Thomites who left the church often attended sporadically, for special events, and remained in touch with their Syrian Christian families and friends. It remains to be seen whether they will be able to provide a similar supportive community for their children with this type of intermittent contact. This will be a dilemma faced by any group of second- and later-generation ethnic Christians who are not able to form their own separate churches.

The Impact of American Evangelicalism on the Mar Thoma Denomination in India

Mar Thoma American parishes are not the only ones to have been impacted by the new dominant forms of American Christianity. The whole denomination has been affected by the spread of nondenominational evangelicalism. As we have seen, the conflict with American Christian ideas is also taking place within Mar Thoma parishes in India. In large metropolitan areas, English-dominant Mar Thoma youth are attracted to evangelical parishes which are linked with American-based churches. Here again the fiercest opposition comes from recent migrants from rural Kerala. The Mar Thoma church is facing trouble even in rural Kerala, earlier its bastion of strength, as Indian Pentecostals and Charismatics have been very successful in gaining adherents from traditional churches. Even many Mar Thoma achens have imbibed conservative, evangelical ideas and the leadership finds itself in a dilemma about how best to deal with this situation. As the new generation churches become more established and institutionalized in Kerala and in other parts of the country, they could potentially have major impacts on older Christian denominations like the Mar Thoma and on interreligious relationships between Christians and other groups. The aggressive proselytizing strategies of these churches are already being blamed for some incidents of violence against Christians by Hindu groups (Baldauf 2005). Many traditional churches like the Mar Thoma find themselves without the resources to counter the global spread of nondenominational evangelicalism. Since these churches are based on very different sociocultural ideas about personhood, autonomy, and spirituality, many might find themselves eventually losing their rich history and traditions.

The New Paradigm and the Impact of the Contemporary Immigration on Mainstream American Churches

How does the new paradigm delinking religion and ethnicity in a post-denominational society shape the relationship between race, religion, and social incorporation for new Christian groups? What impact might this relationship have on nonethnic American churches? The linguistic and cultural barriers faced by immigrants and the fact that they experience ethnicity and religion as intertwined, probably mean that most of this generation will remain within ethnic religious institutions. In a postdenominational society, such ethnic churches are more likely to be spaces of separation from mainstream society than places of integration as in a denominational society. But we have seen that social class matters as well. Immigrants who are well educated (particularly those who have been educated in the United States) and fluent in English may feel comfortable joining mainstream American churches. If ethnic churches continue to focus primarily on meeting the needs of the immigrant generation, more second-generation Americans are likely to leave. Individuals belonging to groups that do not have the option of forming second-generation churches may turn to large evangelical churches for their spiritual needs. Sam George (2015, 5) argues that the overwhelming majority of second-generation Indian American pastors were not serving immigrant churches and that most were drawn to American evangelicalism. According to his survey, over a hundred second-generation Indian American Christians were serving in American evangelical churches and ministries (including several who held leadership positions), and another two hundred who were studying in American seminaries were in the pipeline to work in nonethnic American churches.

Recognizing the limitations of earlier theories of assimilation that projected a homogeneous trajectory and outcome for all immigrants, contemporary models of immigrant integration are more differentiated and contextual and acknowledge that race could pose a potential barrier to integration for contemporary post-1965 nonwhite groups. Yet none of these theories examines how religion might shape social incorporation into American society. Unlike religious minorities, second-generation American Christians have the option of turning to religion, particularly American evangelism with its universalistic message, as a path to inclusion into the wider society. Claiming a Christian identity could also allow such individuals to sidestep their problematic racial location in the United States by adopting a nonracial faith identity (Busto 1996).

However, second-generation East Asian Americans repeatedly mentioned that they left predominantly white evangelical churches because they felt racialized and marginalized in these churches. This is what made them decide to form or join second-generation East Asian American churches.[4] According to Russell Jeung (2005, 74–76), leaders of the second-generation East Asian American evangelical churches that he studied referred to the evangelical homogeneity principle—the idea that the best way to form churches is to focus on homogeneous groups—to justify the racial, cultural, and class homogeneity of their congregations. Other scholars, however, have argued that second-generation Asian Americans who attended ethnic churches felt conflicted about the contradiction between their ethnic separatism and the universalism of evangelical Christian doctrine (Chai 1998; R. Kim 2006; S. Kim 2010). Some attended multiracial churches, but they often formed large minorities within such churches and were still able to have "ethnic fellowship" in such situations (Chai 2004).

We have seen that second-generation Mar Thomites minimized incidents of racism as isolated encounters and reported feeling welcomed and integrated into the evangelical churches that they attended. Unlike East Asian American Christians, second-generation Mar Thoma Christians emphasized their comfort with individuals from a variety of racial and ethnic groups, and the importance of opening their parents' ethnic church to the local community. They also repeatedly stressed that multiracial churches were a mandate found in the Bible. This perspective was not unique to Mar Thoma Christians but was also upheld by other second-generation Indian American Christians influenced by American evangelicalism. I have argued that this may be because evangelical members of small, diverse groups are not able to self-segregate and consequently develop different, interracial, or largely white networks and different perspectives on race and ethnicity compared to members of larger, more homogeneous groups. This is a subject for more research. But clearly it is important not to take the studies of East Asian American Christians as the last word on the interaction between race and religion.

If it is true that smaller groups develop different frameworks for identity when compared to larger groups, seeker-oriented evangelical churches that deemphasize cultural and denominational heritage might potentially provide a route to incorporation for the second-generation members of such groups through an individualistic Christianity. These second-generation individuals could in turn bring about changes in the evangelical churches they join. It may not be a coincidence that many evangelical megachurches have recently embraced multiracialism (Emerson 2009).[5] The literature on multiracial congregations currently focuses on the integration of black members into white churches (Edwards 2008; Emerson and Smith 2000). However, it is likely that more racial minorities will be integrated into these churches in the long term— another reason to examine how American evangelicalism can help new ethnic groups incorporate into the wider society.

While East Asian American urbanites are able to have a de-ethnicized evangelicalism *and* an ethnic community through their second-generation churches, the disentangling of religion and ethnicity means that other second-generation individuals who attend large evangelical churches will have to meet their social and cultural needs and those of their children through secular ethnic get-togethers. However, this is a time- and labor-intensive strategy and is probably not feasible on a regular basis for those who work long hours. It remains uncertain whether later-generation ethnics will consequently experience a loss of the "intrinsic culture" and the communitarian traditions of their ethnic group, and what implications this will have for the group in the long run.

The disentangling of religion and ethnicity could also have wider implications. It could result in the creation of genuine multiethnic and multiracial congregations that, because of their internal diversity and greater resources, can assist ethnic minorities through the ups and downs of life and the process of incorporation more effectively than the ethnoreligious communities of the past. Such multiracial congregations might also transform racial relations within society as a whole. But there is also the danger that multiracial faith assemblies could end up being anonymous and impersonal gatherings, and consequently be unable to provide new ethnics the support they need to successfully integrate into the wider society.

Conclusion: Religion and Global Movement

This book has examined a variety of cases in which religious traditions underwent change as a consequence of being transmitted and transplanted from one global context to another. Specifically, it has demonstrated that this intercultural movement did not just reshape religious and social practices but also affected the community and alliances of the adherents as well as their conception of identity. Syrian Christians in Kerala in the precolonial period were "Hindu in culture, Christian in religion, and Oriental in worship" (Podipara 1973, 107). They were proud of their status as a high-caste group that was allowed to participate in the most prestigious Hindu temple rituals while maintaining their Saint Thomas Christian identity and practices as well as their ties to their East Syrian patriarch. Under the Portuguese, Syrian Christian connections to their cherished patriarch were severed, many of their East Syrian practices were proscribed, and they were brought under the Roman Catholic Church and the pope. They were also prohibited from practicing many of the traditional local customs, which initiated the process of separation of Malankara Syrian Christians from Kerala Hindu society. A breakaway Syrian Christian group rose up in rebellion against Portuguese religious authority and was able to establish ties with a West Syrian Orthodox Jacobite patriarch and come under the Syrian Orthodox church. This led to the first fissure in the Syrian Christian community in over thirteen hundred years and to tensions between Roman Catholic Syrian Christians and Orthodox Syrian Christians. The arrival of Anglican British missionaries led to further schisms among Syrian Christians as some Syrian Orthodox groups "Reformed" under the Anglican influence. It also deepened the separation between Syrian Christians and Hindus as the last elements of ritual cooperation between the two groups were extirpated by Anglicans and Syrian Christian reformers. Anglicans and Syrian Christian reformers attempted to draw boundaries on the basis of religion instead of caste, and attempted to bring Christians of different caste groups together. However, given the continuing importance of caste in Kerala society, these attempts were not very successful.

As a consequence of the alliance with Anglicans, traditional Protestant Christian denominations became the new coalition partners and allies of reformed Syrian Christian groups such as the Mar Thoma, against Roman Catholic and Orthodox groups. At the same time, the Mar Thoma church has tried to maintain its episcopal tradition, communitarian elements, and Eastern corporate worship practices, all of which distinguish the denomination from newer Protestant evangelical groups. This conglomeration of elements has led to confusion and tensions within Mar Thoma parishes in the United States, as both achens and lay members find it difficult to articulate the theology and the distinctness of the Mar Thoma denomination. While most of the immigrant generation remains within Mar Thoma parishes, several of its highly educated members have turned to mainline Protestant denominations, while the second generation is strongly attracted to the theology and contemporary worship of nondenominational evangelical Protestants. Despite the fact that the numbers of Mar Thomites in the United States are relatively small compared to the numbers of Mar Thomites in India, Mar Thoma Americans have impacted the denomination and its functioning in India in many ways. American evangelical and charismatic groups have also brought about changes in the religious landscape of India, affecting the religious paradigms and approaches of traditional Indian churches and the expectations of their membership.

This book makes clear why a global approach is important to our understanding of the movement of religions and people around the world. The biggest limitation of migration studies frameworks is that they currently focus primarily on the one-directional influence of either the home or host society instead of examining the impact of *both* home and host societies on migrants, as well as the impact of migration on home and host societies. Similarly, frameworks of religious change are currently focused on national processes. Given that most religious organizations in the contemporary period operate within global fields and are affected by international migration (Meyer et al. 2011, 243–244), it is important to ensure that our frameworks also take transnational and global dynamics into account to gain a better understanding of the multifaceted processes of religious transformation taking place around the world.

NOTES

1 The segmented assimilation model recognizes that assimilation may be "upward" or "downward" and that racial discrimination can give rise to the self-segregation of minorities and their downward mobility into the underclass (Portes and Zhou 1993). The neo-assimilation perspective focuses on changes in the contemporary U.S. context that enable the blurring, shifting, and crossing of ethnic and racial boundaries, but points out that black and dark-skinned Hispanics might find race to be more of an obstacle to assimilation than the southern Europeans and East Asians who have been able to blur the color line between themselves and whites (Alba and Nee 2003). Finally, the cultural pluralism paradigm emphasizes that multiculturalism and globalization legitimize and facilitate the maintenance of ethnic identities and transnational connections, and that transnationalism may be one way that immigrants try to cope with the racism they encounter in the United States (Basch et al. 1994; Schiller and Fouron 2001).

2 This information is from the National Sample Survey (2010) report, No. 533, "Migration in India: 2007–2008," data from tables 6.1.1 (p. 117) and 6.2.1 (p. 126). These data show that Kerala had the highest proportion of international emigrants (53/1,000) of all states in India. The next highest rate of international emigrants was from Punjab (16.2/1,000).

3 http://marthoma.in.

4 Ibid.

5 For figures on international migration from Kerala, see Zachariah, Mathew, and Rajan 1999, 4; Zachariah 2006, 166, 187; Zachariah and Rajan 2007, 17, 21, 29.

6 The Indian rupee is currently (2016) worth around 1/50th of the U.S. dollar, though this conversion does not provide an accurate picture of its purchasing power in India.

7 The forty-four interviews with members of the immigrant generation included twenty-two men and twenty-two women. Although nurses and their husbands comprised the dominant older immigrant group in most Mar Thoma congregations, more of the professionally educated men and women were willing to speak to me. Consequently I ended up with more interviews with this group: fourteen men and eleven women. In addition, I interviewed nine female nurses and six men who were husbands of nurses. I also talked to two immigrant achens and their wives.

8 The fifty-one interviews included twenty-six men and twenty-five women between the ages of fifteen and forty-four. Except for the teenagers who were still in
high school, those who were interviewed for this project had at least a four-year
college education (a few were still in college) and were in good positions as pharmacists, physiotherapists, engineers, and accountants. Some of the women had
given up their jobs when their children were born.

9 Twenty-six of the interviews in Kerala were with lay Mar Thomites: fourteen men
and twelve women. I also interviewed seven achens (all except two had served a
term in the United States), and four wives of achens. Finally, I interviewed both
the Metropolitan of the Mar Thoma church, Philipose Mar Chrysostom, and
Bishop Zacharias Mar Theophilus, who had been in charge of the North America
and Europe Diocese until 2001. In Bangalore, I interviewed ten Mar Thomites, six
men and four women. One of them was an achen and nine were lay members.

CHAPTER 1. SYRIAN CHRISTIAN ENCOUNTERS WITH COLONIAL MISSIONARIES AND INDIAN NATIONALISM

1 While the Portuguese report the king as a fact, some British commentators have
been skeptical and have indicated that this may have been a king who granted the
Saint Thomas Christians special favors. The Saint Thomas Christian legend is that
the king was a vassal of the king of Cochin and that the dynasty came to an end
at the end of the fifteenth century because the king did not have any heirs. At this
point it was absorbed into the kingdom of Cochin (see Brown 1956, n. 5, 13–14).

2 Nestorianism refers to the belief that Jesus had two natures, one divine and the
other human. Nestorius, a bishop of Constantinople in the fifth century, also
refused to call Mary the "Mother of God."

3 Webb Keane (2007), for example, argues that colonial missionary encounters with
non-Western groups led missionaries to question what constituted the central elements of Christianity—what was essential, and what could be compromised on.

4 The book was titled, *The History of the Church of Malabar, from the time of its being first discover'd by the Portuguezes in the year 1501. The long subtitle of the book,
Giving an account of the persecutions and violent methods of the Roman prelates, to
reduce them to the subject of the Church of Rome: together with the Synod of Diamper, celebrated in the year of Our Lord 1599: with some remarks upon the faith and
doctrine of the Christians of St. Thomas in the Indies, agreeing with the Church of
England, in opposition to that of Rome. Done out of Portuguese into English,* makes
the position of the author amply clear.

5 However, Leslie Brown (1956, 174) indicates that he witnessed some Syrian Christians still observing the practice in the twentieth century.

6 Mar Thoma historical accounts (e.g., see Mathew and Thomas 2005, 43) provide
this information, but both Leslie Brown (1956, 112) and Neill (1984, 328) indicate
that there are doubts that this episcopal consecration took place.

7 Susan Bayly (1989, 268) argues that preserving their high status was in the interests of the Portuguese, who wanted powerful allies.

8 Buchanan comments that but for their liturgy, which includes prayers and scriptural passages, there would have been no "vestige of Christianity left among them" (1819, 120).

9 Apparently the British were initially so keen to make sure that the Church of England was not established in Kerala that when Bishop Middleton received a report that the three missionaries were trying to do this, he went to Cochin to meet with the Metran (Metropolitan). After a two-hour interview with the Metran, at which none of the missionaries were allowed to be present, he satisfied himself that this was not the case (P. Cheriyan 1935, 150–151).

10 Mathew and Thomas (2005, 71) add, "In fairness to the missionaries it may be noted that they admitted Syrians into their Church after considerable hesitation and at the earnest request of the latter. The starting of a branch of the Anglican Church in Travancore was far from the original purpose of the missionaries as is clear from the letters of the missionaries recorded in the Missionary Registers."

11 Christians had customarily joined Nayars to carry an effigy of a sacred horse to a temple at Ayroor in Kerala, but in 1853 the Christians did not participate in this ritual. The Nayars got angry and attacked the Christians and also destroyed their crops. Metropolitan Mathews Mar Athanasius had the local government take legal action against the perpetrators (Philip 1991, 42). In another incident, the Metropolitan saw some Syrian women standing in neck-deep water. On inquiring, he was told that the women were being punished by Nayars because they had not dehusked paddy for the temple. The Metropolitan got the women released and then issued a circular to all the Jacobite parishes indicating that Christians should no longer participate in temple rituals (Philip 1991, 43).

12 This information is from Daniel (1961), discussions with families involved in the St. Thomas Evangelical church, and from https://en.wikipedia.org.

13 Women who marry outside the denomination lose their Mar Thoma membership on the day of their marriage.

CHAPTER 2. THE ROLE OF THE CHURCH IN MIGRATION AND SETTLEMENT

1 The Mar Thoma Church has an additional missionary training center and theological school in Faridabad, near New Delhi, specifically intended to train students working in Mar Thoma mission fields in north India.

2 Original name used here on request.

3 http://marthoma.in.

4 See chapter 1 for a description of the Maramon convention.

5 However, in October 2014 the *Mar Thoma Messenger*, the magazine of the North America and Europe Diocese, had as its theme "Women, Enriching the Church." Mar Theodosius, the bishop of the diocese, indicated that this issue was "an acknowledgement of the fact that the presence of the Mar Thoma Com-

munity was palpable in the lands that we reside in, through the migration of our women for their professional advancement" (Message of October 2014, www.marthomanae.org).

6 Some of the younger unmarried women I talked to similarly said that they had high morals and were turned off by the young second-generation Syrian Christian boys they knew because they were "wild" and had lots of "experiences" (sexual, drinking, smoking). This is why they thought that a man from India would be best for them.

7 This is still available on their North American Diocese website, http://malankara.com.

CHAPTER 3. COUPLING VERSUS DECOUPLING RELIGION AND ETHNICITY IN THE FIRST AND SECOND GENERATIONS

1 This chapter is an amalgamated and revised version of two earlier publications: "Christian by Birth or Rebirth? Generation and Difference in an Indian American Christian Church," in *Asian American Religions: Borders and Boundaries*, edited by Tony Carnes and Fenggang Yang (NYU Press, 2004), 160–181; and "Decoupling Religion and Ethnicity: Second-Generation Indian American Christians," *Qualitative Sociology* 35(4) (2012): 447–468.

2 *Mar Thoma Messenger* (July 2013):32, cited in Varghese (2014, 247).

3 http://sevenmileroadphilly.org.

4 http://sevenmileroadphilly.org.

5 www.crosswaymtc.org.

CHAPTER 4. CLASS, CULTURE, AND THE PERFORMANCE OF GENDERED CHRISTIANITY

1 I also noted that they wore richly embroidered Indian clothes and that several women changed into new outfits for the second part of the day!

CHAPTER 5. RELIGION, SOCIAL INCORPORATION, AND CIVIC ENGAGEMENT AMONG GENERATIONS

1 This chapter draws from "Religion, Social Incorporation, and Civic Engagement: Second-Generation Indian American Christians, *Review of Religious Research* 55(1) (2013):81–104.

2 Foley and Hoge 2007; Kniss and Numrich 2007; Levitt 2008; Stepick, Rey, and Mahler 2009.

3 See Brettell and Reed-Danahay 2012; Ecklund 2006; Foley and Hoge 2007; Kniss and Numrich 2007; Stepick, Rey, and Mahler 2009.

4 See Chen 2002; Jeung 2005; Menjivar 2003.

5 Brettell and Reed-Danahay 2012; Foley and Hoge 2007, 26–27.

6 www.marthomanae.org.

7 See Kniss and Numrich 2007, 26–27; Wong and Iwamura 2007; Ríos 2005.

CHAPTER 6. INTERNATIONAL MIGRATION AND ITS IMPACT ON THE
MAR THOMA DENOMINATION

1   This chapter is a revised version of "The Impact of International Migration on
    Home Churches: The Mar Thoma Syrian Christian Church in India," *Journal for
    the Scientific Study of Religion* 53(1) (2014):109–129.
2   Parish figures from the Mar Thoma denomination's main website, http://mar-
    thoma.in. The discrepancy between the figures mentioned in the Introduction
    and here may be due to the fact that the website figures are not updated or that
    the figures used in the Introduction include congregations in addition to parishes.
3   Stark and Finke 2000, 201; Warner 1993.
4   Stark and Finke 2000, 151–154, 165–166.
5   Stark and Finke 2000, 86, 216, 260–264.
6   www.sharonfellowship.com.
7   www.gfa.org/about.
8   www.douloscollege.org.
9   www.theheavenlyfeast.org.
10 Bhattacharyya 2008; Rahman 2011; see also Miller et al. 2013.
11 Even in the United States, the Mar Thoma leadership claimed that the youth
    who left the church generally returned when they had children. However, I have
    noticed that they tended to overstate the extent to which this took place.

CONCLUSION

1   Original name retained on request.
2   Fisher 2005; Kibria 2008; Kurien 2012; Min 2010; Nayar 2004; Ramji 2008.
3   The CrossWay Facebook page mentions resources from Our Daily Bread, Charles
    Stanley, New Life Worship, Hillsong, and a number of contemporary Christian
    music artists, including Chris Tomlin, Jeremy Camp, and many others.
4   Alumkal 2003; Cha 2001; R. Kim 2006; S. Kim 2010; Jeung 2005.
5   This is not to say that there are no racial problems in evangelical churches. In
    October 2013, in response to some incidents of Asian American caricaturing by
    white evangelical leaders, a group of more than eighty Asian American Chris-
    tian leaders (comprised mostly of East Asian Americans, but also including two
    Indian Americans) released an open letter protesting racial stereotyping of Asian
    Americans by white evangelicals. The letter began with the statement, "We are
    a part of the body, we are North American Christians every bit as much as any
    other North American Christian, and we are weary, hurt, and disillusioned by the
    continuing offensive actions of our fellow brothers and sisters in Christ" (Weber
    2013).

REFERENCES

Alba, Richard, and Victor Nee. 2003. *Remaking the American Mainstream: Assimilation and Contemporary Immigration.* Cambridge: Harvard University Press.

Alba, Richard, Albert J. Raboteau, and Josh DeWind, eds. 2009. *Immigration and Religion in America: Comparative and Historical Perspectives.* New York: NYU Press.

Alexander, Metropolitan Mar Thoma. 1986. *The Mar Thoma Church: Heritage and Mission.* 2nd ed. Manganam, Kottayam: Ashram Press.

Alumkal, Antony W. 1999. "Preserving Patriarchy: Assimilation, Gender Norms, and Second Generation Korean American Evangelicals." *Qualitative Sociology* 22:127–140.

———. 2003. *Asian American Evangelical Churches: Race, Ethnicity and Assimilation in the Second Generation.* New York: LFB Scholarly Publishing.

Apter, Andrew. 1991. "Herskovits's Heritage: Rethinking Syncretism in the African Diaspora." *Diaspora: A Journal of Transnational Studies* 1(3):235–260.

Athyal, Jesudas M. 2015a. Review of "The Impact of International Migration on Home Churches: The Mar Thoma Syrian Christian Church in India." *Focus Online Magazine for the Diaspora Laity of the Mar Thoma Church,* January 2015. http://issuu.com.

———. 2015b. "The Mar Thoma Church: Gender Equality in the Sacred Space." www.patheos.com.

Athyal, Jesudas M., and John J. Thatamanil, eds. 2002. *Metropolitan Chrysostom on Mission in the Market Place.* Tiruvalla: Christava Sahitya Samithy.

Ayyar, L. K. Anantakrishna. 1926. *Anthropology of the Syrian Christians.* Ernakulam: Cochin Government Press.

Baldauf, Scott. 2005. "A New Breed of Missionary: A Drive for Conversions, Not Development Is Stirring Violent Animosity in India." *Christian Science Monitor,* April 1. www.csmonitor.com.

Basch, Linda, Nina G. Schiller, and Cristina S. Blanc. 1994. *Nations Unbound: Transnational Projects, Postcolonial Predicaments, and Deterritorialized Nation-States.* London: Gordon and Breach Science Publishers.

Bayly, Susan. 1989. *Saints, Goddesses and Kings: Muslims and Christians in South Indian Society 1700–1900.* Cambridge: Cambridge University Press.

Bebbington, David W. 1989. *Evangelicalism in Modern Britain: A History from the 1730's to the 1980's.* London: Unwin Hyman.

Bellah, Robert N., Richard Marsden, William M. Sullivan, Ann Swidler, and Steven M. Tipton. 1985. *Habits of the Heart: Individualism and Commitment in American Life.* Berkeley: University of California Press.

Bhattacharyya, Debashis. 2008. "God's Own Country." *Telegraph*, July 13. www.tele-graphindia.com.

Biswas, Soutik. 2010. "Kerala's Love Affair with Alcohol." BBC News, March 12, 2010. http://news.bbc.co.uk.

Bittman, Michael, Paula England, Nancy Folbre, Liana Sayer, and George Matheson. 2003. "When Does Gender Trump Money? Bargaining and Time in Household Work." *American Journal of Sociology* 109:186–214.

Brettell, Caroline B., and Deborah Reed-Danahay. 2012. *Civic Engagements: The Citizenship Practices of Indian and Vietnamese Immigrants*. Stanford: Stanford University Press.

Brines, Julie. 1994. "Economic Dependency, Gender, and the Division of Labor at Home." *American Journal of Sociology* 100:652–688.

Brown, Leslie W. 1956. *The Indian Christians of St. Thomas: An Account of the Ancient Syrian Church of Malabar*. Cambridge: Cambridge University Press.

Buchanan, Claudius. 1819. *Christian Researches in Asia with notices of the translation of the Scriptures into the oriental languages*. 11th ed. Reprint from the University of Toronto Libraries Collection. London: T. Cadell and W. Davies.

Busto, Rudy V. 1996. "The Gospel according to the Model Minority? Hazarding an Interpretation of Asian American Evangelical College Students." *Amerasia Journal* 22(1):133–147.

Cesari, Joselyn. 2004. *When Islam and Democracy Meet: Muslims in Europe and in the United States*. Basingstoke: Palgrave MacMillan.

Cha, Peter T. 2001. "Ethnic Identity Formation and Participation in Immigrant Churches: Second-Generation Korean American Experiences." In *Korean Americans and Their Religions: Pilgrims and Missionaries from a Different Shore*, edited by Ho-Youn Kwon, Kwang Chung Kim, and R. Stephen Warner, 141–156. University Park: Pennsylvania State University Press.

Chai, Karen J. 1998. "Competing for the Second Generation: English-Language Ministry at a Korean Protestant Church." In *Gatherings in Diaspora: Religious Communities and the New Immigration*, edited by Stephen Warner and Judith Wittner, 295–332. Philadelphia: Temple University Press.

———. 2004. "Chinatown or Uptown? Second-Generation Chinese American Protestants in New York City." In *Becoming New Yorkers: Ethnographies of the New Second Generation*, edited by Philip Kasinitz, John H. Mollenkopf, and Mary Waters, 257–279. New York: Russell Sage Foundation.

Chen, Carolyn. 2002. "The Religious Varieties of Ethnic Presence: A Comparison between a Taiwanese Immigrant Buddhist Temple and an Evangelical Christian Church." *Sociology of Religion* 63(2):215–238.

Cheriyan, C. V. 1973. *A History of Christianity in Kerala: From the Mission of St. Thomas to the Arrival of Vasco da Gama, A.D. 52–1498*. Kottayam: C. M. S. Press.

Cheriyan, P. 1935. *The Malabar Syrians and the Church Missionary Society 1816–1840*. Kottayam: Church Missionary Society's Press.

Comaroff, John L., and Jean Comaroff. 1991. *Of Revelation and Revolution: Christianity, Colonialism and Consciousness in South Africa*. Vol. 1. Chicago: University of Chicago Press.

———. 1997. *Of Revelation and Revolution: The Dialectics of Modernity on a South African Frontier*. Vol. 2. Chicago: University of Chicago Press.

Copland, Ian. 2007. "The Limits of Hegemony: Elite Responses to Nineteenth-Century Imperial and Missionary Acculturation Strategies in India." *Comparative Studies in Society and History* 49:637–665.

Cox, Jeffrey. 2002. *Imperial Fault Lines: Christianity and Colonial Power in India 1818–1940*. Stanford: Stanford University Press.

Daniel, K. N. 1961. *Mar Thoma Church in Peril*. Tiruvalla: St. Joseph's Printing House.

Davidson, Allan K. 1990. *Evangelicals and Attitudes to India 1786–1813: Missionary Publicity and Claudius Buchanan*. Oxfordshire: Sutton Courteney Press.

Dhingra, Pawan. 2007. *Managing Multicultural Lives: Asian American Professionals and the Challenge of Multiple Identities*. Stanford: Stanford University Press.

DiMaggio, Paul J. 1998. "The Relevance of Organizational Theory to the Study of Religion." In *Sacred Companies: Organizational Aspects of Religion and Religious Aspects of Organizations*, edited by N. J. Demerath III, Peter Dobkin Hall, Terry Schmitt, and Rhys H. Williams, 7–23. New York: Oxford University Press.

DiMaggio, Paul J., and Walter W. Powell. 1991. "Introduction." In *The New Institutionalism in Organizational Analysis*, edited by Walter W. Powell and Paul J. DiMaggio, 1–38. Chicago: University of Chicago Press.

Durkheim, Emile. 1912. *The Elementary Forms of the Religious Life*. London: George Allen and Unwin.

Ebaugh, Helen R., and Janet S. Chafetz. 1999. "Agents for Cultural Reproduction and Structural Change: The Ironic Role of Women in Immigrant Religious Institutions." *Social Forces* 78:585–612.

———. 2000. *Religion and the New Immigrants: Continuities and Adaptations in Immigrant Congregations*. Walnut Creek, Calif.: AltaMira Press.

———, eds. 2002. *Religion across Borders: Transnational Immigrant Networks*. Walnut Creek, Calif.: AltaMira Press.

Ecklund, Elaine H. 2006. *Korean American Evangelicals: New Models for Civic Life*. New York: Oxford University Press.

Edwards, Korie. 2008. *The Elusive Dream: The Power of Race in Interracial Churches*. New York: Oxford University Press.

Ellingson, Stephen. 2007. *The Megachurch and the Mainline: Remaking Religious Tradition in the Twenty-First Century*. Chicago: University of Chicago Press.

Emerson, Michael. 2009. "Managing Racial Diversity: A Movement toward Multiracial Congregations." Paper presented at the annual meeting of the American Sociological Association, August 10, San Francisco.

Emerson, Michael, and Christian Smith. 2000. *Divided by Faith: Evangelical Religion and the Problem of Race in America*. New York: Oxford University Press.

Fernandes, Leela. 2011. "Unsettled Territories: State, Civil Society, and the Politics of Religious Conversion in India." *Politics and Religion* 4(1):108–135.

Fisher, Timothy N. 2005. "In Church with My Ancestors: The Changing Shape of Religious Memory in the Republic of Armenia and the North American Diaspora." Ph.D. dissertation, University of Southern California, Los Angeles.

Foley, Michael W., and Dean R. Hoge. 2007. *Religion and the New Immigrants: How Faith Communities Shape Our Newest Citizens*. New York: Oxford University Press.

Foner, Nancy, and Richard Alba. 2008. "Immigrant Religion in the U.S. and Western Europe: Bridge or Barrier to Inclusion?" *International Migration Review* 42(2):360–392.

Frykenberg, Robert Eric. 2008. *Christianity in India: From the Beginnings to the Present*. New York: Oxford University Press.

Geddes, Michael. 1694. *The History of the Church of Malabar, from the time of its being first discover'd by the Portuguezes in the year 1501. Giving an account of the persecutions and violent methods of the Roman prelates, to reduce them to the subject of the Church of Rome: together with the Synod of Diamper, celebrated in the year of Our Lord 1599: with some remarks upon the faith and doctrine of the Christians of St. Thomas in the Indies, agreeing with the Church of England, in opposition to that of Rome. Done out of Portuguese into English*. London: n.p.

George, Sam. 2005. *When Women Come First: Gender and Class in Transnational Migration*. Los Angeles: University of California Press.

——. 2015. "The State of Indian American Christianity." Presentation at the Meeting of Indian Christian Theologians and Scholars of Indian Christianity. Berkeley Heights, New Jersey, August 12.

Gillman, Ian, and Hans-Joachim Klimkeit. 1999. *Christians in Asia before 1500*. Ann Arbor: University of Michigan Press.

Glaser, Barney, and Anselm Strauss. 1967. *The Discovery of Grounded Theory: Strategies for Qualitative Research*. New Brunswick, N.J.: Aldine Transaction.

Glynn, Sarah. 2002. "Bengali Muslims: The New East End Radicals?" *Ethnic and Racial Studies* 25:969–988.

Gordon, Milton. 1964. *Assimilation in American Life: The Role of Race, Religion and National Origins*. New York: Oxford University Press.

Gornik, Mark R., and Geomon K. George. 2015. "Passing Down the Faith in the New Immigrant Church." www.faithandleadership.com.

Gouvea, Antonio de. (1606) 2003. *Jornada of Dom Alexis Menezes: A Portuguese Account of the Sixteenth Century Malabar*. Edited and translated into English by Pius Malekandathil. Kochi: LRC Publications.

Greeley, Andrew. 1972. *The Denominational Society: A Sociological Approach to Religion in America*. Glenview, Ill.: Scott Foresman.

Greenstein, T. N. 2000. "Economic Dependence, Gender, and the Division of Labor in the Home: A Replication and Extension." *Journal of Marriage and the Family* 62:322–335.

Harikrishnan, K. S. 2011. "Alcoholism Grips Progressive Kerala." IPSNews.net, January 19. http://ipsnews.net.

Heelas, Paul. 1996. *The New Age Movement: The Celebration of the Self and the Sacralization of Modernity*. Oxford: Blackwell.

Herberg, Will. 1960. *Protestant—Catholic—Jew: An Essay in American Religious Sociology*. Garden City, N.Y.: Anchor Books.

Hervieu-Léger, Danièle. 2006. "In Search of Certainties: The Paradoxes of Religiosity in Societies of High Modernity." *Hedgehog Review* 8:59–68.

Hirschman, Charles. 2004. "The Role of Religion in the Origin and Adaptation of Immigrant Groups in the United States." *International Migration Review* 38:1206–1233.

Hondagneu-Sotelo, Pierrette. 1994. *Gendered Transitions: Mexican Experiences of Immigration*. Berkeley: University of California Press.

———, ed. 2003. *Gender and U.S. Immigration: Contemporary Trends*. Berkeley: University of California Press.

Hough, James. (1839) 2005. *The History of Christianity in India: From the Commencement of the Christian Era*. Vols. I and II. Elibron Classics, reproduction of original published edition. London: R. B. Seeley and W. Burnside.

Houtman, Dick, and Stef Aupers. 2007. "The Spiritual Turn and the Decline of Tradition: The Spread of Post-Christian Spirituality in 14 Countries, 1981–2000." *Journal for the Scientific Study of Religion* 46:305–320.

Jacob, Ron. 2014. "Enthusiasm of Mar Theodosius to Make the Church More Relevant for the Second Generation." In *Beyond the Diaspora: Mar Thoma Church: Identity and Mission in the Context of Multiplicity. A Festschrift in Honor of Rt. Rev. Dr. Geevarghese Mar Theodosius Bishop of the Mar Thoma Church*, edited by K. E. Geevarghese and Mathew T. Thomas, 254–258. Ernakulam: Anaswara Offset Press.

Jenkins, Philip, 2002. *The Next Christendom: The Coming of Global Christianity*. New York: Oxford University Press.

Jeung, R. 2005. *Faithful Generations: Race and New Asian American Churches*. New Brunswick, N.J.: Rutgers University Press.

Joppke, Christian. 1996. "Multiculturalism and Immigration: A Comparison of the United States, Germany, and Great Britain." *Theory and Society* 25(4):449–500.

Juhanon, Mar Thoma Metropolitan. 1968. *Christianity in India: And a Brief History of the Mar Thoma Syrian Church*. 4th ed. Madras: K. M. Cherian.

Keane, Webb. 2007. *Christian Moderns: Freedom and Fetish in the Mission Encounter*. Berkeley: University of California Press.

Keller, Eva. 2005. *The Road to Clarity: Seventh-Day Adventism in Madagascar*. New York: Palgrave MacMillan.

Kerala State Mental Health Authority. *Suicide in Kerala 2010*. www.ksmha.org.

Kibria, Nazli. 2008. "The 'New Islam' and Bangladeshi Youth in Britain and the U.S." *Ethnic and Racial Studies* 31(2):243–266.

Kim, Ai Ra. 1996. *Women Struggling for a New Life: The Role of Religion in the Cultural Passage from Korea to America*. Albany: SUNY Press.

Kim, Rebecca Y. 2006. *God's New Whiz Kids? Korean American Evangelicals on Campus*. New York: NYU Press.

———. 2011. "Critic on Author Meets Critics." Panel discussion of *Preserving Ethnicity through Religion in America: Korean Protestants and Indian Hindus across Generations* by Pyong Gap Min. Annual meeting of the American Sociological Association, August 19, Las Vegas.

Kim, Sharon. 2010. *A Faith of Our Own: Second-Generation Spirituality in Korean American Churches*. New Brunswick, N.J.: Rutgers University Press.

Kniss, Fred, and Paul D. Numrich. 2007. *Sacred Assemblies and Civic Engagement: How Religion Matters for America's Newest Immigrants*. New Brunswick, N.J.: Rutgers University Press.

Kurien, Prema A. 1998. "Becoming American by Becoming Hindu: Indian Americans Take Their Place at the Multicultural Table." In *Gatherings in Diaspora: Religious Communities and the New Immigration*, edited by Stephen Warner and Judith Wittner, 37–70. Philadelphia: Temple University Press.

———. 1999. "Gendered Ethnicity: Creating a Hindu Indian Identity in the U.S." *American Behavioral Scientist* 42(4):648–670.

———. 2002. *Kaleidoscopic Ethnicity: International Migration and the Reconstruction of Community Identities in India*. New Brunswick, N.J.: Rutgers University Press.

———. 2004. "Christian by Birth or Rebirth? Generation and Difference in an Indian American Christian Church." In *Asian American Religions: Borders and Boundaries*, edited by Tony Carnes and Fenggang Yang, 160–181. New York: NYU Press.

———. 2007. *A Place at the Multicultural Table: The Development of an American Hinduism*. New Brunswick, N.J.: Rutgers University Press.

———. 2012. "Decoupling Religion and Ethnicity: Second-Generation Indian American Christians." *Qualitative Sociology* 35(4):447–468.

———. 2013. "Religion, Social Incorporation, and Civic Engagement: Second-Generation Indian American Christians." *Review of Religious Research* 55(1):81–104.

———. 2014a. "Immigration, Community Formation, Political Incorporation, and Why Religion Matters: Migration and Settlement Patterns of the Indian Diaspora." *Sociology of Religion* 75(4):524–536.

———. 2014b. "The Impact of International Migration on Home Churches: The Mar Thoma Syrian Christian Church in India," *Journal for the Scientific Study of Religion* 53(1):109–129.

Kuruvilla, Joe Joseph. 2014. "Ministering to the Youths: Beyond the Diaspora." In *Beyond the Diaspora: Mar Thoma Church: Identity and Mission in the Context of Multiplicity*, edited by K. E. Geevarghese and Mathew T. Thomas, 96–100. Ernakulam: Anaswara Offset Press.

Kwon, Ho-Youn, Kwang Chung Kim, and R. Stephen Warner, eds. 2001. *Korean Americans and Their Religions: Pilgrims and Missionaries from a Different Shore*. University Park: Pennsylvania State University Press.

Lakshman, Arun. 2010. "New Generation Churches 'Poach Devotees' in Kerala." *Rediff.com*, November 23. www.rediff.com.

Lee, Helen. 1996. "Silent Exodus: Can the East Asian Church in America Reverse the Flight of Its Next Generation?" *Christianity Today* 40(9):50–53.

Levitt, Peggy, 2001. *The Transnational Villagers*. Berkeley: University of California Press.

———. 2003. "'You Know, Abraham Was Really the First Immigrant': Religion and Transnational Migration." *International Migration Review* 37(4):847–873.

———. 2008. "Religion as a Path to Civic Engagement." *Ethnic and Racial Studies* 31(4):766–791.

Lincoln, John P. 2008. "Mar Thoma Sabha Mandalam 2008 Meeting." *Mar Thoma Messenger* (October):45.

Madsen, Richard. 2009. "The Archipelago of Faith: Religious Individualism and Faith Community in America Today." *American Journal of Sociology* 114:1263–1301.

Malekandathil, Pius, trans. 2003. *Jornada of Dom Alexis de Menezes. A Portuguese Account of the Sixteenth Century Malabar*. Kochi: LRC Publications.

Mandaville, Peter. 2007. *Transnational Muslim Politics: Reimagining the Umma*. London: Routledge.

Mar Theodosius, Geevarghese. 2000. "Eastern Spirituality and Identity of the Mar Thoma Church." In *The Mar Thoma Church: Tradition and Modernity*, edited by P. J. Alexander, 94–103. Tiruvalla: Malankara Mar Thoma Syrian Church.

Mar Thoma Syrian Church. 2007. *My Lord and My God: A Documentary Film on the Faith Journey of the Mar Thoma Syrian Church*. Delhi: Mar Thoma Syrian Church, Delhi Diocese.

Mathew, Amanda. 2015. "Reflection." Presentation at the Meeting of Indian Christian Theologians and Scholars of Indian Christianity, August 12. Berkeley Heights, New Jersey.

Mathew, C. P., and M. M. Thomas. (1967) 2005. *The Indian Churches of Saint Thomas*. Delhi: ISPCK.

Mattackal, Abraham. 2008. "Faith and Vision of Early Mar Thoma Settlers in North America." In *In the Beginning: Formative Years of Mar Thoma Parishes in North America*, edited by T. M. Thomas and Abraham Mattackal, 217–227. Tiruvalla, Kerala: Christava Sahitya Samithi.

Mattackal, Joseph. 2008. "A Walk through the Memory Lane." In *In the Beginning: Formative Years of Mar Thoma Parishes in North America*, edited by T. M. Thomas and Abraham Mattackal, 95–106. Tiruvalla, Kerala: Christava Sahitya Samithi.

Maurer, Susan. 2010. *The Spirit of Enthusiasm: A History of the Catholic Charismatic Renewal, 1967–2000*. Lanham, Md.: University Press of America.

Menjivar, Cecilia. 2003. "Religion and Immigration in Comparative Perspective: Catholic and Evangelical Salvadorans in San Francisco, Washington D.C., and Phoenix." *Sociology of Religion* 64(1):21–45.

Meyer, Katherine, Helen Rose Ebaugh, Eileen Barker, and Mark Juergensmeyer. 2011. "Religion in Global Perspective: SSSR Presidential Panel." *Journal for the Scientific Study of Religion* 50(2):240–251.

Miller, Donald. 1997. *Reinventing American Protestantism: Christianity in the New Millennium*. Berkeley: University of California Press.

———. 2013. "Foreword." In *Moved by the Spirit: Pentecostal and Charismatic Christianity in the Global South*, edited by Nick Street, 3–5. Los Angeles: Center for Religion and Civic Culture, University of Southern California.

Miller, Donald E., Kimone H. Sargeant, and Richard Flory, eds. 2013. *Spirit and Power: The Growth and Global Impact of Pentecostalism*. New York: Oxford University Press.

Miller, Donald E., and Tesunao Yamamori. 2007. *Global Pentecostalism: The New Face of Christian Social Engagement*. Berkeley: University of California Press.

Min, Pyong Gap. 2010. *Preserving Ethnicity through Religion in America: Korean Protestants and Indian Hindus across Generations*. New York: NYU Press.

Moffett, Samuel Hugh. (1992) 2005. *A History of Christianity in Asia*. Vols. 1 and II. Maryknoll, N.Y.: Orbis.

Mullins, Mark. 1988. "The Organizational Dilemmas of Ethnic Churches: A Case Study of Japanese Buddhism in Canada." *Sociological Analysis* 49(3):217–233.

Narayan, M. G. S. 1972. *Cultural Symbiosis in Kerala*. Calicut: Mathrubhumi Press.

National Sample Survey. 2010. *Migration in India 2007–2008*. NSS 64th Round (July 2007–June 2008). Report No. 533 (64/10.2/2). New Delhi: National Statistical Organization, Ministry of Statistics and Programme Implementation, Government of India.

Nayar, Kamala E. 2004. *The Sikh Diaspora in Vancouver: Three Generations amid Tradition, Modernity, and Multiculturalism*. Toronto: University of Toronto Press.

Neill, Stephen. 1984. *A History of Christianity in India: The Beginnings to AD 1707*. Cambridge: Cambridge University Press.

———. 1985. *A History of Christianity in India 1707–1858*. Cambridge: Cambridge University Press.

New Immigrant Survey. 2003. Conducted by Guillermina Jasso, Douglass Massey, Mark Rosenzweig, and James Smith. http://nis.princeton.edu.

Nossiter, T. J. 1988. *Marxist State Governments in India: Politics, Economics and Society*. London: H. B. Pinter.

Oddie, Geoffrey A. 2000. "India: Missionaries, Conversion, and Change." In *The Church Mission Society and World Christianity 1799–1999*, edited by Kevin Ward and Brian Stanley, 228–253. Grand Rapids, Mich.: Wm. B. Eerdmans.

Park, Jerry Z., and Elaine H. Ecklund. 2007. "Negotiating Continuity: Family and Religious Socialization for Second-Generation Asian Americans." *Sociological Quarterly* 48:93–118.

Parrado, Emilio A., and Chenoa A. Flippen. 2005. "Migration and Gender among Mexican Women." *American Sociological Review* 70:606–632.

Paul, Samuel. 2004. "The Church and Its Institutions: Emerging Issues." *Sabha Tharaka* (September):13–15.

Pew Research Center: Religion & Public Life. 2012. *Asian Americans: A Mosaic of Faiths*. www.pewforum.org.

Pew Research Center: Religion & Public Life, and Pew Hispanic Center. 2007. *Changing Faiths: Latinos and the Transformation of American Religion*. http://pewform. org.

Philip, A. T. 1991. *The Mar Thoma Church and Kerala Society*. Thiruvananthapuram: Juhanon Mar Thoma Study Centre.

Podipara, P. 1973. "Hindu in Culture, Christian in Religion, Oriental in Worship." In *The St. Thomas Christian Encyclopedia of India*, edited by G. Menachery, 107–112. Vol. 2. Madras: B. N. K. Press.

Podipara, Placid J. 1971. *The Thomas Christians*. London: Darton, Longman & Todd.

Portes, Alejandro, and Min Zhou. 1993. "The New Second Generation: Segmented Assimilation and Its Variants." *Annals of the American Academy of Political and Social Science* 530:73–96.

Pothan, S. G. 1963. *The Syrian Christians of Kerala*. Bombay: Asia Publishing House.

Purkayastha, Bandana. 2012. "Intersectionality in a Transnational World." *Gender and Society* 26:55–66.

Putnam, Robert. 2000. *Bowling Alone: The Collapse and Revival of American Community*. New York: Simon & Schuster.

Rae, George Milne. 1892. *The Syrian Church in India*. Edinburgh: William Blackwood and Sons.

Rahman, Shafi. 2011. "Independent Churches Mushroom across India Attracting Foreign Funds." *India Today*, April 30. http://indiatoday.intoday.in.

Ramji, Rubina. 2008. "Creating a Genuine Islam: Second Generation Muslims Growing Up in Canada." *Canadian Diversity* 6(2):104–109.

Ríos, Elizabeth D. 2005. "'The Ladies Are Warriors': Latina Pentecostalism and Faith-Based Activism in New York City." In *Latino Religions and Civic Activism in the United States*, edited by G. Espinosa, V. Elizondo, and J. Miranda, 197–217. New York: Oxford University Press.

Robbins, Joel. 2004. *Becoming Sinners: Christianity and Moral Torment in a Papua New Guinea Society*. Berkeley: University of California Press.

Roof, Wade Clark. 1999. *Spiritual Marketplace: Baby Boomers and the Remaking of American Religion*. Princeton, N.J.: Princeton University Press.

Roy, Oliver. 2004. *Globalized Islam: The Search for a New Umma*. New York: Columbia University Press.

Salih, Ruba. 2004. "The Backward and the New: National, Transnational, and Post-National Islam in Europe." *Journal of Ethnic and Migration Studies* 30:995–1011.

Samuel, Charles. 2015. "The Indian Church Must Die." http://charlessamuel.com.

Sargeant, Kimon Howland. 2000. *Seeker Churches: Promoting Traditional Religion in a Nontraditional Way*. New Brunswick, N.J.: Rutgers University Press.

Sauvaget, C., K. Ramdas, J. M. Fayette, G. Thomas, S. Thara, and R. Sankaranarayanan. 2009. "Completed Suicide in Adults of Rural Kerala: Rates and Determinants." *National Medical Journal of India* 22(5):228–233.

Scaria, Joe. 2010. "Kerala Seeing Increasing Number of Divorces." *Economic Times*, November 17. http://articles.economictimes.indiatimes.com.

Schiller, Nina G., and Georges E. Fouron. 2001. *Georges Woke Up Laughing: Long-Distance Nationalism and the Search for Home*. Durham: Duke University Press.

Schmidt, Garbi. 2002. "Dialectics of Authenticity: Examples of Ethnification of Islam among Young Muslims in Sweden and the United States." *Muslim World* 92:1–17.

Schurhammer, George, SJ. 1934. *The Malabar Church and Rome during the Early Portuguese Period and Before*. Trichinopoly: St. Joseph's Industrial School Press.

Shanavas, S. 2012. "Till Divorce Do Us Part." *Sunday Indian* (Delhi), March 22. www.thesundayindian.com.

Shaw, Rosalind, and Charles Stewart. 1994. "Introduction: Problematizing Syncretism." In *Syncretism/Anti-Syncretism: The Politics of Religious Synthesis*, 1–24. New York: Routledge.

Shenk, Wilbert R. 2009. "Ancient Churches and Modern Missions in the Nineteenth Century." In *India and the Indianness of Christianity: Essays on Understanding, Historical, Theological, and Bibliographical in Honor of Robert Eric Frykenberg*, edited by Richard Fox Young, 41–58. Grand Rapids, Mich.: Wm. B. Eerdmans.

Smith, Christian. 1998. *American Evangelicalism: Embattled and Thriving*. Chicago: University of Chicago Press.

Smith, Timothy L. 1978. "Religion and Ethnicity in America." *American Historical Review* 83 (December):1155–1185.

Stark, Rodney, and Roger Finke. 2000. *Acts of Faith: Explaining the Human Side of Religion*. Berkeley: University of California Press.

———. 2005. *The Churching of America 1776–2005: Winners and Losers in Our Religious Economy*. New Brunswick, N.J.: Rutgers University Press.

Stepick, Alex, Terry Rey, and Sarah J. Mahler. 2009. *Churches and Charity in the Immigrant City: Religion, Immigration and Civic Engagement in Miami*. New Brunswick, N.J.: Rutgers University Press.

Stewart, Charles. 2005. "Relocating Syncretism in Social Science Discourse." In *Syncretism in Religion: A Reader*, edited by Anita Maria Leopold and Jeppe Sinding Jensen, 264–285. New York: Routledge.

Stock, Eugene. 1899. *The History of the Church Missionary Society: Its Environment, Its Men and Its Work*. Vol. 1. London: Church Missionary Society (printed by Gilbert & Rivington).

Strauss, Anselm. 1987. *Qualitative Analysis for Social Scientists*. Cambridge: Cambridge University Press.

Subramanyam, Sanjay. 1998. *The Career and Legend of Vasco Da Gama*. New York: Cambridge University Press.

Suh, Sharon. 2004. *Being Buddhist in a Christian World: Gender and Community in a Korean American Temple*. Seattle: University of Washington Press.

Taylor, Charles. 2007. *A Secular Age*. Cambridge, Mass.: Harvard University Press.

Thomas, Joseph. 1997. "Mar Thoma Syrian Church and Its Missionary Concerns." In *Gleanings: The Mar Thoma Church: Its Faith, Practice and Mission*, edited by M. J. Joseph, 44–58. 2nd ed. Bangalore: St. Paul's Press.

Thomas, T. M. 2008a. "Story of Kerala Migration in the 20th Century." In *In the Beginning: Formative Years of Mar Thoma Parishes in North America*, edited by T. M. Thomas and Abraham Mattackal, 27–30. Tiruvalla, Kerala: Christava Sahitya Samithi.

———. 2008b. "Establishing Congregations in New York and Other Cities of North America." In *In the Beginning: Formative Years of Mar Thoma Parishes in North America*, edited by T. M. Thomas and Abraham Mattackal, 31–42. Tiruvalla, Kerala: Christava Sahitya Samithi.

Thomas, T. M., and Abraham Mattackal, eds. 2008. *In the Beginning: Formative Years of Mar Thoma Parishes in North America*. Tiruvalla, Kerala: Christava Sahitya Samithi.

Tomlinson, Matthew, A. 2009. *In God's Image: The Metaculture of Fijian Christianity*. Berkeley: University of California Press.

Tovey, Philip. 1995. "Abraham Malpan and the Amended Liturgy of CMS." *Indian Church History Review* 29(1):38–55.

Usdansky, Margaret L. 2011. "The Gender Equality Paradox: Social Class, Preferences and Couples' Division of Paid and Unpaid Labor." *Journal of Family Theory & Review* 3:163–178.

Varghese, Baby. 2004. *West Syrian Liturgical Theology*. Burlington, Vt.: Ashgate.

Varghese, Lal. 2008. "Colonia Mar Thoma—Our Mission Field in Mexico." *Mar Thoma Messenger* (July):12–15.

———.2014. "Commitment to Mar Thoma Church and Ardor for Giving It a Global Identity—Mar Theodosius." In *Beyond the Diaspora: Mar Thoma Church: Identity and Mission in the Context of Multiplicity. A Festschrift in Honor of Rt. Rev. Dr. Geevarghese Mar Theodosius Bishop of the Mar Thoma Church*, edited by K. E. Geevarghese and Mathew T. Thomas, 243–253. Ernakulam: Anaswara Offset Press.

Varghese, Shawn. 2015. "My Apology to the Mar Thoma Church." February 15. https://shawnvarghese.wordpress.com.

Vásquez, Manuel A. 2008. "Studying Religion in Motion: A Networks Approach." *Method and Theory in the Study of Religion* 20:151–184.

Vattakunnel, Betty. 2014. "Mar Theodosius and New Generation." In *Beyond the Diaspora: Mar Thoma Church: Identity and Mission in the Context of Multiplicity. A Festschrift in Honor of Rt. Rev. Dr. Geevarghese Mar Theodosius Bishop of the Mar Thoma Church*, edited by K. E. Geevarghese and Mathew T. Thomas, 259–262. Ernakulam: Anaswara Offset Press.

Verghese, Paul. 1967. *The Joy of Freedom: Eastern Worship and Modern Man*. London: Lutterworth.

———. 1973. "The Church in Kerala at the Coming of the Portuguese." In *The St. Thomas Christian Encyclopedia of India*, edited by George Menachery, 32–36. Vol. 2. Madras: B. N. K. Press.

Vertovec, Stephen. 2004. "Migrant Transnationalism and Modes of Transformation." *International Migration Review* 38(3):970–1001.

Vertovec, Steven, and Susanne Wessendorf, eds. 2010. *The Multiculturalism Backlash: European Discourses, Policies, and Practices*. London: Routledge.

Visvanathan, Susan. 1993. *The Christians of Kerala: History, Belief and Ritual among the Yacoba*. Delhi: Oxford University Press.

Waldinger, Roger. 2015. *The Cross-Border Connection: Immigrants, Emigrants, and Their Homelands*. Cambridge: Harvard University Press.

Warner, Lloyd W., and Leo Scrole. 1945. *The Social Systems of American Ethnic Groups*. New Haven: Yale University Press.

Warner, Stephen R. 1993. "Work in Progress toward a New Paradigm for the Sociological Study of Religion in the United States." *American Journal of Sociology* 98(5):1044–1093.

Warner, Stephen R., and Judith G. Wittner. 1998. *Gatherings in Diaspora: Religious Communities and the New Immigration*. Philadelphia: Temple University Press.

Waters, Mary C. 1999. *Black Identities: West Indian Immigrant Dreams and American Realities*. New York: Russell Sage Foundation.

Weber, Jeremy. 2013. "'Stop Stereotyping Us,' Demand Distressed Asian American Evangelical Leaders." *Christianity Today*, October. www.christianitytoday.com.

West, Candace, and Sarah Fenstermaker. 1995. "Doing Difference." *Gender and Society* 9:8–37.

West, Candace, and Don H. Zimmerman. 1987. "Doing Gender." *Gender and Society* 1:125–151.

Williams, Raymond Brady. 1988. *Religions of Immigrants from India and Pakistan: New Threads in the American Tapestry*. Cambridge: Cambridge University Press.

———, ed. 1992. "Sacred Threads of Several Textures: Strategies of Adaptation in the United States." In *A Sacred Thread: Modern Transmission of Hindu Traditions in India and Abroad*, 228–257. Chambersburg, Pa.: Anima Publications.

———. 1996. *Christian Pluralism in the United States: The Indian Immigrant Experience*. Cambridge: Cambridge University Press.

Wong, Janelle, and Jane Iwamura. 2007. "The Moral Minority: Race, Religion, and Conservative Politics in Asian America." In *Religion and Social Justice for Immigrants*, edited by Pierrette Hondagneu-Sotelo, 35–49. New Brunswick, N.J.: Rutgers University Press.

Wuthnow, Robert. 1988. *The Restructuring of American Religion: Society and Faith since World War II*. Princeton, N.J.: Princeton University Press.

Wuthnow, Robert, and Stephen Offut. 2008. "Transnational Religious Connections." *Sociology of Religion* 69(2):209–232.

Yang, Fenggang. 1999. *Chinese Christians in America: Conversion, Assimilation and Adhesive Identities*. University Park: Pennsylvania State University Press.

———. 2004. "Gender and Generation in a Chinese Christian Church." In *Asian American Religions: The Making and Remaking of Borders and Boundaries*, edited by Tony Carnes and Fenggang Yang, 205–222. New York: NYU Press.

Yang, Fenggang, and Helen Rose Ebaugh. 2001. "Transformations in New Immigrant Religions and Their Global Implications." *American Sociological Review* 66(2):269–288.

Yep, Jeanette, Peter Cha, Paul Tokunaga, Greg Jao, and Susan Cho Van Riesen. 1998. *Following Jesus without Dishonoring Your Parents*. Downers Grove, Ill.: Intervarsity Press.

Zachariah, K. C. 2006. *The Syrian Christians of Kerala: Demographic and Socio-Economic Transition in the Twentieth Century*. New Delhi: Orient Longman.

Zachariah, K. C., and S. Irudaya Rajan. 2007. "Migration, Remittances and Employment: Short-Term Trends and Long-Term Implications." Working Paper 395. Trivandrum: Centre for Development Studies.

Zachariah, K.C., E. T. Mathew, and S. Irudaya Rajan. 1999. "Impact of Migration on Kerala's Economy and Society." Working Paper 297. Trivandrum: Centre for Development Studies.

Zhou, Min, and Carl L. Bankston III. 1998. *Growing Up American: How Vietnamese Children Adapt to Life in the United States*. New York: Russell Sage Foundation.

INDEX

Abraham Mar Thoma, 65, 67

access: to Hindu sacred spaces and rites, 9, 36, 243, 244; to thirumenis, 86, 154

achens, 17, 18, 84, 141, 146, 161, 167, 212; background of, as barrier to change, 204–205, 226; and building projects, 202, 205; and financial support of home church in India, 175, 179; linguistic and cultural fluency of, 125, 193, 205; mediation of parish conflicts by, 82; overseas postings, 199–201, 202–203, 229; provide vocational guidance, 75–76; salaries and benefits in America, 199–201; short terms of, 126, 202–203, 229; theological training of, 72–75, 197, 212; wives of, 155, 200. *See also* marriage: of priests

adaptation, immigrant, 13. *See also* incorporation

Addai, apostle, 36

Ahatallah, bishop, 49–50

alcoholism, in Kerala, 206

All People's Church, Bangalore, 210, 211

altar, 17, 69, 144, 159–161, 164, 228

"Altar Boys and Covenant Girls" program, Mar Thoma church, 105

Anglicans, 7, 20, 30, 64, 68, 165, 222; attempts to establish church in India, 29–30; initial presence in Kerala, 53–56; Mar Thoma church in full communion with, 22, 29–30, 72; merged into CSI, 71; missionaries, 9, 15, 19, 29–30, 53–60, 67–68, 244, 249nn9–10

anti-institutional religion, 12. *See also* nondenominational churches

Antioch, Patriarch of, 50, 59, 62, 63

Antiochan Christians, 58

antiritualism, 64

apostolic succession, 52, 55, 62, 212

archdeacons, 39

arranged marriages, 92, 98

assemblies and conventions, of Mar Thoma church, 65, 69, 75, 86, 97

assimilation theories, 2, 11, 109, 241, 247n1. *See also* incorporation

auricular confession, 38, 53, 57, 62

Babylon, patriarch of, 9, 41

"back stage" vs. "front stage," in gender performance, 143

Bailey, Benjamin, 30, 57, 58

Baker, Henry, 57, 58

baptism, 1, 38, 126, 127, 139, 212

Bayly, Susan, 34–35, 36, 52, 248n7

Believers Church, Tiruvalla, 207–208

Bharatiya Janata Party (BJP), 169, 170, 171

Bible, 104, 116, 156–157; applicable to normal day's life, 125, 135; as basis for liturgy, 141; centrality of, in Mar Thoma church, 66; and limited women's church roles, 159–161, 162; multiracial churches mandated by, 129, 242; personal reading and group study of, 70, 112, 145, 184; at Sunday services, 59; vernacular translations of, 29, 54

Bible colleges, 208, 222

Bible Study Fellowship, 96, 115, 132

bishops, 9, 175, 229; access to, 86,
154; celibacy of, 38, 62; familiar
with American context of church,
193; Metropolitan, 16, 69; said to
"dominate" Mandalam, 204. *See also*
thirumenis
BJP (Bharatiya Janata Party), 169, 170, 171
"born again" experience, 1, 109, 135, 210
Brahmins, 9, 15; converted to Christianity,
33, 34
bridge-church, Mar Thoma church as, 16,
21, 65
Brown, Leslie, 35, 36, 52, 248nn5–6
Buchanan, Claudius, 53–56
building projects, achens', 202, 205

campus evangelism, and the second generation, 96, 113, 142, 188
Carmelite missionaries, 50, 51
cassanars/cattanars, 41, 44, 49, 50, 52. *See
also* achens
caste system, 36, 52; attempts to reform,
244; high status of Syrian Christians
(*see* status); low-caste converts, 39, 58;
and pollution by lower-caste contact,
47, 222 (*see also* pollution; untouchability)
Catholic Church, 68, 95, 230–231; civic
engagement, intergenerational differences in, 173; Kerala seminary, 39; Portuguese importation of, 27–28, 38–58,
67–68, 243; and the Synod of Diamper,
9. *See also* Synod of Diamper
Cayo, Saint, 43
Chafetz, Janet S., 152
Chaldean church, 38
Chandy, bishop, 50
chanting, 17, 121
charismatic Christianity, 13, 68, 216;
churches in India, 239, 244; transnational, 207, 214, 219
"checkbook" outreach to India, 183–184,
190, 236

Cheppattu Mar Dionysius (Mar Thoma
XII), 59, 61, 62
children, 140; changes in relations with,
and migration, 206; exposure to
Malayalam television serials, 223; in
Kerala cultural "bubble," 225; Mar
Thoma membership for sake of, 117–
119, 131–132, 163, 251n11; in nursing
families, 91–92, 147; in professional
families, 91–92, 153
Chinese American Christians, 13, 142,
156, 230. *See also* East Asian American
Christians
Christ: identity in, 134; men as symbols of,
161; modeling of, 185, 186, 187; personal
relationship with, 109, 115, 124, 176, 235.
See also God
Christ for the Nations, seminary, 139
Christian identity, 3, 9, 15, 171, 193, 243;
and civic engagement, 174–175, 188–
189, 193; and class differences, 144;
intergenerational differences in, 109,
111, 112–117, 144; transcending ethnicity
and race, 189, 194
Christianity: American evangelical model, 111, 188; essential, and
missionaries, 248n3; importance of
intellectual understanding of, 116;
"Sunday," 125
Christian Researches in Asia (Buchanan),
53
Christians, attacks against, in India, 170,
172, 224, 240
Chrysostom, Metropolitan. *See* Philipose
Mar Chrysostom
churches: dual parish attendance, 140;
ethnic (*see* ethnic churches); immigrant perspective on role of, 117–122;
for second generation, 122–127; *vs.*
sects, 213
Church Missionary Society (CMS), xi, 29,
30, 57
Church of North India (CNI), 71–72

God: controlling all aspects of believer's life, 116; in Eastern tradition, 16; personal relationship with, 111, 122. *See also* Christ

Gospel for Asia (GFA), 208

Gouvea, Antony de, 36, 39, 40, 41, 42, 46, 54

Graham, Billy, 111

Heavenly Feast, Kottayam megachurch, 208

hegemony, Gramscian, 31

Herberg, Will, 11

heresy: achens said to preach, 127; elimination of, 28, 48, 68

Hindus: active evangelism towards, discouraged, 135; Brahmin converts to Christianity, 33–37, 34; Christian participation in spaces and rites of, 9, 36, 62–63, 243; influences of, in Syrian Christian churches, 28, 33, 69; lower-caste, Mar Thoma outreach to, 174; pollution standards, 9, 20

Holy Communion. *See* Eucharist

home as "back stage" arena, 143

home country: and international migration, 20–22, 24, 25–26, 222, 245; loyalties to, legitimized by multiculturalism, 232

homogeneity principle, in evangelizing, 241

homosexuality, 126; LGBT Mar Thomites, 165–166

host societies, 245

housework, gendering of, 87–89, 102, 151, 162, 231

hymns, Malayalam, 121

hypocrisy, 185

idavakas, 60, 66

identity: in Christ, 134 (*see also* Christian identity); cultural, 119; ethnic, 3, 51, 223, 225; faith, nonracial, 241; Indian, 171, 175; Mar Thoma, 174–175, 188, 220, 237; Orthodox, 104; religious, 74, 119, 223; youth, 179–180

ideology of gender: egalitarian, 88 (*see also* feminism); evangelical, in the second generation, 156–166, 168; transnational persistence of, 167

images, in worship, 36, 38, 52, 53, 62

immigrants, 10, 88, 124, 191, 236, 240; alleged hypocrisy of, 185; civic incorporation and engagement of, 25, 170, 173–175; desire to preserve cultural traditions, 119–121, 132, 147, 189, 192; ethnic *vs.* religious identification, 109, 112–113; men, dominant in church life, 145; nurses and husbands (*see* nurses); parishes dominated by, and local engagement, 177–181; professional families, 25, 90, 91–92; on role of the church, 117–122, 122; settlement struggles, 87–94; sponsorship of, 78, 106–107, 223

Immigration Act of 1965, 19, 21, 77

incorporation, of immigrants: civic, 25; "new paradigm" of religion and ethnicity, 231–232, 240–243; role of religion in, 10–11. *See also* assimilation theories

India: attacks against Christians in, 170, 172, 224, 240; "checkbook" outreach to, 183–184, 190; foodways, and the second generation, 189; nondenominational evangelical churches branches in, 142; Pentecostal and charismatic churches in, 239, 244; Supreme Court of, 218; urban evangelical missions, 111

Indian American Christians, relative diversity among, 14

Indian Emergency, 67

Indian identity: of immigrants, 175; as Kerala Christian, 171

Indian independence movement, 24, 66–67, 69

individualistic religion, 12, 64, 194, 233; and evangelism, 66, 68, 193, 242

information technology boom, and second-wave immigration, 21

ABOUT THE AUTHOR

Prema A. Kurien is Professor of Sociology at Syracuse University and author of two award-winning books, *Kaleidoscopic Ethnicity: International Migration and the Reconstruction of Community Identities in India* and *A Place at the Multicultural Table: The Development of an American Hinduism*. She is currently working on her next book, *Race, Religion, and Citizenship: Indian American Political Advocacy*.